GRAVE NEW WORLD

GRAVE NEW WORLD

THE END OF GLOBALIZATION,
THE RETURN OF HISTORY

STEPHEN D. KING

YALE UNIVERSITY PRESS
NEW HAVEN AND LONDON

For information about this and other Yale University Press publications, please contact:

U.S. Office: sales.press@yale.edu   yalebooks.com

Europe Office: sales@yaleup.co.uk   yalebooks.co.uk

Set in Minion Pro by IDSUK (DataConnection) Ltd

Printed in the United States of America

Library of Congress Control Number: 2017936404

ISBN 978-0-300-21804-6

A catalogue record for this book is available from the British Library.

10 9 8 7 6 5 4 3 2 1

To Yvonne, Helena, Olivia and Sophie

CONTENTS

CONTENTS

PROLOGUE
A Victorian Perspective on Globalization

. . . we have now reached the third stage in our history, and the true conception of our Empire.

What is that conception? As regards the self-governing colonies we no longer talk of them as dependencies. The sense of possession has given place to the sense of kinship. We think and speak of them as part of ourselves, as part of the British Empire, united to us, although they may be dispersed throughout the world, by ties of kindred, of religion, of history, and of language, and joined to us by the seas that formerly seemed to divide us. But the British Empire is not confined to the self-governing colonies and the United Kingdom. It includes a much greater area, a much more numerous population in tropical climes, where no considerable European settlement is possible, and where the native population must always outnumber the white inhabitants . . . Here also the sense of possession has given way to a different sentiment – the sense of obligation. We feel now that our rule over these territories can only be justified if we can show that it adds to the happiness and prosperity of the people . . .

In carrying out this work of civilization we are fulfilling what I believe to be our national mission, and we are finding scope for the exercise of those faculties and qualities which have made us a great governing race . . .

No doubt, in the first instance, when those conquests have been made, there has been bloodshed, there has been loss of life among the native populations, loss of still more precious lives among those who have been sent out to bring these countries into some kind of disciplined order [but] . . . You cannot have omelettes without breaking eggs; you cannot destroy the practices of barbarism, of slavery, of superstition, which for centuries have desolated the interior of Africa, without the use of force . . . Great is the task, great is the responsibility, but great is the honour: and I am convinced that the conscience and the spirit of the country will rise to the height of its obligations, and that we shall have the strength to fulfil the mission which our history and our national character have imposed upon us.

. . . the tendency of the time is to throw all power into the hands of the greater empires . . . But, if Greater Britain remains united, no empire in the world can ever surpass it in area, in population, in wealth, or in the diversity of its resources . . .

Extracts from a speech by Joseph Chamberlain, Secretary of State for the Colonies, at the annual dinner of the Royal Colonial Institute, 31 March 1897

INTRODUCTION
The Andalucían Shock

ONE-WAY TRAFFIC

Globalization is often regarded as 'one-way traffic'. In the modern age, we think of extraordinary advances in technology that allow us to connect in so many remarkable – and increasingly inexpensive – ways. We can communicate verbally and pictorially through WhatsApp, Twitter and Facebook. We can talk to each other via FaceTime and Skype. We can search for recipes and the structure of the human brain through Google. We can purchase chicken madras and salmon nigiri over the internet and have them brought to our homes via local delivery services. We can stream music for free thanks to Spotify and watch our favourite artists and cat videos on YouTube or Vevo. We can download television programmes and movies to watch at our convenience. We can more easily pry into the affairs of the rest of the world (and, equally, the rest of the world can more easily pry into our affairs).

Seen through these technological advances, it is easy to believe that globalization is inevitable; that distances are becoming ever shorter; that national borders are slowly dissolving; and that, whether we like it or not, we live in a single global marketplace for goods, services, capital and labour.

IT'S NOT JUST ABOUT TECHNOLOGY

Technology alone, however, does not determine globalization, and nor does it rule out competing versions of globalization at any one moment in time. If technology was the only thing that mattered, the Western Roman Empire – among other things, an incredibly sophisticated technological and logistical infrastructure – would never have come to an ignominious end in AD 476; the Chinese, with their superior naval technologies, would have been busily colonizing the Americas in the early sixteenth century, preventing Spain and, by implication, the rest of Western Europe from gaining a foothold; the British Empire would today still be thriving, thanks to the huge advantages it gained from the Industrial Revolution; the Cold War – which ultimately offered two competing versions of globalization associated with an uneasy nuclear stand-off – would never have happened; and today's 'failed states' – suffering from disconnections both internally and with the rest of the world – would be a contradiction in terms. Globalization is driven not just by technological advance, but also by the development – and demise – of the ideas and institutions that form our politics, frame our economies and fashion our financial systems both locally and globally. When existing ideas are undermined and institutional infrastructures implode, no amount of new technology is likely to save the day.

Our ideas and institutions shift with alarming regularity. Spanish *conquistadors* of the early sixteenth century – bounty-hunters hell bent on extracting silver from the New World, regardless of the human cost – would have been surprised to discover that Spain, at one point Europe's superpower, is now one of the poorer Western European nations. The Ottomans of the sixteenth and seventeenth centuries – who had threatened to conquer Vienna and, by implication, much of the rest of Europe

– would have been amazed to see how their empire, which had stretched from the Balkans into the Middle East and North Africa, completely imploded after the First World War (even if the seeds of its downfall were sown many years before). Victorians would be shocked to find that their beloved British Empire – which provided the essential foundations for nineteenth-century globalization – had more or less disappeared by the late 1940s, by which time the UK itself was on the brink of bankruptcy. Those many fans of the Soviet economic system during the 1930s Depression years would doubtless be astonished to discover that the entire edifice began to crumble following the fall of the Berlin Wall in 1989.

SOUTHERN SPAIN

Even when patterns of globalization endure for many centuries, they can break down remarkably quickly, leading to dramatic changes in fortune. Consider, for example, the history of Andalucía in southern Spain, a story that veered from one seemingly permanent political structure (Islam) to another (Christianity) within just a handful of years.

In AD 711, a Muslim Berber force travelled from North Africa across the Mediterranean to reach southern Spain. Six years later, and thanks to the Berbers' defeat of the hitherto-ruling Christian Visigoths, Córdoba had become the capital of what was known as al-Andalus. The conquering Moors then set about building their symbols of power. In 784, construction began on the Grand Mosque of Córdoba. By 987 – and following three further development stages – the mosque was complete. A truly remarkable building, it was designed above all to be a symbol of lasting Islamic dominance. Yet, following the defeat of the Almoravids by the Almohads, the centre of Islamic power later transferred from Córdoba to Seville, just under a hundred miles away. Inevitably, a new mosque was required and, in 1171, it was provided: topped off by its minaret, known today as the *Giralda*, Seville's Almohad Mosque was a marvel of the Moorish world.

For the citizens of southern Spain, it would have been easy to believe that medieval 'globalization' was ultimately dependent on the spread of Islam, a way of life which appeared to be intellectually, technologically and culturally much more advanced than anything Christian Europe had to offer. Yet within a handful of years, Islamic rule in the Iberian Peninsula had descended into chaos. In 1213, following the death of the ruling caliph, his 10-year-old son took over. This inevitably triggered infighting among the grown-ups, each of whom jockeyed for power. Worse, the young caliph died a decade or so later without leaving a single heir: at a stroke, the ruling conventions of Moorish Spain had been totally undermined. For the northern Christian kings, this was too good an opportunity to miss. By 1236, they had taken control of Córdoba. Twelve years later, they had their hands on Seville. Córdoba's mosque was 'converted' into a cathedral, while Seville's mosque was demolished (apart from the *Giralda*, which became a bell tower), to be replaced by what to this day remains the world's largest cathedral.

The ultimate irony, perhaps, is that Seville Cathedral – or, to give it its full Spanish name, Catedral de Santa María de la Sede – houses the remains of Christopher Columbus. In 1492, the year in which Columbus discovered the New World, the Moors were finally expelled from the Iberian Peninsula, following the start of the Inquisition in 1478 (doubtless a surprise to the remaining Moors: after all, nobody expects the Spanish Inquisition. . .). By then, Islamic power was being consolidated farther east.

AFTER COLUMBUS

Columbus had inadvertently discovered a new Western European-led and mostly Christian path towards global political and economic expansion. The next five hundred years witnessed the increasing dominance of so-called Western powers: either those based in Europe or those whose new populations were mostly sourced from Europe. And while these powers were often in conflict with each other, they all ultimately shared the same view of the rest of the world: it was there to be discovered, exploited and colonized for their individual and collective benefit. It was the beginning of what might loosely be described as 'post-Columbus' globalization.

Yet while there were attempts to create lasting stability – ranging from the Peace of Westphalia in 1648 through to the Congress of Vienna in 1814–15 – post-Columbus globalization was always vulnerable to imperial rivalries. For a while, the British Empire, in all its pomp, appeared to provide an answer: its enthusiasm for free trade – enforced by the long arm of the Royal Navy – opened up a remarkable web of commercial connections worldwide. Other nations, however, understandably wanted their share of the spoils, most obviously the Russians in the nineteenth century and the Germans in the first half of the twentieth. Eventually – and, in hindsight, inevitably – post-Columbus globalization collapsed, to be replaced by war, revolution and isolationism. Only after the Second World War was it able to re-emerge, albeit under the shadow of the Cold War. This time the US was, in effect, both globalization's leading architect and its main sponsor, even if Washington now rejected the empire-building it had partly sponsored during the nineteenth century.[1] The emergence of the US as the world's dominant superpower was, in many ways, the apotheosis of post-Columbus globalization, signalling the triumph of Western liberal democratic values and free-market capitalism.

At the beginning of the twenty-first century, however, post-Columbus globalization is in serious trouble. Economic power is shifting eastwards and, as it does so, new alliances are being created, typically between countries that are not natural cheerleaders for Western political and economic values. There are signs that pre-Columbus versions of globalization – in which power was centred on Eurasia, not the West – are making a tentative reappearance. The US is no longer sure whether its priorities lie across the Atlantic, on the other side of the Pacific or, following the election of Donald Trump as president in 2016, at home rather than abroad. Indeed, President Trump confirmed as much in his January 2017 inauguration speech, stating that 'From this day forward, it's going to be only America first.' Free markets have been found wanting, particularly following the global financial crisis. Support and respect for the international organizations that provided the foundations and set the 'rules' for post-war globalization – most obviously, the International Monetary Fund, the European Union and the United Nations Security Council (whose permanent members anachronistically include the UK and France, but not Germany, Japan, India or Indonesia) – are rapidly fading. Political narratives are becoming increasingly protectionist. It is easier, it seems, for politicians of both left and right to blame 'the other' – the immigrant, the foreigner, the stranger in their midst – for a nation's problems. Voters, meanwhile, no longer fit into neat political boxes. Neglected by the mainstream left and right, many have opted instead to vote for populist and nativist politicians typically opposed to globalization. Isolationism is, once again, becoming a credible political alternative. Without it, there would have been no Brexit and no Trump.

THE END OF POST-COLUMBUS GLOBALIZATION

In combination, these political and economic forces suggest that globalization, at least of the post-Columbus kind, is simply not inevitable. In this book – a deliberate mixture of economics, history, geography and political philosophy – I make six key claims:

- First, economic progress that reaches beyond borders is not, in any way, an inescapable truth. Globalization can all too easily go into reverse.
- Second, technology can both enable globalization and destroy it.
- Third, economic development that reduces inequality between nation states but appears to increase it within those states inevitably creates a tension between a desire for overall gains in global living standards and a yearning for economic and social stability at home.

- Fourth, the desire for domestic stability may be undermined by huge twenty-first-century migration flows.
- Fifth, the international institutions that have helped govern globalization's advance are losing their credibility: rightly or wrongly, globalization is increasingly seen to work for the few, not the many. Creating new twenty-first-century institutions to combat this perception will not be easy, however, particularly given the potential clash in values between what might be described as Western democracies and Eastern autocracies.
- Sixth (and as the Western powers are belatedly beginning to recognize), there is more than one version of globalization. As US relative economic power declines, so other nascent superpowers will be looking to reshape the world around them in ways that serve their own interests and reflect their own histories. If the Cold War was ultimately a binary rivalry, the twenty-first century is likely to see multiple rivalries, closer in nature to the imperial disputes of the nineteenth century. Indeed, President Xi's speech in Davos in January 2017 only served to reinforce the sense that globalization is up for grabs.

There have been many cheerleaders for globalization, but ultimately my conclusion is that the world is most certainly not flat, and nor can it be.[2] Economics and politics are both heavily contoured and constantly changing, particularly so when borders are involved. And, as I argue throughout this book, we are all, in some sense, slaves to our own versions of history. For those of us living in the West, we have found it all too easy to claim that our own good fortune will continue and that, in time, it will inevitably spread far and wide. It's time to wake up to reality.

POST-WAR SUCCESS, TWENTY-FIRST-CENTURY FAILURE

Part One explains both why globalization was, for so many post-war years, a means towards rising wealth, and why, later, it seemingly became more of a curse than a blessing. As the twentieth century drew to a close, it seemed as though Western free-market capitalism and liberal democracy had triumphed. At the end of the Cold War, it was easy to believe that we could all enjoy, to augment a notorious phrase, 'peace and prosperity in our time'.

It was not to be. Even before the global financial crisis, there were already signs of trouble: the crisis itself just made things worse. Why, after so many years of rising incomes for the many, was globalization suddenly in trouble? Put another way, why did we ever think we had discovered the secrets behind ever-rising prosperity? What went so right in the years after the Second World War – a period during which economies became both richer and increasingly integrated with each other – and why did it all seem to be going so wrong at just the point when lasting success was, for many observers, seemingly guaranteed?

NATION STATES VERSUS GLOBALIZATION

Part Two examines the inevitable tension between globalization and the existence of nation states. For globalization to work, nation states need to accept reductions in sovereignty for the greater good. But who decides what is the greater good?

In the nineteenth century, the imperial powers shared out the responsibility. Some performed the role better than others. Yet none was enthusiastic about the rights of their colonial subjects. Globalization flourished economically and financially, yet politically it was both unfair and unstable.

As, one by one, empires collapsed, the twentieth century saw the nation state emerge as the 'default' political arrangement, thanks in part to the philosophical and practical support provided by successive US presidents (and, less helpfully, the arbitrary carve-up by the retreating imperial powers of the Middle East and Africa). Nation states, however, sit uneasily with a globalized world. From Hobbes to Montesquieu and through to James Buchanan with his 'theory of clubs', it is not at all obvious that what might loosely be defined as the 'national interest' will always be consistent with the 'global interest'. Montesquieu, in particular, argued that a democratic nation would only survive if the vast majority of its citizens thought their interests sat comfortably with those of the state as a whole. If instead some of those citizens began to think their interests could more easily be pursued by taking advantage of others – via the exertion of political power – the 'spirit of inequality' would begin to undermine the social contract.

Yet modern-day globalization appears to be conjuring up exactly this spirit of inequality. Rising income and wealth inequality has not helped – although it is worth noting that, even in those countries where inequality of living standards has not really risen much (notably in continental Europe), support for globalization is waning. But of greater importance is, perhaps, the sense that 'we're not all in this together'. In the modern age, the spirit of inequality takes many forms: the growing income gap among those countries that pooled their monetary sovereignty in the Eurozone; the absence of significant income gains for many millions of Western workers, even as a lucky few have become unimaginably rich; the extraordinary progress of the Chinese economy, thanks in part to China's ability to attract investments by Western companies that might, in an earlier age, have created jobs and raised wages in the US or Europe; the increased competition in some – but not all – labour markets, thanks to the impact of both technology and immigration; and the emergence of elites, which too often appear to be deciding our collective futures to suit their own interests, whether we like it or not.

It would be wrong, however, to think that globalization is struggling simply because it sits uncomfortably with the interests of nation states. As other parts of the world have flourished economically, so competing frameworks for globalization have emerged, reflected in China's desire to, in effect, re-create a Eurasian Silk Road and Russia's increasing exertion of power in the Middle East. New institutions are challenging the international status quo, including the fledgling Asian Infrastructure

Investment Bank – backed by China – and the Shanghai Cooperation Organization – ultimately a Sino-Russian entity which potentially offers not just closer economic ties, but also closer security ties. In the West, we lazily talk about the 'international community', supposedly a like-minded collection of countries with similar moral and ethical outlooks. It turns out, however, that there is really no such thing. There are, instead, rival communities that, in difficult economic times, may increasingly struggle to agree on a common course of action, particularly given their very different historical perspectives and, in many cases, their inability to reach agreement on unresolved territorial disputes.

THE TWENTY-FIRST-CENTURY CHALLENGES

Part Three uses the prism of the past to gaze into the future, focusing on three crucial challenges to globalization: migration, technology and money.

Globalization in its purest form would ultimately be a world without borders, without independent nation states, with the dominant institutions of government operating at the global level. In this – imaginary – world there would be free movement of goods, services, capital and people, precisely the 'Four Freedoms' enshrined within the European Union. There would also be a single currency and a single central bank: with perfectly functioning markets, there would be no need for currency adjustment.

Already, however, we know that the European Union is struggling politically with two of its 'Four Freedoms', namely the free movement of capital and of people. The Eurozone crisis, in abeyance at the time of writing, but still unresolved, partly stems from Europe's inability to cope with the consequences of the free flow of capital across its internal borders. The Syrian conflict, meanwhile, has revealed severe challenges regarding the free movement of people, particularly given the weak points in the Schengen area's common external border.

Yet, relative to historical patterns of migration, the number of Syrian migrants entering the European Union has been tiny. If migration had a high point, it was back in the nineteenth century, when rising incomes in Europe, together with the falling cost of a transatlantic berth, paved the way for a mass exodus of people to the New World. Syria may eventually represent only the foothills of a twenty-first-century migration crisis. In sub-Saharan Africa, where the infant mortality rate is falling more rapidly than the fertility rate, a 'baby boom' on a totally unprecedented scale is on the way. Alongside rising real incomes, we may be on the cusp of witnessing an extraordinary migration of African people northwards, across the Mediterranean to Europe – in search of a better life – whether Europe is ready or not.

Technology is often regarded as the key driver of modern-day globalization, largely through its ability to demolish barriers associated with distance, time and cost. Yet technology has a dark side. The use of social media is undermining existing political arrangements. Despite its name, the Islamic State of Iraq and Syria (ISIS) is a classic example of a non-state actor that has been able to gain support via social media. The cybersphere has created opportunities for nations to attack and undermine each other in virtual reality. Mainstream political parties – on either side of the Atlantic – have effectively been hijacked by mavericks (and their supporters). And, in many cases, the mavericks have succeeded by forcibly expressing their opposition to globalization on social media, while being economical with the truth.

Money, meanwhile, has become a means of conducting economic warfare, in a twenty-first-century version of coin clipping aimed at the foreign investor. For all the talk of central bankers kick-starting economic growth, monetary stimulus has increasingly ended up creating only winners and losers both within and across borders – a process that has served to create an even bigger gulf between policymakers and the citizens they are supposed to serve.

TECHNOCRATIC SOLUTIONS, OBLIGATIONS AND MORALITY

Part Four argues that many of the 'solutions' to the problems associated with globalization are simply too technocratic. The decline of post-Columbus globalization is, in part, a reflection of its lack of democratic accountability. It is also, importantly, a result of what might best be described as a lack of global 'leadership', a reflection not just of an increasingly insular approach from the US, but also of the emergence of credible rivals in other parts of the world who – unlike Western Europe and Japan after the Second World War – see no reason to bow to Washington, particularly given America's 'pick 'n' mix' approach to global values: not everyone, after all, enthuses about Iran–Contra, the Second Gulf War or the treatment of prisoners in Guantanamo Bay.

Globalization's demise, however, is not only about the return of global power games. Both before and (more obviously) after the global financial crisis, it has simply failed to deliver prosperity for all. This reflects profound weaknesses that go far beyond market forces, even though market forces themselves have been – occasionally – incredibly destructive. Obligations that we take for granted within nation states tend too often to be ignored across borders. How should creditors in one country relate to debtors in another? Why should taxpayers in a single country be on the hook for a bank's global misdemeanours? What social rights should immigrants enjoy if they haven't paid their taxes? In the absence of a global tax system, how realistic is it to demand that globalization's winners compensate its losers, particularly if they come not just from different countries, but from different continents?

My version of the future is not quite as terrifying as that contained in Aldous Huxley's *Brave New World*: there are no human 'hatcheries', no chemically engineered economic castes and no official promotion of hallucinogenic drugs to encourage a shallow and hedonistic lifestyle. My story is, however, deeply unsettling. Many of the values and beliefs that the Western world embraced following the end of the Second World

War are rapidly crumbling. In particular, we placed our faith in markets and technology, lazily assuming that, with the Cold War at an end, the rest of the world would embrace supposedly universal truths associated with liberal democracy and free markets. Yet many countries have done no such thing. Worse, Western nations themselves are deeply divided, unsure as to whether they should carry on supporting international institutions and reaching out to the rest of the world, or should instead hunker down, opting for an insular approach that, even if initially seductive, has proved eventually to be hugely destructive.

The book begins, however, with Lincoln Steffens, a man who would have disappeared from the history books altogether had he not uttered a phrase that encapsulates our utopian tendency to believe that, within the right framework, human progress is inevitable.

Part One

PARADISE LOST

7

FALSE PROPHETS, HARSH TRUTHS

NEW MODEL ECONOMIES

Lincoln Steffens was one of the pioneering muckrakers. Hailing from California, he first made his mark as an 'investigative journalist' in New York in the early 1900s. He came to know everyone – from Theodore Roosevelt and Woodrow Wilson through to William Randolph Hearst and James Joyce. His chosen mission was to expose corruption wherever he found it. In early twentieth-century America, there was no shortage of targets, with Wall Street, big business and municipal governments at the top of the list.[1]

Steffens eventually became disillusioned with his muckraking efforts. Scandals typically led only to short-term reform. Venality, it seemed, was pretty much a fact of life, at least in the United States. Like other intellectuals of his generation, Steffens became increasingly fascinated by more radical approaches to political and social reform. If corruption was endemic in Western society, perhaps it was time for more 'scientific' solutions.

During a trip in March 1919 to what was to become the Soviet Union, Steffens thought he had found the answer. Unlike other fans of the Marxist-Leninist experiment, who chose to ignore the brutality associated with the embryonic Soviet regime, Steffens accepted that life in the 'workers' paradise' was not exactly easy. Short-run 'evil', however, was a price worth paying for long-run 'hope'.

So impressed was Steffens by the design of the Soviet system that, on his return to the United States, he famously proclaimed 'I have seen the future, and it works.'

It is easy to see why he was so enthralled. In the immediate aftermath of the First World War, much of the West found itself in the midst of economic and political chaos. The United States economy succumbed to an eighteen-month depression beginning in 1920, its citizens enduring both falling output and severe deflation. Weimar Germany suffered from hyperinflation between 1921 and 1924, a consequence of the absurd reparation conditions imposed by the allied victors under the Treaty of Versailles. Bundles of Marks were carried around in wheelbarrows, and cigarettes became a more useful means of exchange. Government debt in the UK had jumped from a mere 25 per cent of national income before the outbreak of hostilities in 1914 to a remarkable 181 per cent in 1923, triggering years of financial upheaval and austerity. The nineteenth century's pre-eminent world power found itself, both politically and economically, in severe relative decline.

For a while, Steffens' claim seemed to be remarkably prescient. We now know that, between 1920 and 1930, Soviet living standards rose by more than 150 per cent, compared with gains of 42 per cent for Germany, 20 per cent for the UK and 12 per cent for the US.[2]

Not surprisingly, many regarded Soviet industrialization under Lenin and Stalin as a near-miraculous process. Naive luminaries were totally seduced. In a letter to the *Manchester Guardian* published on 2 March 1933, George Bernard Shaw and 20 co-signatories angrily wrote:

Particularly offensive and ridiculous is the revival of the old attempts to represent the condition of Russian workers as one of slavery and starvation ... We ... are recent visitors to the USSR ... Everywhere we saw a hopeful and enthusiastic working-class, self-respecting, free up to the limits imposed upon them by nature and a terrible inheritance from the tyranny and incompetence of their former rulers, developing public works, increasing health services, extending education, achieving the economic independence of women and the security of the child and ... setting an example of industry and conduct which would greatly enrich us if our system supplied our workers with any incentive to follow it ... We urge all men and women of goodwill to take every opportunity ... to support the movements which demand peace, trade and closer friendship with an understanding of the greater Workers' Republic of Russia.[3]

Shaw and his fellow travellers presumably had not stumbled across the Gulag. Nor had they recognized that, in Stalin's 'Through the Looking Glass' ethical world, the best way to survive was to denounce others before they could denounce you.[4]

Steffens and Shaw were far from stupid. Nevertheless, they were too easily seduced by the Soviet system, blinded by the iniquities they saw at home: corruption, unemployment, inequality, inflation and austerity. For them, capitalism had failed. The Soviet system provided, through their blinkered eyes, a vision of the future.

It was not to be. Soviet living standards rose relative to those in the US in the interwar period – from 20 per cent in 1920 to 35 per cent in 1938 – only to return to 21 per cent in the immediate aftermath of the Second World War. They rose again during the Cold War, reaching a peak of 38 per cent of American incomes in 1975, before falling to 31 per cent as the Berlin Wall came down in 1989. The Soviet version of economic progress – the one that Steffens and Shaw believed in so passionately – just didn't deliver the goods.

HOW THE WEST DIDN'T WIN

Still, it would be wrong to suggest that the proponents of communism in its various forms were the only ones unable to see clearly into the future. In 1909, Norman Angell published the first edition of *The Great Illusion*, in which he argued that, thanks to nineteenth-century globalization and the resulting economic interdependency, war between the major nations of the world would be futile. Many regarded his book as the best argument in favour of continued peace, and therefore concluded that war was simply impossible (Angell himself wasn't so optimistic). Yet thanks to the shooting skills of Gavrilo Princip in Sarajevo five years later, it turned out that no amount of political or economic logic could prevent a catastrophic conflagration. The First World War turned the world upside down economically, financially and politically. The Ottoman and Austro-Hungarian empires disappeared without trace, while the British Empire began what proved to be its terminal decline.

Eighty years on, as the Soviet states began to crumble, Francis Fukuyama, the eminent political scientist, argued that:

> The most remarkable development of the last quarter of the twentieth century has been the revelation of enormous weaknesses at the core of the world's seemingly strong dictatorships . . . liberal democracy remains the only coherent political aspiration . . . liberal principles in economics – the 'free market' – have spread, and have succeeded in producing unprecedented levels of material prosperity, both in industrially developed countries and in countries that had been part of the impoverished Third World.[5]

More than two decades after the publication of Fukuyama's *The End of History* – both as a 1989 short paper[6] and a 1992 weighty tome – its claims no longer appear to be quite so secure. The link between liberal democracy and economic advance, frequently espoused by Western politicians, is not so obvious given the rapid economic growth of China, a nation that shows no sign of abandoning its one-party principles. Fukuyama himself now writes about both political order and political decay, presciently drawing attention to perceived fault lines in American society:

> The American political system has decayed over time because its traditional system of checks and balances has deepened and become increasingly rigid. With sharp political polarization, this decentral- ized system is less and less able to represent majority interests but gives excessive representation to the views of interest groups and activist organizations that collectively do not add up to a sovereign American people.[7]

Certainly, the American people are today no longer quite so enthusiastic about activities on Capitol Hill. The proportion of Americans polled who have either 'a great deal' or 'quite a lot' of confidence in Congress dropped from 42 per cent in 1973 – when Gallup first asked the ques- tion – to just 8 per cent in 2015, an approval rating lower than for any other institution, including banks, organized labour, newspapers, the criminal justice system, television news and big business. Liberal democracy may be a coherent aspiration, but in the US it seems there is little appetite for the current batch of democratically elected politicians or the gridlocked system they claim to represent: one reason why Donald Trump – political outsider, property developer and reality TV star – was elected US president in November 2016.

In what was a mostly conciliatory acceptance speech, Mr Trump stated that 'the forgotten men and women of our country will be forgotten no longer'. Why had they been forgotten? Why had they been left behind? For Trump, the explanation was simple: too many people had suffered as a result of free trade deals, Chinese competition, Mexican immigration and Islamic terrorism. It was time to reject globalization in all its many forms. Trump's answer was to build walls, both physical and metaphorical, to protect the forgotten people.

MR PUTIN'S POPULARITY

Outside the United States, it is far from obvious that liberal democracy really is 'the only coherent political aspiration' or that the collapse of Soviet communism has somehow proved that Western political and economic values are universal. Vladimir Putin first became Russian president in 2000. After eight years, he 'stepped down' to become Russia's prime minister under Dmitry Medvedev. Four years later, Putin was back in charge. By the summer of 2015, his approval rating was the highest it had ever been.[8] Nine out of ten Russians thought favourably of Putin's presidency, thanks in large part to developments in Ukraine. Specifically, 87 per cent of Russians were in favour of the annexation of Crimea, which just so happens to be mostly populated by ethnic Russians.

The West's decision to impose sanctions on Russia only bolstered Putin's popularity, even if the sanctions – alongside a collapse in energy prices – contributed to the Russian economy's contraction in late 2014 and 2015. It is hard to believe that Putin's many supporters are craving the imminent arrival of liberal democracy, despite their economic hardship. They instead appear to prefer their 'strongman', an image Putin chooses to reinforce by riding bare-chested on a horse or plumbing the Black Sea's depths in a submersible off the Crimean coast.

WHAT HAPPENED TO THE ARAB SPRING?

The hoped-for transition to liberal democracy in the Middle East and North Africa has simply not materialized. In November 2003, President George W. Bush – sticking to the *End of History* theme – told an appreciative audience at the National Endowment for Democracy that the US was:

working closely with Iraqi citizens as they prepare a constitution, as they move toward free elections and take increasing responsibility for their own affairs . . . This is a massive and difficult undertaking – it is worth our effort, it is worth our sacrifice, because we know the stakes. The failure of Iraqi democracy would embolden terrorists around the world, increase dangers to the American people, and extinguish the hopes of millions in the region. Iraqi democracy will succeed – and that success will send forth the news, from Damascus to Teheran – that freedom can be the future of every nation. The establishment of a free Iraq at the heart of the Middle East will be a watershed event in the global democratic revolution.[9]

Twelve years later, large swathes of Syria were not much more than a bombsite. The murderous ISIS – the antithesis of liberal democracy – had at one point taken control of around 50 per cent of both Syria and Iraq in its attempt to re-establish a caliphate. And, even as it was forced to retreat in the Middle East, its followers brought terror to the streets of Europe, with outrages committed in Paris, Nice and Brussels, among others. The equally violent President Assad, an old-fashioned Middle Eastern hard man who was well aware of what had already befallen Saddam Hussein and Hosni Mubarak, clung on to power in Damascus, increasingly dependent on the support of Russian forces. Western governments couldn't quite work out which side was morally more repugnant. Meanwhile, millions of Syrian refugees sought sanctuary either in neighbouring countries or, as time went by, in the European Union. They were not always guaranteed a warm welcome.

The Muslim Brotherhood's Mohammad Morsi, elected president of Egypt in 2012 following the Arab Spring, was deposed in a coup in June 2013 after violent protests. His Freedom and Justice Party was banned from the 2014 elections, and a year later Morsi was handed a provisional death sentence. In November 2016, the Egyptian Court of Cassation revoked the sentence, but Morsi still faced the prospect of serving three prison sentences: 20 years, 40 years and life.[10]

Libya, meanwhile, was left divided among competing warlords – none, it seems, favourably disposed to the principles of liberal democracy or, indeed, to the European nations that helped put them into power following the overthrow of Colonel Gaddafi in October 2011. Hamas's victory in the January 2006 election meant that Gaza was controlled by what Israel, the European Union and the US regarded as a terrorist organization. The Palestinian Authority – which retained control over the West Bank – was not particularly happy either.

THE RISE OF CHINA

In the Middle East and North Africa, the failure to establish liberal democracy is often seen as a hindrance to economic development (other than for the oil-producing Gulf States, which happily benefited from high economic rents until oil prices collapsed in 2015). The absence of liberal democracy in other parts of the world, however, appears to have been a blessing. On some measures, the People's Republic of China is now the biggest economy in the world. Hundreds of millions of Chinese have been dragged out of poverty under a one-party – nominally communist – system. Even if the heady growth rates of the last 30 years are unlikely to be repeated, China's rapid expansion sits uneasily with the idea that all nations will naturally converge on liberal democratic values. That unease becomes more pronounced when China's economic progress is compared with democratic India's more measured advance. In the mid-1970s, per capita incomes in China overtook those in India. By 2010, the average Chinese citizen enjoyed an income more than double that of his or her Indian counterpart.

Admittedly, China might prove to be yet another casualty of the so-called 'middle-income trap'. Recent history is certainly not encouraging. In the second half of the twentieth century, only a handful of what might loosely be described as 'non-Western' countries successfully managed to achieve typical Western living standards: Japan, South Korea, Hong Kong, Singapore, Taiwan and, at a pinch, Israel.[11] Despite huge progress, China's per capita incomes in 2015 were still only 25 per cent of those in the US, less than the Soviet Union managed – relatively – in the 1930s and the 1970s. Averages, however, can be misleading. Living standards in Beijing and Shanghai are fast approaching those more typically found in the developed world, even as those in China's southern provinces – most obviously Yunnan and Guizhou – languish at levels more commonly associated with the world's poorer nations. Parts of China have had spectacular economic success – but not all.

China's economic advance may not be uniform, but it is nevertheless creating new gravitational pressures in the Asian region. For better or worse, China is simply too big to be ignored. And, with the US no longer willing to sponsor trade deals in the region – with the much-heralded Trans-Pacific Partnership killed off by Donald Trump[12] – Asian leaders are understandably rethinking their approach to the Middle Kingdom, some with more trepidation than others. Japan, more than most, feels distinctly uneasy about its neighbour; yet in late 2016, the Philippines (erstwhile ally of the US and a country historically involved in serious territorial disputes with China), recognized – thanks to President Duterte, a man not known for hiding his opinions – that engagement with the world's most populous economy was too good an opportunity to miss.

LATIN AMERICA'S WOES

Following the failure of its currency board at the end of the 1990s – an arrangement in which the peso was supposedly fixed against the US dollar for all time – and its subsequent return to Perónist policies under the Kirchners, Argentina appeared unwilling to subscribe fully to the Western model of faith in free markets and respect for property rights.

Argentina, however, was an exception (alongside Venezuela, albeit from a rather different political perspective). Other large Latin American economies were keen to get a slice of the free-market action. Mexico signed up to the North American Free Trade Agreement on 1 January 1994. Although unfortunately timed – Mexico suffered its so-called 'tequila crisis' that year – its deal with the US and Canada underscored its enthusiasm for free-market values. Brazil, meanwhile, successfully managed to get a grip on inflation – thanks, in part, to the introduction of the so-called '*Real* plan' in the mid-1990s. Standing at almost 3,000 per cent in 1990 and 2,000 per cent in 1994, Brazilian inflation badly needed to come down. And it did, dropping like a stone to a low of around 3 per cent in 1998.

Yet, in the twenty-first century, Latin America's progress has at best been patchy. Strong gains in Brazilian living standards in the years both preceding and immediately after the 2008 global financial crisis were followed by a very deep and long-lasting recession. This huge reversal revealed that the Brazilian economy's progress had depended more on temporarily inflated commodity prices (thanks to China's post-financial crisis boom) and 'hot money' inflows from the US (a reflection of the Federal Reserve's money-printing escapades) than on any lasting improvements in productivity and competitiveness. Mexico's economy, much more closely aligned with America's, collapsed in line with its northern neighbour's during the financial crisis – and, like the US economy, made only moderate progress thereafter. For an emerging market hoping to see its living standards slowly converge with those of the developed world, this was profoundly disappointing. In 1990, Mexico's per capita incomes were 35 per cent of those in the US; by 2015, they had dropped to only 31 per cent of those north of the border.

One almost inevitable consequence of this economic disappointment was an increase in political turmoil, revealing that Latin America was still struggling to build robust liberal democratic institutions able to function well under stress. In September 2016, Brazilian President

Dilma Rousseff was impeached, following an attempt to channel funds from state banks into government coffers in a bid to massage the recession-hit fiscal numbers. The Western model of free markets and democracy had been either poorly applied, badly misunderstood or found wanting. Whatever the answer, Latin America hadn't delivered the goods.

DEMOCRACY, IMPERIAL BUREAUCRACY AND RIGHT-WING POPULISM: THE EUROPEAN QUESTIONS

In Europe, economic failure has placed extraordinary pressure on liberal democratic values, which, all too frequently, appear to have been undermined to ensure the euro's future. With the onset of the Eurozone's financial crisis in 2010, European policymakers had to make up the Eurozone's rules on an almost daily basis in an attempt to prevent the collapse of the financial system and, perhaps, the euro's ultimate fragmentation. Largely to protect German and French banks (and, by implication, the entire credit system) it was deemed essential that Southern European governments should not be allowed to default to their Northern European creditors: instead, Southern European citizens would have to accept painful austerity, in some cases on a multi-year basis. Admittedly, Southern European nations had borrowed stupid amounts from their Northern European creditors, but equally, those creditors had lent stupid amounts: the burden of adjustment, however, fell in large part on the debtors alone.

In Greece's case, the situation deteriorated rapidly, as the economic costs of austerity proved considerably greater than the International Monetary Fund and others had forecast when budget cuts were first implemented. Alexis Tsipras's anti-austerity Syriza party won a parliamentary election in January 2015 on the basis that Greece could both stay in the euro and escape from painful austerity. It turned out to be an impossible dream. The Greek people quickly discovered that other

European nations were in no mood for compromise. Detailed austerity measures were imposed upon the Greek people – including pension adjustments, increases in VAT and the sequestration of €50 billion of public assets in a special privatization fund – that in normally functioning democracies would be the prerogative of the domestic political process alone.

Greece's plight was, in many ways, a throwback to the nineteenth century. Egypt – at the time a loose cog in the Ottoman Empire – suffered similarly embarrassing financial humiliation in the 1870s. Having borrowed heavily from European creditors as part of an ambitious modernization programme inspired by the construction of the Suez Canal, the Cairo government eventually defaulted. Fearful that Egypt would otherwise face the wrath of Europe's imperial powers – and keen to restore its modernization programme sooner rather than later – Cairo's leaders acquiesced to the appointment of two European financial 'watchdogs'. Their initial austerity demands were largely ignored, leading to a complete breakdown of trust. London and Paris eventually established a tougher 'Dual Control' system – which understandably provoked a nationalist backlash and an army revolt.[13]

To be fair, it has not all been reverse gear in Europe. For many years, former Soviet satellites appeared to have found a home in the European Union's welcoming democratic arms. Poland, for example, went from strength to strength economically following the fall of the Berlin Wall in 1989. Between 1990 and 2015, Polish per capita incomes more than doubled, thanks in large part to major institutional reforms associated with Poland's efforts to join the EU, a feat it eventually accomplished in 2004. The contrast with Ukraine – stuck in a no man's land between the European Union and Russia – is striking. In the early 1990s, Ukraine and Poland had roughly similar living standards but, after two decades of both relative and absolute economic decline, Ukrainian per capita incomes had dropped to less than 40 per cent of those in Poland by 2015.[14]

Yet even in Poland – one of the most visible beneficiaries of Central Europe's reorientation – developments following the global financial crisis raise doubts about the European Union's 'common values'. The victory of the right-wing Law and Justice party in the October 2015 parliamentary elections led to big questions about, oddly enough, law and justice: Jarosław Kaczyński, leader of the Law and Justice party, was accused of making 'political' appointments to the ostensibly independent Constitutional Tribunal. Religious tolerance, meanwhile, appeared to be under threat: an effigy of an Orthodox Jew was burnt in Wrocław, a warning that Poland's anti-Semitic past was in danger of encroaching on its present, while in a radio interview doubtless designed to reassure Poles that they were in no danger of being overrun by Muslim refugees, Kaczyński observed that: 'The church and its teachings are the foundations of Polishness. And everyone, even if they are not believers, has to accept it. Any hand raised against the church is also a hand raised against Poland.'[15]

On the other side of Europe, the UK voted on 23 June 2016 to leave the European Union. The vote was, however, remarkably close: a little under 52 per cent of voters opted for Brexit, whilst the rest preferred to remain in the EU. The Brexiteers appeared to represent a broad church: some saw departure from the EU as a way to flee from the uncertainties of globalization, while others saw Britain's exit as an opportunity to escape the EU's protective embrace, in the process opening up new opportunities to engage with the rest of the world.

Given the deep divisions revealed within British society, it is likely that disengagement from the European Union will prove to be both tricky and prolonged. The last time England attempted to break away from Europe was in the 1530s, when Henry VIII initiated the English Reformation in order to divorce Catherine of Aragon. Battles between Protestants and Catholics (the equivalent of Brexiteers and Remainers) raged for the next 150 years. James II, the last (and short-lived) Catholic king of England, Scotland and Ireland, was crowned in 1685, but deposed three years later thanks to the Glorious Revolution, in which Protestant powerbrokers put William of Orange (son-in-law and nephew of James, but, importantly, a Protestant) on the throne alongside James's daughter, Mary. Only then did the Protestants effectively secure their victory; and only then was the primacy of parliament properly established. When it comes to Europe, breaking up is hard to do.

MAYBE THE FUTURE ISN'T BRIGHT AFTER ALL

Elsewhere, there are occasional nuggets of good news. Cuba may be emerging from Fidel Castro's brand of salsa communism. Investors have flocked to Vietnam. Myanmar is no longer completely shunned. Even Iran may be coming in from the cold. Nevertheless, hopes that Western values would spread far and wide have been overplayed.[16] According to Freedom House, countries with a decline in freedom outnumbered those with an increase in every single year between 2006 and 2014.[17]

Back in the 1920s and 1930s, Lincoln Steffens and George Bernard Shaw thought they had seen the future. They hadn't. Soviet communism ultimately failed to deliver. In an earlier, supposedly more peaceful era, Norman Angell's supporters hoped that common sense would prevail, that war would be futile because it would be mutually destructive. Economic interdependency was so great that only a madman would go to war. Having suffered brain damage at birth, Kaiser Wilhelm II unfortunately went on to prove the point.[18] Francis Fukuyama admitted in 1992 that he could not guarantee the end of history. For him, the biggest objection came from Nietzsche, 'who believed that modern democracy represented not the self-mastery of former slaves, but the unconditional victory of the slave and a kind of slavish morality . . . The last man had no desire to be recognized as greater than others, and without such desire no excellence or achievement was possible.'[19]

Yet, as Soviet communism collapsed, Fukuyama's disciples were convinced that Western liberal democracy – and Western free-market capitalism – had triumphed. Why? Why, given a litany of false prophets throughout recorded history, were Western observers so convinced that the world's political and economic rivalries could finally be put to rest?

One answer is that, as human beings, we cannot help but believe in mankind's progress. Adam Smith described his 'four stages of history': the age of hunters, the age of shepherds, the age of agriculture and the age of commerce. Karl Marx – heavily influenced by Hegel's view that all reality could be rationalized – thought there were six stages: primitive communism, the slave society, feudalism, capitalism, the 'first phase' of communism (which Lenin termed socialism) and, finally, communism's 'higher phase', in which there would be no states, no classes and no property. Just imagine.

Another answer is simply that the enemy in the Cold War had been defeated. Soviet regimes in Eastern Europe quickly became members of the European Union, the Russian Empire crumbled, Belarus, Georgia and Ukraine became independent states – as did those in Central Asia – and Russia itself was forcibly converted into a free-market capitalist society through a massive sale of state assets at knock-down prices. With the Soviet Empire defeated – and Soviet communism's reach around the world rapidly shrinking – democracy and free-market capitalism had self-evidently triumphed. Even better, as more and more nations signed up to the Western model, there was every chance that the world would become a lot wealthier: after all, if the Western model had defeated all comers, it made sense for everyone else to sign up to its economic and political programme.

A more nuanced answer, however, has to go back to 1944, one year before the end of the Second World War, when a new international architecture was being created, supposedly to ensure lasting economic success under American hegemony or, at the very least, American enlightened self-interest. That architecture is now showing severe signs of subsidence.

This is, perhaps, not the end of history after all. Western-led globalization is in big trouble. We may be witnessing the collapse of the postwar international economic and political order. What follows may eventually lead to the re-emergence of imperial rivalries, a throwback to the nineteenth century. In the short term, however, the world is likely to be increasingly chaotic. As such, huge challenges lie ahead for the West.

2

THE NEW IMPERIUM

PASSING OF THE BATON

It was 1944 when the Allies – more specifically, the Americans and British – began to think properly about a post-war international economic and financial order. They certainly did not want to go back to the chaos of the 1930s, a decade of depression, devaluation and default, and nor did they ultimately wish to impose huge costs on a defeated Germany.[1] Instead, they hoped to create a system that would avoid both the 'beggar-thy-neighbour' behaviours of the 1930s and the hardships imposed on the defeated nations, which resulted from the iniquitous post-First World War Treaty of Versailles. The Americans had a further ambition. They hoped also to get rid of the nineteenth-century empires, which, in their view, had substantially contributed to the carnage seen in the first half of the twentieth century. That meant, in particular, dismantling the British Empire. It is no mere chance that the conditions Washington laid down for helping the British financially during and after the Second World War were notably tough.

The Bretton Woods Conference – which took place in July 1944 in the Mount Washington Hotel in Bretton Woods, New Hampshire – appeared to represent a marked departure from previous behaviour. There was a strong desire to avoid the foolishness of the interwar period, during which time attempts to return to the gold standard at pre-war exchange rates had led to both painful austerity and ultimate economic and financial chaos. Having re-joined the gold standard in 1925 – a year after John Maynard Keynes had termed gold 'a barbarous relic'[2] – the UK was eventually forced to devalue sterling in 1931, thanks to a perilously weak balance of payments position made worse as the world plunged into recession at the beginning of that decade.

As it turned out, sterling's departure proved to be an unexpected blessing, insulating the UK from the very worst of the economic and financial collapse taking place elsewhere. Yet the Americans did not see it that way: from their perspective, Britain's actions were the start of what today would be described as 'currency wars'. Post Second World War, such financial instability was to be avoided.

There was an equally strong desire to rid the world of the protectionist practices that had swamped the world economy in the 1930s. Part of this was a pure belief in the benefits of free trade, a return to British liberal values of the nineteenth century. Also, however, it was an attempt by the Americans to drive another nail into the coffin of the British Empire, which had managed to survive the traumas of the Great Depression through the adoption in 1932 of Imperial Preference, a protectionist policy based on the principle of 'home producers first, empire producers second and foreign producers last'.[3] Given that Congress had pushed through the infamous Smoot–Hawley tariff in 1930 – which arguably triggered the wholesale move to protectionism in the years that followed – it was a bit rich of the Americans to complain. Still, at the end of the Second World War, the US was rich and had a large trade surplus, whereas Britain was more or less bust. As John Maynard Keynes discovered during the Bretton Woods negotiations, cleverness was no substitute for diplomacy and deep pockets.

THE BEDROCK OF INSTITUTIONAL GLOBALIZATION

These ambitions – driven primarily by American self-interest – led to the creation of three institutions that became the bedrock of post-war economic and financial globalization: the International Monetary Fund (IMF), the World Bank – eventually a supercharged aid agency, but initially designed to facilitate post-war reconstruction – and, two years after the end of the Second World War, the General Agreement on Tariffs and Trade (otherwise known as GATT, the precursor to the World Trade Organization).

The IMF was to be run by an American. Unfortunately, the only one in contention – Harry Dexter White, Keynes' Bretton Woods nemesis – was rumoured to be a Soviet spy.[4] President Truman decided that a Belgian, Camille Gutt, would have to do instead. Ever since, the IMF has been headed by a European: one Spaniard, one Dutchman, one German and a remarkable five French men and women (to be precise, one woman, Christine Lagarde). The World Bank, in contrast, has always been headed by an American (the latest incumbent, Dr Jim Yong Kim, was born in South Korea, but went with his family to the US at the age of five). Both institutions, however, are based in Washington and both depend financially on America's deep pockets.

While the IMF's design was still on the drawing board, a fundamental disagreement emerged between the British view (in effect, that of Keynes) and the American view (championed by White). The British saw the Fund as a simple international clearing house, providing short-term credit to those countries which, temporarily, had encountered a balance of payments difficulty. Like a bank overdraft facility, the funds would be provided automatically, with no questions asked. Keynes thought this could only be achieved through the issuance of a new international currency, which he termed *bancor*. This would both sever direct links with gold – thereby reducing the risks of deflation in the event of a gold shortage, as had been seen in the late nineteenth century and, more painfully, in the 1920s and 1930s – and limit the influence of the US dollar (and, by implication, American economic ambitions).

The Americans – who at the time had a healthy balance of payments surplus and the world's dominant currency – understandably feared that they would be on the hook for all sorts of expansionist excesses elsewhere in the world (Keynes himself was not to be trusted on this score). White had no desire to make the US a passive 'creditor of last resort', as Keynes appeared to be suggesting. At the Bretton Woods conference, White effectively sidelined Keynes in order to push his own plans through. There was to be no *bancor*, no other newly created international currency and no automatic overdraft facility. Instead, there was going to be a new monetary system, in which dollars would be linked to gold (and in theory would be as good as gold), where countries would only be able to adjust their exchange rates with IMF approval (an attempt to prevent a repeat of the competitive devaluations of the 1930s), and where the Fund could impose 'conditionality' on those countries that needed financial help.

As the Fund's biggest economy, the US also paid in the largest 'quota' or subscription. That in turn initially gave it a 33 per cent share of the vote. As important decisions required a four-fifths majority, the US therefore had a blocking veto. Whenever decisions were made, debtor nations alone – countries with balance of payments deficits – were the ones that typically had to adjust their domestic policies. Thanks to its veto, the US, the world's major surplus nation, had immunity, even if Washington itself might on occasion have been responsible for the build-up of international financial imbalances. The IMF became, at first, a US creditor's charter: with persistent capital outflows (the flipside of its balance of payments current account surplus) the US had become the world's premier banker.

Admittedly, the US was not in complete control. While it could block the actions of others, it was equally possible that the others could block Washington's own initiatives: after all, enough smaller countries could form their own 'superminority' in order to veto decisions that might otherwise have gone through.[5] And over time, US influence has diminished: in 2016, the US vote share had dropped to around 16 per cent. Nevertheless, the principles established in the IMF's early days still very much applied at the beginning of the twenty-first century: in particular, it was still better to be a creditor than a debtor (unless, like the US, you happened to be the issuer of the world's principal reserve currency).

THE RED MENACE AND THE DEEP POCKETS

Despite the best of intentions, the IMF and the World Bank simply did not have the financial firepower to deliver a sustainable post-war settlement. In particular, the IMF's job was to manage only temporary balance of payments distortions, specifically to keep the financial wheels of world trade well oiled. It could do nothing of significance to help rebuild war-torn Europe, which was basically bust. Yet, following George Kennan's famous 'long telegram' to the US secretary of state in February 1946, Washington felt obliged to act.

At the time, Kennan was deputy head of the US mission in Moscow. His suspicion of Soviet ambitions – and, indeed, his recognition that Moscow was equally suspicious of Western ambitions – led him to advocate a policy of containment against potential Soviet expansion. At the end of his 5,500-word missive, he reached five conclusions. Of these, from Europe's point of view, the fourth was particularly pertinent:

(4) We must formulate and put forward for other nations a much more positive and constructive picture of sort of world we would like to see than we have put forward in past. It is not enough to urge people to develop political processes similar to our own. Many foreign peoples, in Europe at least, are tired and frightened by experiences of past, and are less interested in abstract freedom than in security. They are seeking guidance rather than responsibilities. We

should be better able than Russians to give them this. And unless we do, Russians certainly will.[6]

A little over a year later, the US reached into its deep financial pockets. The catalyst was Secretary of State George Marshall's Harvard speech of 5 June 1947:

The truth of the matter is that Europe's requirements for the next three or four years of foreign food and other essential products – principally from America – are so much greater than her present ability to pay that she must have substantial additional help or face economic, social, and political deterioration of a very grave character.

The remedy lies in breaking the vicious circle and restoring the confidence of the European people in the economic future of their own countries and of Europe as a whole. The manufacturer and the farmer throughout wide areas must be able and willing to exchange their products for currencies the continuing value of which is not open to question.[7]

The European Recovery Plan – better known as the 'Marshall Plan' – ran for four years from April 1948. The numbers involved were staggering: the US provided $13 billion in aid, worth almost 5 per cent of US national income in 1948 and around $130 billion in 2015 dollars. At America's insistence, the money was to be allocated by the Europeans themselves through the Organisation for European Economic Co-operation (OEEC). Four GATT rounds in just nine years – all aimed at reducing trade tariffs – also helped to kick-start economic activity: Geneva in 1947 (pre-dating Marshall), Annecy in 1949, Torquay in 1950 and Geneva (again) in 1956.

There were, however, several strings attached. To keep Soviet communism at bay, European nations were encouraged to embrace free-market principles. That meant getting rid of unnecessary regulations, abolishing price controls, supporting free trade and, bit by bit, rebuilding Europe on principles consistent with Washington's strategic ambitions. There was to be no return to the sovereign rivalries that had led to hostilities in the first half of the century: economic interdependency was to be paramount, and empire-building was to be but a distant memory.

Moreover, the Americans were in no mood to offer 'special favours' to wartime allies. This was especially problematic for the newly elected Labour government in Britain: its odd mix of socialist ambitions (nationalization, free healthcare for all, a generous social safety net) and imperial nostalgia was anathema to Washington. Westminster may not have realized it at the time, but ultimately the British government was making a choice: its enthusiasm for high levels of social welfare kept it financially disabled well into the 1950s, a result that left it increasingly dependent on US financial help and less able to prop up its empire, much of which disappeared in no more than a puff of smoke in the late 1940s. The ultimate humiliation, however, came in 1956, when, in a joint action with France and Israel, British soldiers seized the Suez Canal, recently nationalized by Egypt's charismatic leader, President Gamal Abdel Nasser. The British had not told Washington beforehand – largely because the White House would likely have objected – and nor had they bargained on Washington's subsequent wrath. President Eisenhower threatened the withdrawal of financial support to Britain. This, given the country's precarious balance of payments position, would have meant a humiliating devaluation of sterling and lasting international opprobrium. In the event, British troops were withdrawn, Anthony Eden, the British prime minister, fell on his sword, and to all intents and purposes, the British Empire was consigned to history.

The Marshall Plan did not solve all the problems. Both the French franc and the Italian lira ratcheted downwards in the late 1940s, eventually triggering a wholesale devaluation of European currencies against the US dollar in September 1949. However, it proved to be an essential building block for a new (Western) European economy, which in the 1950s and 1960s delivered extraordinary gains in living standards. Such was its success that by 1960 both the Americans and the Canadians wanted a piece of the action. The Organisation for European Economic Co-operation became the Organisation for Economic Co-operation and Development (OECD), more informally known as the 'rich nations' club'. In 2016, it had 35 members worldwide, up from the OEEC's 18 (European) members in 1948.

ODE TO JOY

A second essential building block for a new Europe was the establishment of the European Coal and Steel Community (ECSC) under the 1951 Treaty of Paris, inspired by the Schuman Declaration – named after the eponymous French foreign minister – the previous year. The Declaration was a combination of the noble and the practical:

> The contribution which an organized and living Europe can bring to civilization is indispensable to the maintenance of peaceful relations . . .
>
> . . . Europe will not be made all at once, or according to a single plan. It will be built through concrete achievements which first create a de facto solidarity. The coming together of the nations of Europe requires the elimination of the age-old opposition of France and Germany. Any action taken must in the first place concern these two countries.
>
> . . . [T]he French Government proposes . . . that Franco-German production of coal and steel as a whole be placed under a common High Authority, within the framework of an organization open to the participation of the other countries of Europe. The pooling of coal and steel production should immediately provide for the setting up of common foundations for economic development as a

first step in the federation of Europe, and will change the destinies of those regions which have long been devoted to the manufacture of munitions of war, of which they have been the most constant victims.

The solidarity in production thus established will make it plain that any war between France and Germany becomes not merely unthinkable, but materially impossible.[8]

Initially, six countries joined the ECSC – France, Germany, Italy, Belgium, Luxembourg and the Netherlands. In 1957, those countries went on to sign the Treaty of Rome, the agreement which led to the creation of the European Economic Community in January 1958. Some 34 years later, thanks to the Maastricht Treaty,[9] what started off as a seemingly humble arrangement involving coal and steel became the European Union.

By then, the original 6 members had become 12, with the UK, Ireland and Denmark joining in 1973, Greece in 1981, and Spain and Portugal in 1986. By 2015, membership was up to 28 nations, with many Eastern European countries – formerly under the Soviet yoke – now part of a Union with a total population of over 500 million citizens, making it the third most populated 'country' in the world after China and India. A year later, the EU suffered its first major membership reversal, following the outcome of the UK 'Brexit' referendum.

TWELVE MUSKETEERS

The third essential building block was the one with teeth. The North Atlantic Treaty was signed in April 1949. The 12 founding nations[10] adopted a *Three Musketeers* approach to their collective defence, with Article 5 of the Treaty stating that 'an armed attack against one or more of them . . . shall be considered an attack against them all'. At first, the concept that became NATO was not much more than words on a piece of paper, but following the outbreak of the Korean War in June 1950, a new sense of urgency, in the light of a perceived Soviet threat, led to the establishment of the Supreme Headquarters Allied Powers Europe (SHAPE), initially based in France, but, following de Gaulle's 1966 decision to withdraw from NATO, thereafter located in Belgium.

NATO was not there merely to handle the growing Soviet danger. It was designed also to foster deeper European political integration and to counter any threat of a return of the nationalist militarism that had led to so much death and destruction in the first half of the twentieth century. It worked for one simple reason: the US felt compelled to have a permanent military presence in Europe. In 1950, just over 120,000 American troops were stationed in Europe. In 1955 – which marked the peak in terms of manpower – there were 413,000. Of these, the lion's share – around 270,000 – was stationed in West Germany. There were also, however, around 55,000 troops in France, 47,000 in the UK and a few thousand in Italy, Portugal and Spain.[11]

WILSON'S VISION

The end of the Second World War marked an extraordinary change relative to the American position of splendid isolationism in the late nineteenth century and its unenthusiastic involvements in world affairs in the first half of the twentieth century. Following the American Civil War, the US had few serious military ambitions – other than on its border with Mexico – and little in the way of an army or navy. By the 1880s, the American army was smaller than Bulgaria's.[12] An 1881 official review of the navy's seafaring power revealed that only around 50 vessels were operational – even though the fleet was supposed to amount to 140 ships – and, of those that could set sail, only 17 had hulls clad in iron. It was all rather pathetic. Still, there was little interest in getting involved in silly wars elsewhere in the world. As President Cleveland noted in 1885: 'It is the policy of neutrality, rejecting any share in foreign broils and ambitions upon other continents and repelling their intrusion here.'[13]

Admittedly, Theodore Roosevelt adopted a more aggressive worldview, warning of endemic weaknesses in countries that were overly 'humanitarian' – in particular, that they could 'invite destruction . . . by some less-advanced [civilization]'. To prove his point, he commanded his 'Great White Fleet' to circumnavigate the world, which it duly did between 1907 and 1909. By the end of the First World War, however, Woodrow Wilson was offering a rather different view. Championing the principle of self-determination, he argued that 'Self-governed nations do not fill their neighbor states with spies or set the course of intrigue to bring about some crucial posture of affairs which will give them an opportunity to strike and make conquest.'[14]

For him, successful self-governed nations would have ethnic and linguistic unity: a fine idea if the aim was merely to break up empires, but absolutely hopeless if the result was stranded minorities, human rights abuses and ethnic cleansing. In an interwar European context, the imposition of self-determination left a still very large Germany surrounded by a variety of much smaller – and less powerful – states: rather than contending with the might of the Russian Empire or a rather more friendly but still muscular Austro-Hungarian Empire, Germany now only had to worry about Poland, Lithuania and the Czech Republic – easy pickings, it turned out, for a future German megalomaniac (of Austrian birth) who was keen to bring stranded ethnic Germans back into the fold.

Wilson, of course, hoped that future conflicts could be avoided through the creation of the League of Nations. The results proved disastrous. The Senate voted against US membership in 1919; Germany, Japan and Italy eventually walked away; and the Soviet Union, which only joined in 1934, was promptly (and rightly, although possibly illegally) expelled in 1939 for invading Finland.

The US may have been as reluctant to involve itself in the Second World War as it had been to take part in the First World War, but its involvement was ultimately an opportunity to rewrite the world order and, for that matter, America's part within it. This was not fully recognized at the time. Following the Japanese attack on Pearl Harbor on 7 December 1941, Winston Churchill was privately thankful: 'It was . . . a blessing that Japan attacked the United States and thus brought America wholeheartedly and unitedly into the war. Greater good fortune has rarely happened to the British Empire than this event.'[15]

Churchill's relief, however, was not fully justified: having faced the Axis threat on its own, Britain's survival was now more or less guaranteed, but its empire was about to crumble. A new superpower was on the scene.

US attitudes as the war ended were, in many ways, a revival of the Jeffersonian doctrine in favour of an 'empire for liberty'. In Thomas Jefferson's own words:

> We feel that we are acting under obligations not confined to the limits of our own society . . . we are acting for all mankind . . . circumstances denied to others, but indulged to us, have imposed on us the duty of proving what is the degree of freedom and self-government in which a society may venture to leave its individual members.[16]

In other words, the US had a moral purpose. Its job was to demonstrate the value of freedom and democracy to countries far and wide, consistent with the much later arguments of Fukuyama and the *End of History*. After the Second World War, the Jeffersonian approach was given economic, financial and military backbone. This was not just a return to the Wilsonian principles that supported self-determination; it was also a response to the interwar economic and political failures and, importantly, to the perceived threat from the Soviet Union. The US could no longer afford to be insular – and no longer did it want to be. The institutions it either helped create (the IMF, the World Bank, GATT and NATO) or nurture (thanks to the Marshall Plan, what eventually became the European Union) provided a framework in which industrialized nations were able to flourish both economically and politically. The US may have been a reluctant imperium, but whatever its misgivings, its economic, financial and military strengths gave it the chance to reshape the world in its own image. For many years – even with pitfalls along the way – the approach seemed to work. Under US tutelage, many parts of the world experienced an economic transformation.

3

RELATIVE SUCCESS

A MIRACLE?

At first sight, increases in living standards in the industrialized world in the decades following the end of the Second World War seem to be nothing short of remarkable. The US itself did well, its per capita incomes more or less doubling between 1950 and 1980. Others successfully pursued their own versions of the American Dream. In 1950, German per capita incomes were a mere 41 per cent of those in the US. By 1980, they had risen to 76 per cent. French per capita incomes in 1950 were 54 per cent of those in the US. Thirty years later, they were up to 79 per cent. Italian incomes went from 33 per cent to 70 per cent. On the other side of the world, Japanese incomes jumped from a mere 20 per cent of those in the US to 72 per cent.

Not all industrialized countries made as much progress, but that was largely because they had not experienced the level of destruction faced by war-torn Japan or the continental European nations that had been overrun by troops and bombs. UK living standards in 1950 were 73 per cent of those in the US, dropping marginally to 70 per cent by 1980.

Swiss citizens began the 1950s with incomes around 95 per cent of those in the US; by 1980, they had reached parity with their American cousins. Canadians slowly closed the gap with their southern neighbours, while Australian average incomes stayed at around 78 per cent of those in the US.

A FRACTURED WORLD

Countries and regions elsewhere in the world had a completely different experience. Behind the Iron Curtain, nations struggled to make any significant economic progress. Czechoslovaks, who had enjoyed considerable economic success in the interwar period, saw their average living standards fall from 37 per cent of those in the US in 1950 to 33 per cent in 1980. Poles, Hungarians and Soviet citizens made modest gains, but in relative terms were left for dust by the more dynamic Western European nations: their incomes per capita were still only between 30 and 35 per cent of those in the US in 1980. Over the same period, the incomes of the eight largest economies in Latin America rose only modestly compared with those in the US: on average up from 28 per cent to a still paltry 32 per cent. Chinese and Indian citizens were impoverished throughout, their average living standards stranded at only around 5 per cent of those in the US. Shockingly, incomes in some sub-Saharan African nations fell not only relative to those in the US, but also in absolute terms: citizens of Angola, the Central African Republic, Chad, Somalia and Uganda were worse off in 1980 than their parents had been in 1950. The decades following the Second World War may have witnessed remarkable economic progress in some parts of the world, but sadly the experience was not universal.

BUSINESS AS USUAL

Oddly enough, the success of the industrialized nations in the decades following the end of the Second World War could be seen merely as a return to business as usual. Constant fighting in the first half of the twentieth century, interspersed with periods of economic and financial chaos, had left most European nations licking their wounds. Yet, within a handful of decades, many had returned to the relative positions seen at the beginning of the twentieth century, when Norman Angell was writing about the futility of war. Consider, for example, the living standards of typical Northern Europeans[1] and Americans. In 1900, per capita incomes in Northern Europe averaged around 75 per cent of those in the US. Having dropped to a mere 35 per cent in 1945, they were back to around 75 per cent by 1980.

The economic success of the industrial nations owed a lot to the influence of the key post-war institutions – the IMF, GATT, NATO and, later, the European Union. First, they helped undo much of the damage caused by the protectionism and isolationism that spread during the interwar period. Second, their existence dramatically reduced the chances of conflict in continental Europe: the peace that followed contributed hugely to lasting economic success. Third, their presence made it less likely that countries would do 'dumb things': successive effective GATT rounds made trade restrictions seem almost unethical, while the IMF's supportive presence ensured that trade finance was mostly available even when countries were suffering from temporary balance of payments difficulties.

This did not mean that chaos could be ruled out altogether. Rather, when chaos threatened, it could be dealt with more easily, even if the occasional nation state suffered a degree of political humiliation along the way.

FOR A FEW DOLLARS MORE . . .

One potential source of chaos from the very beginnings of Bretton Woods was the likelihood that eventually the US would not be able to meet its commitment to exchanging dollars for gold on demand at the preestablished rate. All governments occasionally have to make use of the printing press, typically to finance costly military ventures. In the UK, where price data are available all the way back to the seventeenth century, inflation reached double digits during the War of the Spanish Succession (1701–14), the early stages of the Napoleonic Wars (specifically, the War of the Second Coalition, 1799–1802) and the two twentieth-century world wars. For the US, big inflationary shocks were associated with the Revolutionary War (1775–83), the Civil War (1861–65), the tail end of the First World War and both the early stages of US involvement in the Second World War and the war's immediate aftermath. There was also a temporary spike during the Korean War (1950–53).

From the mid-1950s through to the early 1960s, US inflation was very well behaved – good news for US citizens and equally good news for the health of the global financial system. Stable monetary conditions in the US left central bank reserve managers around the world confident that US dollars could be swapped for gold at the prevailing fixed exchange rate of $35 per ounce.

That all changed, however, as the US got itself more heavily involved in Vietnam. Although problems had been bubbling away in what was formerly French Indochina for years – and American advisers had been involved there since the early 1950s – it was not until 1965 that a serious US troop presence was established. As the costs of the Vietnam War escalated, so inflation began to pick up. Lyndon B. Johnson's 'Great Society' ambitions and the small matter of a journey to the moon added (rocket) fuel to the fire. By the end of the 1960s, inflation was threatening to hit 6 per cent, higher than at any point since the Korean War. Rapid increases in domestic demand also meant that the US was in danger of losing its 'creditor nation' status: its balance of payments current account surplus had shrunk to a mere $399 million in 1969, down from $6.8 billion five years earlier.

Foreign holders of dollars were becoming increasingly restless. More dollars were held in reserve abroad than could be redeemed for American gold. According to the IMF, 'In 1966, foreign central banks and governments held over 14 billion US dollars. The United States had $13.2 billion in gold reserves, but only $3.2 billion of that was available to cover foreign dollar holdings. The rest was needed to cover domestic holdings.'[2]

Put another way, the entire financial system was vulnerable to a public sector version of a bank run. If other nations thought there was any risk that their dollar holdings would be devalued, they would sensibly demand that their reserves should immediately be converted into gold. If, however, everyone thought that way, then devaluation would become inevitable. The link between dollars and gold established by Harry Dexter White in the 1940s was ultimately an act of faith: by the mid-1960s, however, faith was in short supply. In 1968, the US decided no longer to redeem privately held dollars for gold. Three years later, President Nixon announced live on US radio and television, in what became known as the 'Nixon Shock', that:

> We must protect the position of the American dollar as a pillar of monetary stability around the world . . .
>
> In recent weeks, the speculators have been waging an all-out war on the American dollar. The strength of a nation's currency is based on the strength of that nation's economy – and the American economy is by far the strongest in the world. Accordingly, I have directed the Secretary of the Treasury to . . . suspend temporarily the convertibility of the dollar into gold or other reserve assets, except in amounts and conditions determined to be in the interest of monetary stability and in the best interests of the United States . . .
>
> Let me lay to rest the bugaboo of what is called devaluation.
>
> If you want to buy a foreign car or take a trip abroad, market conditions may cause your dollar to buy slightly less. But if you are among the overwhelming majority of Americans who buy American-made products in America, your dollar will be worth just as much tomorrow as it is today.

The effect of this action, in other words, will be to stabilize the dollar.

Now, this action will not win us any friends among the international money traders. But our primary concern is with the American workers, and with fair competition around the world.

To our friends abroad, including the many responsible members of the international banking community who are dedicated to stability and the flow of trade, I give this assurance: The United States has always been, and will continue to be, a forward-looking and trustworthy trading partner. In full cooperation with the International Monetary Fund and those who trade with us, we will press for the necessary reforms to set up an urgently needed new international monetary system. Stability and equal treatment is in everybody's best interest. I am determined that the American dollar must never again be a hostage in the hands of international speculators.

I am taking one further step to protect the dollar, to improve our balance of payments, and to increase jobs for Americans. As a temporary measure, I am today imposing an additional tax of 10 percent on goods imported into the United States. This is a better solution for international trade than direct controls on the amount of imports.

This import tax is a temporary action. It isn't directed against any other country. It is an action to make certain that American products will not be at a disadvantage because of unfair exchange rates. When the unfair treatment is ended, the import tax will end as well.

As a result of these actions, the product of American labor will be more competitive, and the unfair edge that some of our foreign competition has will be removed. This is a major reason why our trade balance has eroded over the past 15 years.[3]

Nixon's statement was remarkable in many ways. The idea that the dollar's vulnerability simply reflected the behaviour of speculators was absurd – unless, that is, President de Gaulle's earlier decision to swap all

French dollar reserves into gold meant that he, too, was a speculator. The claim that the US economy was the strongest in the world was a deliberate act of obfuscation: it may have been the world's *biggest* economy, but a combination of rising inflation and a worsening balance of payments position suggested that it was far from being the strongest. The suggestion that American-produced goods would cost roughly the same as before conveniently ignored the fact that many of those goods had import content, which, thanks to a weaker dollar and a higher import tariff, would now be more expensive. And the idea that the US would remain a forward-looking and trustworthy trading partner was, on the face of it, delusional.

AVOIDING THE 1930S

This was classic 1930s 'beggar-thy-neighbour' behaviour. Yet what followed was not a 1930s outcome. The Bretton Woods exchange rate system totally fractured in 1973, but unlike in the 1930s, the currency upheavals that followed did not lead to a deep depression, even if John Connally, the combative US Treasury secretary, had famously told his European counterparts that 'the dollar may be our currency but it's your problem' – a sentiment echoed by Nixon when he rebuked H.R. Haldeman, his chief of staff, saying 'I don't give a shit about the [Italian] lira.'[4]

True, all currencies lost value against gold – hardly a surprising outcome given that the Americans had basically severed the link between the historically trustworthy metallic store of value and fiat money. The US dollar itself dropped in value from $36 per ounce in 1970 to $615 per ounce ten years later. But there was also a new-found degree of flexibility. Some currencies ended up stronger than others, largely reflecting varying national tolerances for inflation. The Germans and Swiss hated inflation: their tougher approach to monetary policy helped the German mark and Swiss franc to rise against the US dollar by 93 per cent and 157 per cent respectively, a disinflationary process that kept German and Swiss inflation at around 5 per cent per year through the decade – very low by the standards of the day. The Japanese yen rose a more modest 58 per cent, leaving the Japanese economy with an average inflation rate of 9 per cent. Sterling was more or less unchanged against the US dollar between the beginning and the end of the decade: over the ten years, the UK suffered an annual inflation rate of approaching 14 per cent. The Italian lira, meanwhile, fell almost 27 per cent against the US dollar and also ended up with an inflation rate close to 14 per cent.

THE IMF RIDES TO THE RESCUE

With all this monetary chaos, it would be reasonable to think that the IMF would be in trouble, perhaps heading in monetary terms towards oblivion, in much the same way as the League of Nations had done in diplomatic terms four decades earlier. Yet, as the 1970s progressed, it became increasingly apparent that, with a move to floating exchange rates, the IMF's role was, if anything, strengthening.

First, the dollar's heightened volatility meant that reserve managers elsewhere in the world craved an alternative monetary store of value that would be neither dollars nor gold. The IMF's Special Drawing Rights (SDRs) – known colloquially as 'paper gold' – proved to be just the ticket. Representing a basket of major currencies, they allowed reserve managers to escape the heightened dollar volatility associated with the vagaries of US monetary policy.

Second, with the abandonment of the fixed currency regime, the IMF's 'surveillance' role was bolstered: most major industrialized countries were understandably fearful that a world of floating currencies could lead to a series of 'beggar-thy-neighbour' outcomes, particularly given the heightened opportunity for currency manipulation. With a newly enhanced surveillance role thanks to a Second Amendment agreed to by its Interim Committee in 1976 (whose members decided that Jamaica would be a nice place to meet), the IMF was fast becoming the world's financial policeman.

Third, the quadrupling of oil prices at the end of 1973 – triggered by an oil embargo imposed by Arab nations on Western nations regarded as being overly sympathetic to Israel following the Yom Kippur War of that year – had left the world facing a huge 'petrodollar' problem. Saudi Arabia and other oil producers suddenly had more dollars than they knew what to do with. These petrodollars were increasingly recycled through the world financial system, leading to the creation of so-called 'external imbalances' – large and, in some cases, unsustainable balance of payments deficits, particularly in Latin America – that in time would require treatment by the IMF.

Fourth, even as oil prices rose, the slowdown in global economic activity in the 1970s meant that many commodity-producing nations – particularly those in Latin America and Africa – were suddenly faced with severe income losses and, as a consequence, severely weakened balance of payments positions. Aggregate demand for IMF financing arrangements went up dramatically in the late 1970s, even as industrialized nations discovered that they could escape the IMF's clutches by using their exchange rates as 'shock absorbers'. The IMF, meanwhile, was usefully able to respond: having sold a third of its gold reserves in the late 1970s at a remarkably inflated price, it suddenly had very deep pockets.

Fifth, even though most industrialized countries rather liked their new-found monetary freedom, a select few still managed to end up in terrible financial trouble. In 1976, both the UK and Italy had to go 'cap in hand' to Washington. Yet, despite the apparent ignominy of needing its help, the Fund proved useful as a way of forcing through tough but necessary economic and financial decisions that might otherwise have disappeared in a puff of political smoke.

SPLINTERS IN THE CABINET

Perhaps the strongest evidence for this comes from the fraught discussions that took place within the British Cabinet in 1976, a few weeks after Denis Healey, the chancellor of the exchequer, had been forced to abandon a trip to Hong Kong, turning back from Heathrow as the financial markets seemingly went into meltdown. According to the minutes of the Cabinet meeting that took place on 23 November, Jim Callaghan, the prime minister, observed that:

> The Cabinet faced a very serious question: did they think that they could and should afford to pay the price the IMF were asking for a loan; and, if not, what were the consequences? If they failed to reach agreement with the IMF, the Government faced the risk of the exchange rate falling out of control, with reserves totally inadequate for the purposes of intervention, with implications for prices and unemployment which could break the partnership between the Government and the unions. On the other hand, if an agreement were reached on the lines at present envisaged by the IMF, this too could strain the Government's relationship with the trade union movement beyond breaking point and put the Social Contract at risk.[5]

Summing up the discussion, Callaghan went on to note: 'There was widespread agreement that the Government must have the loan from the IMF . . . Nevertheless many of the Cabinet at present felt that the scale of the public expenditure cuts at present proposed was too great to accept.'[6]

Two days later, the bickering in the Cabinet continued, with some – notably Tony Benn, the secretary of state for energy – urging a completely different approach. Benn submitted to Cabinet his own proposals the following week. He wanted a national recovery plan based on import quotas, exchange controls, government-directed investment and substantial interest rate cuts (amidst all this, Benn appeared totally to ignore the UK's inflation problem). In other words, Benn wanted to impose a 'siege economy'.[7]

On 15 December, Denis Healey announced a mini-budget that contained a whopping £2.5 billion of spending cuts. The next day, *The*

Times noted that 'the announcement of his economic measures was greeted with calls from both sides for his [Healey's] resignation'. Later, however, Healey declared the negotiation of the IMF loan a pyrrhic defeat.[8] All along, he had wanted to push through tough measures, but had been unable to do so thanks to opposition from within the Cabinet and across the union movement. In his eyes, therefore, the IMF was rather handy: it helped him deliver a policy package that, in his view, Britain badly needed, even if others simply refused to listen.

NEW CUSTOMS . . . NO CUSTOMS

Meanwhile, another organization established in the 1940s was also doing its bit to prevent a repeat of the Great Depression. The GATT Tokyo round lasted from 1973 to 1979, with the participation of a remarkable 102 countries.[9] Customs duties were cut by around one-third across the world's major industrial markets, bringing the average tariff on tradable goods down to 4.7 per cent. The negotiators also attempted to introduce a process of 'harmonization', which basically meant that higher tariffs had to be cut by proportionately more than lower tariffs. All of this was a far cry from the 1930s, when Smoot–Hawley and Imperial Preference ruled the roost. Admittedly, the outcome of the Tokyo round was far from perfect: only a handful of major industrialized countries signed up to many of the agreements – on, for example, subsidies, import licensing and government procurement – suggesting that multilateralism was but a distant dream. Still, unlike the 1930s, protectionism was mostly held at bay.

Ultimately, the post-war institutions offered an international framework for stability, backed by American dollars and military hardware. Even when stability was threatened – most obviously via the Nixon Shock – the institutions were able to adapt to new challenges. By the end of the 1970s, the IMF was stronger than ever before, even if the fixed exchange rate system conjured up in Bretton Woods had been consigned to the scrap heap. Successive GATT rounds had managed to keep protectionism at bay. And, with the European Economic Community's enlargement in 1973, what had originally been a cross-border economic arrangement designed primarily to stop France and Germany from fighting again was fast becoming a major economic, political and social force.

A NEW 'CONCERT OF EUROPE'?

The apparent stability seen during this period carried echoes of an earlier era. Following the Napoleonic Wars, the so-called 'Concert of Europe' was designed to prevent another European-wide conflict. Made up of Europe's nineteenth-century superpowers – Austria, Prussia, Russia, the United Kingdom and, after a decorous breathing space, France – the continent-wide wars that had started with the French Revolution and ended with the Battle of Waterloo had seemingly been put to bed. Over the next hundred years there were plenty of European 'skirmishes', including the Crimean War of 1853–56, in which the Russians were defeated by an unlikely combination of British, French, Ottomans and Sardinians, and the Franco-Prussian War of 1870–71, in which the French were, not for the last time, humiliated by superior German forces. Until 1914, however, there was no European-wide conflict.

This had important implications for Europe's influence in the rest of the world. Freed from continental threats, Europe's 'peripheral' superpowers – the United Kingdom in the west and Russia in the east – were able to expand their global influence, indulging in what became known as the 'Great Game', a term coined by Arthur Conolly, an intelligence office of the 6th Bengal Light Infantry. Through the nineteenth century, the Russians gained control of (among others) Georgia, Armenia, Azerbaijan and outer Manchuria, thanks to wars against the Persians and Ottomans and deals with China's Qing dynasty. The British, meanwhile, became masters of the Indian subcontinent, turned Singapore into a thriving hub for trade in Southeast Asia, made inroads into coastal China and, thanks to Admiral

Lord Nelson's destruction of the Spanish fleet at Trafalgar in 1805, expanded trade with the former Spanish-American Empire unimpeded. The end to war meant not only the beginnings of peace, but also a revolution in world trade. Gone was the costly mercantilist model of the eighteenth and early nineteenth centuries, when empires vied for control of the world's shipping lanes. In its place was a new, British-led embrace of free trade. And Britain, not surprisingly, was the biggest beneficiary. Between 1700 and 1800, British living standards rose by 39 per cent. Over the next hundred years, they more than doubled. By 1900, alongside Switzerland, Great Britain was one of the two richest countries in the world.

If there was a balance of power equivalent to the Concert of Europe after the Second World War, it was between the US and the Soviet Union. Yet, although the Cold War led to a huge increase in weaponry on both sides, there was no balance of power in the economic sphere. The post-war US economic model worked, whilst the Soviet alternative did not. It was not just a reflection of the superiority of free-market capitalism. Importantly, the US had abandoned the insular approach of the late nineteenth and early twentieth centuries. As with the British after the Congress of Vienna, the US and the institutions it supported became the guarantors of trade and finance throughout the industrialized world – an approach that worked extremely well, particularly for the US itself. In the second half of the twentieth century, American living standards tripled, having already doubled in the first half. And, as with the British a century earlier, America's commercial reach extended far and wide, in part reflecting the ubiquity of its global brands. These became a symbol, at least in American minds, of so-called 'soft power' – the idea that the US was capable of winning hearts and minds all over the world with its sugary drinks, its animated characters and its manufactured gizmos.

Joseph Nye, the originator of the term, describes soft power thus:

A country may obtain the outcomes it wants in world politics because other countries – admiring its values, emulating its example, aspiring to its level of prosperity and openness – want to follow it. In this sense, it is also important to set the agenda and attract others in world politics, and not only to force them to change by threatening military force or economic sanctions. This soft power – getting others to want the outcomes that you want – co-opts people rather than coerces them.[10]

And if soft power is partly about brand recognition – in effect, a way of demonstrating to the rest of the world the advantages of a free-market capitalist system – the US ruled supreme. According to *Forbes*, of the top 20 most valuable global brands in 2016, 15 were American.[11] Of those, ten were associated with technology and social media: Apple, for example, was in the top spot, Google was second, Microsoft third and Facebook fifth. Yet, arguably, America's most successful brands are not so much these johnny-come-latelies, but rather those that have withstood the test of time. In the top ten, three stand out: Coca-Cola in fourth position, Disney in eighth and General Electric (GE) in tenth.

Coke was first invented in 1886 and first listed on the New York stock exchange in 1919. Walt Disney Productions was incorporated in 1938 and listed in 1957. GE was created from a merger between Edison Electric and Thomson-Houston Electric in 1892, and was one of the founding members of the Dow Jones Industrial Average in 1896. It soon dropped out; but, having re-joined in 1907, it has not looked back.

Each of these companies has extraordinary global reach. Coca-Cola's success partly stemmed from supplying American GIs with refreshment during the Second World War. Thereafter, its presence became increasingly global: by 1959, there were 1,700 bottling operations supplying more than 100 countries. Its increasing presence behind the Iron Curtain – Hungary and Yugoslavia in 1968, Poland in 1972 and the first Soviet bottling plant in 1985 – only served to emphasize the remarkable dominance of the world's most famous secret recipe. The Chinese got their first taste of the 'Real Thing' in 1978, while Deng Xiaoping was still in the middle of consolidating his power base. By 2015, Coke was selling

1.7 billion 'products' to its thirsty customers each and every day. Roughly half those sales were outside North America.[12]

Disney, meanwhile, increasingly invested abroad, most visibly in Disneyland Paris, Hong Kong Disneyland and Disney Resorts in both Tokyo and Shanghai. Alongside its 200 US stores, there are now also 40 in Japan and 80 scattered through countries in Western Europe. And, while it received a rather poor critical reception in China, Disney clearly thought that *Mulan* – a 1998 animation based on a Chinese poem – might establish a foothold in what promised to be a lucrative new market. As it turned out, the Chinese – like everyone else – preferred the earlier *Lion King*.

As for GE, its success was partly based on the sheer breadth of its operations and, over the long haul, its inventions and innovations. Every two seconds, an aircraft powered by one of its jet engines takes off somewhere in the world. Having invented the X-ray machine at the end of the nineteenth century and having been a pioneer in the development of the electric locomotive, it is now responsible for a good proportion of the world's hospital equipment and rolling stock. And its tinkering with light bulbs continued long after Thomas Edison, its co-founder, invented the incandescent bulb in 1879: like it or loathe it, fluorescent strip lighting was a GE innovation in the 1930s.

TEETH

The US's dominance was not, however, merely a consequence of the success of its brands, even if those brands helped the US achieve its worldwide reach. According to the Reputation Institute, the US does not make it into the 'top 20' most reputable countries, even though its northern neighbour, Canada, is ranked number one.[13] There is a rather obvious reason for this. Unlike Canada – and, for that matter, all the other countries in the top 20 – the US enjoys formidable military clout. Americans may like to think that soft power matters, but for many others it is hard power that makes the difference.

The numbers are staggering. As the Berlin Wall came down in 1989, the US accounted for around 35 per cent of global military spending. There was a temporary spike during the first Gulf War, followed by a further, more sustained increase following the 'War on Terror', George W. Bush's response to 9/11: by 2010, US military spending had risen to over 41 per cent of the global total. It faded thereafter – a combination of cuts in US defence spending and increases by, among others, China and Russia – but nevertheless, the US remained the world's dominant military power. In 2014, only four countries worldwide spent more per capita on their military than the US: Saudi Arabia, the United Arab Emirates, Oman and Israel. China, the second-biggest military power, had a military budget roughly one-third of America's, while Russia's budget was only half of China's.[14]

However, as the British discovered during the twentieth century, economic and military pre-eminence does not last forever. In 1880, the UK had the largest national income among the European Great Powers, enjoyed by far the highest per capita income among those powers, had by some margin the biggest share of world manufacturing output (eclipsing not only the UK's European rivals, but also the US) and by far the most impressive collection of warships: 650,000 tons, compared with 271,000 for France, 200,000 for Russia, 169,000 for the US, 100,000 for Italy and a measly 88,000 for Germany.[15] It was on the verge of creating the biggest empire – in terms of both land mass and population – the world had ever seen. Nor was its empire all 'hard power': it created legal systems, opened trading routes, established giant bureaucracies (notably in India), constructed rail networks and brought cricket to the masses. None of this, however, was enough to ensure the British Empire's survival. As it crumbled, the world succumbed to a prolonged economic and social spasm.

We may be on the verge of something similar today.

4

PRIDE AND THE FALL

ON THE MARCH

When the Berlin Wall came down, it was easy enough to believe that countries previously shackled to Soviet communism would choose the American way. And those hitherto stuck in 'no man's land', frozen like rabbits in the headlights of an on-going Cold War and unable to choose between the US and the Soviet Union, could now link up with the best the West had to offer. Everyone was now free to join in. Globalization was on the march. The Jeffersonian doctrine was becoming truly universal.

And when, a decade or so later, Osama bin Laden's suicidal henchmen launched their murderous attack on New York and Washington, it seemed perfectly reasonable for George W. Bush to warn that 'There are thousands of these terrorists in more than 60 countries' and, later in the same speech, to inform Congress and the world that 'we will pursue nations that provide aid or safe haven to terrorism. Every nation in every region now has a decision to make: Either you are with us or you are with the terrorists.'[1]

He received a standing ovation.

This was strong stuff, an understandable emotional reaction to Al Qaeda's repeated terrorist atrocities.[2] Ultimately, the Bush philosophy relied on the idea that the world was populated by good guys and bad guys; and, moreover, that all right-thinking nations would see the world through the same lens as the US. It depended on that peculiar combination of hard and soft power that the US had cultivated in its attempts to reshape the world in the American way. And, for a time, the world lent the US a sympathetic ear.

THE CRACKS APPEAR

All the while, however, something wasn't quite right. The developed world was already showing signs of relative economic decline. Even as China, India and others were beginning their economic resurgence, European growth rates in the 1980s were heading downwards. Japan had an even worse experience a decade later. The US itself began to slow at the beginning of the new millennium. Elsewhere in the world, free-market philosophies were seemingly contributing to financial instability: most striking was the Asian Crisis of 1997/98 – which hit Thailand, South Korea, Indonesia, Malaysia and Hong Kong hard, even as communist China emerged relatively unscathed – and the broader emerging-market upheavals that followed. The phrase 'Washington Consensus' – which originally referred to a ten-point plan involving, *inter alia*, fiscal discipline, tax reform, trade liberalization, open cross-border capital markets, property rights and privatization[3] – was reinterpreted pejoratively as a symbol of US 'neo-liberalism', leading to huge criticism of the post-war Washington-based institutions that, in earlier decades, had done so much to foster economic stability. Multilateral trade talks stalled. The GATT Uruguay Round was the last to be completed, back in 1994. The World Trade Organization (WTO), GATT's successor, failed to complete a single multilateral trade agreement, with the doomed Doha Round – Uruguay's successor – seemingly preserved in aspic, a relic of an earlier, more optimistic age. The second Gulf War – which ultimately deposed Saddam Hussein – created both a rather modest 'coalition of the willing' and what might be best described as a 'coalition of the very doubtful', a large number of nations that regarded the invasion as an act of folly. Ultimately, only three countries – the UK, Australia and Poland – provided troops to fight on the ground alongside the armies of their American commander-in-chief. Meanwhile, ahead of the invasion, 3 million protesters gathered in Rome, the biggest anti-war rally on record.[4]

Yet none of these has proven as big a threat to the post-war economic order as the financial crisis of 2007/08.

FROM THE NEW CONVENTIONAL WISDOM TO THE GLOBAL FINANCIAL CRISIS

The financial crisis represented the biggest economic and financial setback the Western world had faced since the 1930s, when George Bernard Shaw and his colleagues were extolling the virtues of Soviet communism. The crisis served to undermine almost all the 'cherished beliefs' that had become part of the conventional wisdom over the previous 30 years.

Those beliefs stemmed from an intellectual revolution beginning in the 1970s that came to dominate economic and political thinking through to the early twenty-first century. Its progenitors economically were, more than anyone else, Milton Friedman and Friedrich Hayek. Both believed in free choice, a market economy, sound money and small government. Their views had already been embraced – with limited success – by late 1970s policymakers, rightly frustrated over the apparent inability of standard Keynesian macroeconomic policies to solve the twin evils of unemployment and inflation. In 1979, Jimmy Carter appointed Paul Volcker – a believer in the tenets of Friedman's monetarism – to head the US Federal Reserve. In the UK, Jim Callaghan and Denis Healey tentatively introduced monetary targeting – much to the irritation of the trade unions – in 1977. It was not, however, until the election of Margaret

Thatcher as the UK's prime minister in 1979 and, a year later, Ronald Reagan's election as president of the US that things really began to change: no amount of novel economic ideas would be likely to get off the ground without some form of democratic endorsement.

Thatcher and Reagan were not just enthusiastic supporters of monetarism. They also, it turned out, shared a deep antipathy towards government. As Reagan put it – in a more memorable way than Hayek ever managed – 'The nine most terrifying words in the English language are "I'm from the government and I'm here to help".'[5]

Even then, the early years were touch and go: in 1981, Ronald Reagan sacked around 13,000 American air traffic controllers who went on strike in violation of the terms of their contracts, while even in her second term in office Margaret Thatcher was engaged in a ferocious battle with Britain's coal miners. By the late 1980s, however, Reagan and Thatcher had won: the private sector had triumphed – at least philosophically – over the public sector, markets had succeeded where central planning had failed, macroeconomic policy was aimed at price stability, not full employment, and economic growth was to be achieved through 'supply-side' reform, not Keynesian-style demand management. Importantly, following Thatcher's lead with her very early decision to abolish exchange controls, capital markets were to be subject to the discipline provided by international investors. There was to be no hiding place from the market and, by implication, no hiding place from international finance.

This collection of beliefs began to spread like wildfire. Those who attempted to head off in a different direction were, all too often, humbled by the invisible hand of international capitalism. In the early 1980s, President Mitterrand tried to impose his brand of socialism on the French economy: a vast array of companies were nationalized, the minimum wage was raised, a solidarity wealth tax was introduced and social benefits were increased. The intention was to reduce unemployment. Instead, the franc ended up being devalued on no fewer than three separate occasions, leading to ever-higher inflation and inexorably rising unemployment. Two years into his presidency, Mitterrand was forced into a U-turn with the adoption of the *tournant de la rigueur* (the austerity turn). Thereafter, France adopted the so-called *franc fort* policy, a largely successful attempt to emulate the German Bundesbank's pre-existing commitment to monetary rigour. Indeed, without the French commitment to a strong and stable franc, it is doubtful that the euro would ever have become a reality.

A decade or two later, it was easy to believe that 'free-market capitalism' – if not liberal democracy – had triumphed. The evidence seemed to be everywhere: Deng Xiaoping's reforms had paved the way for Western and Japanese capital to pour into China; the Berlin Wall had come down; Latin American economies had embarked on 'free-market' and 'sound-money' reforms which were bringing hitherto excessive inflation to heel; Western Europe was completing the 'single market', built on the so-called 'four freedoms' (free movement of goods, services, capital and labour – principles first established, if not acted upon, in the 1957 Treaty of Rome); and the 'commanding heights' of industry were, in the majority of countries, rapidly being privatized.

When corporate scandals did come along – the Savings and Loans, Long Term Capital Management and Enron crises in the US; the Guinness, Bank of Credit and Commerce International, Barings and Maxwell affairs in the UK; the Yamaichi and Long Term Credit Bank shocks in Japan – it didn't seem to matter too much: corporate wrongdoing and outright greed alone appeared not to have the capacity to throw economies off course. Better still, it seemed as though the free-market system – upon which an increasingly globalized world depended – had inbuilt resilience, precisely because it was able to detect and painlessly remove its 'rotten apples'.

Policymakers themselves happily bought into this new world order. Keynesian demand-management policies were discarded. UK-based economists who had previously rejected the central 'sound-money' tenets of Thatcherism found themselves latter-day converts to the cause, even if they mostly did so under Tony Blair's later Labour administration, long after the tough decisions had already been made.[6] Low inflation was increasingly regarded not just as a good thing in its own right, but also as a way of reducing the risk of nasty recessions. As Olivier Blanchard, a French academic who later became the IMF's chief economist, put it in 2001: 'the decrease in output volatility [in the US] was associated with – and may have largely been caused by – the decrease in inflation volatility that occurred around the same time'.[7] Three years later, Ben Bernanke, later to become chairman of the Board of Governors of the Federal Reserve, reinforced this claim, saying that:

> improved monetary policy has likely made an important contribution not only to the reduced volatility of inflation (which is not particularly controversial) but to the reduced volatility of output as well ... This conclusion on my part makes me optimistic for the future, because I am confident that monetary policymakers will not forget the lessons of the 1970s.[8]

Meanwhile, UK Chancellor of the Exchequer Gordon Brown claimed that he had abolished 'boom and bust'. 'Fiscal orthodoxy' became *de rigueur*: small budget deficits – or, even better, budget surpluses – were desirable both to free up funds that could be used more efficiently by private companies (which were supposedly more likely to be subject to market discipline) and to minimize any chance that governments and central banks could go back to the printing presses of the 1970s (even if, in the event, fiscal orthodoxy proved easier to promise than to deliver).

FASHION

Intoxicating stuff, admittedly, but how much of this represented objective economic and political truth, and how much of it was merely a statement of the latest economic and political fashion? Some – who frankly should have known better – were convinced that it was the former. Robert Lucas, the Nobel laureate in economics, argued in 2003 that:

> Macroeconomics was born as a distinct field in the 1940s as part of the intellectual response to the Great Depression . . . My thesis . . . is that macroeconomics in this original sense has succeeded: Its central problem of depression prevention has been solved, for all practical purposes, and has in fact been solved for many decades.[9]

With the benefit of hindsight, however, it is a lot easier to argue in favour of the latter.

Fashion is an odd thing. It not only encourages people to dress in similar ways, but it also frowns on people who don't. In the early 1970s, most people under 30 had long hair and wore flared jeans. Those who didn't were regarded as 'square' and had no chance of enjoying, for example, a slow dance at the local disco: they were outcasts, the fashion equivalents of François Mitterrand's economic policies in the early 1980s. Fashion dictated not only what to wear, but also what not to wear. There were obvious – and possibly unpleasant – consequences of being a fashion loser, even if no exchange rate collapses were involved.

No one, however, would claim that flares were 'objectively' better than drainpipes. Before long, Johnny Rotten's Sex Pistols came along, suggesting to some that spiky hair and selected body-piercings were the way to go. Moreover, flares too easily ended up caught in one's bicycle chain, giving teenage punks a certain practical advantage – even if, thanks to the tight fit of their jeans, they presumably suffered from restricted blood circulation.

There is little 'truth' in fashion. In economics, however, fashion too often masquerades as truth. To quote John Maynard Keynes:

> Practical men who believe themselves to be quite exempt from any intellectual influence, are usually the slaves of some defunct economist.

Madmen in authority, who hear voices in the air, are distilling their frenzy from some academic scribbler of a few years back.[10]

It was fashionable to believe that the economic cycle had been tamed; that low inflation would secure lasting prosperity; that governments the world over would happily choose to sign up to the new 'free-market' conventions; that ever-larger cross-border capital flows would ensure a more efficient allocation of resources with, potentially, gains for all; and that the best way to achieve rapid increases in living standards was to follow the 'free market and low inflation' mantra. Yet the economic fashionistas had failed to spot one rather obvious problem. If enough people believed that the world's fundamental economic problems had been solved, they would begin to take risks that, collectively, would make the world a much more dangerous place.

This was hardly a new idea. In his *General Theory*, Keynes famously talked about so-called 'animal spirits', noting that:

Even apart from the instability due to speculation, there is the instability due to the characteristic of human nature that a large proportion of our positive activities depend on spontaneous optimism rather than mathematical expectations, whether moral or hedonistic or economic. Most, probably, of our decisions to do something positive, the full consequences of which will be drawn out over many days to come, can only be taken as the result of animal spirits – a spontaneous urge to action rather than inaction, and not as the outcome of a weighted average of quantitative benefits multiplied by quantitative probabilities.[11]

Later, Hyman Minsky formulated a theory of financial crises which turned out to be eerily prescient. In Minsky's world, a sustained economic expansion leads eventually to euphoria, a point at which excessive risk-taking is financed by ever-higher levels of debt. As a result, the financial structure goes from 'robust' to 'fragile'. Interest rates eventually rise, maybe because of a perceived inflationary threat or a shortage of available funds. Overextended debtors then find themselves in trouble and have no choice but to attempt the liquidation of highly illiquid assets. Panic selling spreads, leading to a meltdown in asset prices and the possibility of recession.[12]

In Minsky's world, the process of liquidation is brutal, but also essential. This leads to an unfortunate conclusion. If a central bank steps in to prevent bankruptcies – via aggressive interest rate cuts and generous 'lender of last resort' activities – the subsequent recovery will be even more financially fragile. Over a number of economic cycles, the degree of financial fragility rises to such an extent that monetary easing and lender of last resort facilities eventually begin to lose their potency. A debt-deflation downward spiral threatens to take hold. Falling prices raise the real value of outstanding debts, triggering even more liquidation and, eventually, a total collapse in economic activity.

Seen through Minsky's eyes, the 'Great Moderation' was always going to end in tears. Central bank actions designed to limit downswings – or, indeed, to prevent downswings from happening altogether – only served to increase financial fragility and thus the risk of an eventual economic and financial meltdown. The financial system was allowed to expand to a size that ultimately proved to be highly destabilizing. As the system grew, so faith in finance rose. Many bankers genuinely saw themselves as Masters of the Universe, seemingly unaware that Tom Wolfe's sobriquet was hardly intended to be a compliment.[13]

Regulators, meanwhile, were foolishly confident that the regulations they had imposed would severely limit the chances of major failures. The authors of Basel I, signed in 1988 and enforced in 1992, regarded corporate lending as more risky than mortgage lending, and mortgage lending, in turn, as more risky than lending via investments in triple-A-ranked mortgage-backed securities. The regulators took the – superficially sensible – view that the riskier the class of asset, the more capital a bank would have to hold. But Basel I was indifferent about the quality of lending *within* asset classes (prompting profit-maximizing banks to lend more in any one category to riskier customers, who would pay higher interest rate spreads) and it was overly dependent on the judgements of ratings agencies, which, on too many occasions, had no more understanding of the inherent riskiness of innovative financial assets – collateralized debt obligations, for example – than anybody else. The architects of Basel II, produced in 2004 but still not fully implemented as the global financial crisis got going, were more sceptical about the value that ratings agencies could add. Yet, remarkably, they preferred to rely on banks' own internal risk models to gauge the riskiness of the activities banks were engaged in. Even without the inevitable conflict of interest this approach was still problematic: whether the models were internally constructed or independently generated, they were typically based on too limited a time period and thus said very little about the robustness of a particular institution in the event of, for example, a housing meltdown. And both Basel I and II focused too much on capital and not enough on liquidity. Banks only had to demonstrate that they would be able to survive a shutdown of wholesale funding for a week or so: in 2007 and 2008, wholesale markets shut for months.

Put another way, regulators, alongside central bankers and the banking industry at large, happily suffered from a sense of euphoria, a legal high, a sense that nothing could go wrong. They weren't outsiders looking in on a Minsky world: they were, collectively, very much part of that world.[14]

UNDERMINING THE NEW WISDOM

The financial crisis was not, however, a story about euphoria alone. It stemmed from a combination of factors, each of which challenged what had become conventional thinking over the previous three decades.

Markets themselves were failing, thanks in part to asymmetric information: the ultimate investors in US sub-prime mortgages were often blissfully unaware of the risks they were taking, largely because the underlying nature of their risky investments was typically camouflaged through the copious use of collateralized debt obligations and other innovative financial 'disguises'.[15]

Incentives were badly skewed: those who made commission from selling risky products were typically able to pass the risk on to others – often thousands of miles away – using 'pile 'em high and sell 'em cheap' tactics.

Excessive Chinese savings, a reflection of a poorly functioning domestic capital market, found their way into the US Treasury market, reducing the yield on treasuries and thus encouraging others to hunt for higher returns on – inevitably riskier – assets.

Higher interest rates designed to contain inflationary pressures often triggered upward currency movements which, in turn, spurred hot money inflows that served only to increase domestic financial instability.

The Federal Reserve found itself turning into a reluctant central bank for the global economy: as capital market behaviour converged across borders, the US central bank's monetary decisions had an increasingly magnetic impact on monetary and financial conditions in other parts of the world, leaving policymakers elsewhere increasingly impotent, even as the Fed focused primarily on developments only within the US itself.[16]

THE GLOBAL FINANCE REVOLUTION

Underneath all these challenges was a revolution in global finance. In the heyday of late nineteenth-century globalization, foreign holdings of capital amounted to around 20 per cent of global income. Half of those stocks were owned by the British, who could rightly claim to be bankers to the world. In the first half of the twentieth century, thanks to two world wars, foreign capital ownership collapsed. By 1945, it was down to a mere 5 per cent of a (by then) rather higher level of global income. By

1980, the figure had risen to 25 per cent, thus overtaking the pre-First World War peak. Thereafter, there was a massive acceleration. By 2000, latest estimates suggest that foreign assets were 110 per cent of global income. By 2007 (the year in which the financial cracks first began to appear), the figure had leapt to over 200 per cent, before falling back to a – still very high – 190 per cent by 2014.[17]

Moreover, ownership had become very diffuse: at the beginning of the twenty-first century, the US accounted for only a quarter of foreign assets, implying the absence of a single centre of finance equivalent to London before the First World War. This lack of financial 'concentration' reflected three key developments: the huge growth of the (offshore) eurodollar market in the 1960s and 1970s (a response to increased demand for US dollar holdings free from America's regulatory clutches); the two big oil shocks of the 1970s that left countries in the Arab world with huge surplus savings in search of a home somewhere else in the world; and China's persistent current account surpluses in the 1990s and beyond, which led to a huge increase in (mostly US dollar) Chinese foreign exchange reserves.

When the world succumbed to the financial crisis, it was rather like watching the end of *The Wizard of Oz* in slow motion. The crisis itself was the equivalent of Toto pulling away the curtain, exposing a series of underlying truths that few previously had wanted to recognize. The scale of the crisis revealed that policymakers' and investors' strongly held convictions were often no more than acts of faith, based on a series of quasi-religious beliefs. As with Dorothy, it was time to wake up to reality.

So what was hiding behind the curtain? The pace of economic growth was much slower than had previously been assumed. For most countries in the developed world, the rate of increase in living standards had begun to slow long before the onset of the financial crisis. The crisis itself – and its aftermath – simply reinforced the point. Slower growth, however, meant that tax revenues were a lot lower than expected, leaving budgetary authorities with a whole bunch of new constraints and, in time, awkward political choices. It also meant that income and wealth inequality – previously camouflaged by euphoria associated with the supposed end of boom and bust – became much more relevant politically.

THE RETURN OF NATIONAL SELF-INTEREST

The 'Great Moderation' wasn't so great after all. Low and stable inflation provided no guarantees of a longer and smoother economic cycle. Indeed, to the extent that low and stable inflation had encouraged excessive risk-taking, economies had become increasingly exposed to financial, rather than price, instability. Greater financial instability, in turn, revealed the ineffectiveness of international economic and financial governance.[18] Thanks to the huge increase in cross-border asset holdings, losses made in one part of the world too often had to be paid for by taxpayers in another part of the world. Not surprisingly, taxpayers didn't like it.

As individual nations strove to minimize their share of those losses, so international cooperation was replaced in many cases by a revival of national self-interest. Those Asian nations that got caught with excessive balance of payments deficits during the 1997/98 crisis mostly decided to run surpluses thereafter – which inevitably meant that deficits elsewhere had to get bigger. Ahead of the global financial crisis, many of the biggest deficits appeared in Southern Europe. Yet, just as Asia had discovered a decade earlier, private sector creditors from other nations turned their backs on the likes of Spain and Greece at the first sign of trouble. Thereafter, the governments of creditor nations (most obviously Germany, but also the Netherlands and Finland) alongside the so-called Troika (the European Commission, the European Central Bank and, reluctantly, the IMF) demanded that the 'borrower nations' should shoulder the burden of adjustment. Austerity imposed upon the debtors was seen to be the best way of minimizing the creditors' losses – and preserving the stability of the financial system – even though the creditors themselves had been part of the problem, too happy to send their savings to other parts of the world without thinking carefully enough about how those savings would be invested.

When losses did arise, it turned out that market forces were of no real use. Fear of a financial meltdown left governments seemingly with no choice but to bail out those banks and other financial institutions that might otherwise have gone bust. The desire to prevent deposit flight – which could have led to economic and financial failures on a par with the Great Depression – meant that current and future taxpayers were now on the hook. Government debt levels inevitably soared, leading in some cases to sovereign bond crises.

The post-war Bretton Woods institutions – and their offshoots – had not kept pace with the internationalization of market forces. Whilst the OECD had broadened its membership, it was still primarily a 'rich man's club', unable to cope with the growing influence of, for example, China or India. The European Union had created a single market and a shared currency, but lacked the key arrangements that most successful common currency areas – nation states, in other words – take for granted: a common budget, fiscal transfers, a banking union and some form of political union. The IMF was still hamstrung by US dominance – a legacy of Bretton Woods – and was struggling to reshape itself for a world of massive savings imbalances and ever-larger balance of payments disequilibria. Many poorer nations began to lose faith, particularly given that they were now seemingly the only ones forced to undergo the disciplines associated with the IMF's sometimes draconian programmes.

Ultimately, none of these international institutions could easily cope with the extraordinary growth of cross-border capital flows: when it all went wrong, the buck stopped here, there and everywhere. Everyone was responsible, yet no one was responsible.

More than anything, the crisis revealed a fundamental mismatch between, on the one hand, the global economy and markets and, on the other, the interests of nation states and non-state actors. The crisis was thus as much a crisis about governance and institutions as it was about economic and financial losses. Markets had failed, the dark side of globalization had been revealed, and no one knew what to do. Suddenly, free-market capitalism – part of the 'end of history' bedrock – found itself in the dock.

Part Two

STATES, ELITES, COMMUNITIES

5

GLOBALIZATION AND NATION STATES

The market-led model of globalization ultimately depended on the idea that, left to their own devices, increasingly internationalized markets could generate outcomes that were both in everybody's self-interest and in societies' collective interests. Yet, following the financial crisis, it was no longer obvious that this idea was in any way credible. Indeed, Alan Greenspan, former chairman of the Federal Reserve and for much of his life a cheerleader for market forces, was forced to admit as much while giving evidence to the US House Committee on Oversight and Government Reform in October 2008: 'Those of us who have looked to the self-interest of lending institutions to protect shareholders' equity, myself included, are in a state of shocked disbelief.' Markets cannot function easily in a vacuum. They need to operate within some kind of institutional framework. But which one?

THE NINETEENTH-CENTURY FRAMEWORK: IMPERIAL POWER

The nineteenth-century model of globalization ultimately relied on the existence of international institutions within which markets were able to flourish. In a very simplistic sense, those institutions were basically empires. One reason why London could be banker to the world was that, in the nineteenth century, the typical British financier hoped that wherever his money went, it was likely to be protected by the very long arm of (English) law, enforced, if necessary, by the very long reach of the Royal Navy.[1]

Admittedly, it wasn't empires alone. There were serious attempts to link (Western) nations together in ways designed to foster closer international political and economic cooperation and reduce the chances of conflict. Jeremy Bentham, the great utilitarian philosopher, argued in favour of an international legal system. Richard Cobden, a member of parliament for the Radicals, was the greatest proselytizer of free trade during the Victorian era, arguing that its pursuit was ultimately the best way to guarantee liberty. Giuseppe Mazzini, the Italian politician and thinker, argued that (republican) nation states were fully consistent with greater international cooperation, largely because they fostered universal values of duty and obligation.[2] Karl Marx thought that – whichever state they came from – members of the proletariat should rise up against the bourgeoisie, a view that inspired the creation of International Socialism and the associated rejection of the ruling elites that had re-established their hold over power – via the Congress of Vienna – at the end of the Napoleonic era.[3] Doubtless Marx would have been disappointed to discover that, on the eve of the First World War, the proletariat were attracted more to patriotism and jingoism than to the joys of cross-border working-class comradeship and the red flag.[4]

Some – but not all – of these ideas contributed to the creation of new arrangements and conventions: the International Court of Justice in The Hague, the Geneva Convention and – for an increasingly global monetary system – a near-universal adoption of the gold standard (adherence to the gold standard was the nineteenth-century equivalent of today's industrialized countries opting for a 2 per cent inflation target: if everyone else opts for it, you'd be odd not to). Yet for all this apparently greater cooperation, progress was, at best, mixed. Closer linkages were intended only for the 'civilized nations' – the cosy club of Western colonial powers.[5] 'Barbaric nations' – which included south-eastern European states and principalities that only won their independence from the Ottoman Empire towards the end of the nineteenth century – were to be treated as second-tier societies and, where necessary, forcibly occupied to allow the great powers to pursue their individual and collective interests. 'Savage nations' were to be colonized, most obviously reflected in the late nineteenth-century 'Scramble for Africa', a race that, more than anything, revealed that Europeans themselves were capable of immense savagery in the name of civilization.[6]

There were rules and procedures aplenty but their interpretation varied enormously. Cobden's civilized belief in free trade, for example, was too often expropriated by others in a bid to gain commercial advantage in parts of the world that had no desire to open up their societies to avaricious Europeans. The creation of treaty ports in China, for example, only occurred thanks to Britain's victory over China's Qing Empire in the First Opium War (1839–42). It was far from obvious that encouraging a large number of Chinese subjects to become hooked on opium in order to enable British consumers to get their hands on fine Chinese porcelain was quite what Cobden had in mind.

NINETEENTH- AND EARLY TWENTIETH-CENTURY DARWINIAN MARKETS

Meanwhile, attitudes towards markets operating within the 'civilized world' through much of the nineteenth century were basically Darwinian. What mattered was survival of the fittest. Financial crises were a fact of life. Banks regularly went bust, sometimes leaving their depositors without so much as a penny or a dime. Panics were both plentiful and painful. The US suffered seven financial crises in the nineteenth century. The UK endured at least five. Depositors often lost the shirts on their backs. There was little in the way of deposit insurance. Lender of last resort facilities – inspired by Henry Thornton and Walter Bagehot – were designed primarily to prop up the monetary system as a whole and not to prevent insolvent institutions from failing.[7]

In other words, markets were allowed to work. They rewarded success and punished failure. Those planning to put their money into a bank for safe-keeping had to think long and hard about the likelihood of ever seeing their hard-earned savings again. As a result, banks continuously had to advertise their supposed safety and robustness, one reason why banking halls constructed in the nineteenth century were, in many cases, on the grandest of scales.

One such example is 14 rue Bergère in Paris, purchased by the Comptoir National d'Escompte de Paris in the 1860s and now owned by BNP Paribas. The architect Edouard Corroyer was brought in at the end of the 1870s to turn the original grand edifice into something still more impressive. He succeeded with considerable aplomb. The revamped building provided a remarkable mixture of medieval and High Gothic styles. The main banking hall had a floor partly made of glass – a first in its day – allegedly to demonstrate to sceptical would-be customers that there really were large vaults directly below. Inside the bank, there was what might best be described as a rudimentary, yet still remarkably imaginative, air-conditioning system. A casual passer-by was more likely to think he had stumbled across a palace than a financial institution.

None of this, however, prevented the Comptoir from ending up in serious trouble following the suicide of Eugène Denfert-Rochereau, a patron of the bank, in 1889, and associated large losses on the copper market. Fortunately, the Comptoir was rescued by other French banks over the following few months, thus preventing it from becoming a late nineteenth-century version of Lehman Brothers. Nevertheless, despite its impressive appearance, the Comptoir's financial foundations turned out to be remarkably weak. Like a magician, it could pull off an impressive illusion, but underneath it all, its financial prowess depended too much on assorted sleights of hand.

THE BACKLASH AGAINST GLOBALIZATION

No matter how robust it might have seemed, nineteenth-century globalization couldn't last. The Industrial Revolution – and its associated laissez-faire values – led to the rise of a middle class that no longer wanted to act in deference to ruling elites: within this newly emergent group of educated people were social reformers who regarded free markets with considerable suspicion – an entirely understandable response, given the emergence of the workhouse and debtors' prisons. Labour became increasingly organized and, in the process, began to push for higher wages, better working conditions and greater job security, particularly in the face of heightened competition from abroad.

Meanwhile, as empires fragmented – both before and after the First World War – the formation of new nation states led to increased ethnic and cultural tensions both within and across borders. Japan's economic success following the Meiji Restoration in the 1860s paved the way, eventually, to victory in the Russo-Japanese War of 1904–05, suggesting that European superpowers could no longer treat the rest of the world as their plaything. US economic success had been delivered largely behind protectionist doors – at least with regard to trade with the rest of the world – suggesting that Cobden-style liberalism was not the only viable model of economic development. Huge cross-border movements of labour – from 'Old Europe' to the New World – contributed to a massive shift in relative economic power. In the 1860 census, the first in which US statisticians decided it was worth including Native Americans in their calculations, the population of the US amounted to just over 31 million. On the eve of the First World War, it was around 100 million. By then, over 13 per cent of the population was foreign born.

Financial globalization limped on after the First World War, but the end was nigh. Although most countries returned to the gold standard in the 1920s – in a vain attempt to suggest that there had been a return to 'business as usual' – the system completely fell apart in the 1930s. The UK – the centre of the financial world on the eve of the First World War – left in 1931, the Americans in 1933 and the French and Italians in 1936. In the midst of the Depression, there was also a decisive move away from a focus on the free market, by then increasingly seen as a major contributor to both systemic financial collapse and the rapid erosion of business and consumer confidence. As President Roosevelt put it in his first 'fireside chat' on 12 March 1933, 'After all, there is an element in the readjustment of our financial system more important than currency, more important than gold, and that is the confidence of the people.'[8]

NOT FOR THE LAST TIME, THE BANKS

Roosevelt was faced with bank failures in the US on a totally unprecedented scale. In the 1920s, up to a thousand (typically very small) bank failures occurred in any one year; most years had considerably fewer. In 1930, however, there were 1,350 failures, followed by 2,293 in 1931, 1,453 in 1932 and an astonishing 4,000 in 1933. Relative to the nineteenth-century experience, this was a banking crisis totally off the scale. The peak of the panic was reached on the day of Roosevelt's inauguration at the beginning of March 1933. Visitors to Washington found notes in their hotel rooms informing them that cheques drawn on out-of-town banks were no longer acceptable. With state after state declaring a bank holiday, something had to be done.

The answer came partly in the form of deposit insurance. As an emergency measure in direct response to the March meltdown, Congress agreed to offer insurance protection to each depositor up to a maximum of $2,500 ($44,800 in 2015 US dollars) in the hope that bank runs would be stymied. In July of the following year, the level of protection was raised to $5,000 ($89,000 in 2015 US dollars). The policy worked, to the extent that the financial system was stabilized and confidence returned. It also, however, introduced moral hazard. Thanks to deposit insurance, most depositors no longer had to worry about what their bank was up to: their money was safe, come what may. At a stroke, market discipline had been removed, largely because an increasing number of politicians, legislators and members of the public no longer thought markets were working for them.[9] It marked a sea change in attitudes – one that was to prevail for the next 40 years.

GLOBALIZATION ABHORS A VACUUM

The late nineteenth-century and early twentieth-century experience shows that globalization cannot operate in a vacuum. There needs to be a framework. Back then, the relevant framework was a combination of empire and (at least for the British variety) a commitment to free trade. Yet the framework ultimately crumbled. A late nineteenth-century observer able to travel into the future (not so difficult to imagine, given that H.G. Wells published *The Time Machine* in 1895) would have been amazed to discover that, just 40 years later, the certainties of the Victorian era had gone up in smoke: empires were on their knees, the gold standard had gone, markets were no longer to be trusted, nationalism was in the ascendancy (helped by a poisonous cocktail of racism and eugenics), protectionism was rife and – for good or ill – governments were increasingly interfering in daily life. In the UK, for example, tax revenues jumped from around 10 per cent of national income before the First World War to over 20 per cent in its immediate aftermath: they have steadily risen thereafter, thanks to ever-increasing dependence on state, rather than market, provision.[10]

The world had changed – but, from a Victorian businessman's perspective, not obviously for the better. Change, however, was inevitable: the imperial arrangements of the late nineteenth century could not cope with the new economic, financial and political realities. Instead, chaos ruled.

And it is quite possible that the US-led post-Bretton Woods arrangements of the late twentieth century are unable to cope with the new economic, financial and political realities of the early twenty-first century.

THE TWENTIETH-CENTURY MODEL: DEFINING THE NATION STATE

In contrast to the imperial arrangements of the nineteenth century, the increasingly dominant institution of the twentieth century was the nation state, thanks in large part to the Wilsonian – and hence American – belief in self-determination, consistent with Washington's desire to stymie the imperial ambitions of the nineteenth-century superpowers which, from a US perspective, had been largely responsible for the death and destruction during the First World War. American sponsorship, in turn, meant that the stability of the system depended on the acceptance by others that the US was 'first among equals'.

Admittedly, defining a nation state is not easy. From a Western European perspective, it might once have been regarded as an area with a common ethnicity, a dominant language, a mythologized history and a unifying religion.[11] At the beginning of the twenty-first century, with the rise of multi-polar societies, this is clearly not the case. With only very few exceptions – American Samoa, Macau and Yemen, for example – countries have some degree of ethnic mix: fairly modest in the majority of Western European countries, but extremely large in many African nations (Uganda, Liberia, Madagascar and Congo top the list). Many countries have no difficulty functioning in the absence of a common language: Belgians just about get on with each other using a combination of Flemish and French; the Swiss happily get by with a mixture of French, German, Italian and Romansh; the US is full of people who contentedly communicate in both English and Spanish. Those states that function less well – at least when judged by standard measures of human development – can find themselves at either end of the language spectrum: almost all Haitians speak a local Creole, while there are more than a hundred languages spoken in Tanzania. As for a common religion, one of the very few countries that appear to have completely managed it is Serbia – and that was for all the wrong reasons. Those with the greatest religious diversity, meanwhile, can sometimes be among the most successful in terms of human development: the US, Australia and New Zealand fall into this category, in part because many of their citizens – from a wide range of religious and cultural backgrounds – can cite a shared immigrant bond.[12]

A NATION STATE'S PURPOSE

Despite all these inconsistencies, it is nevertheless still possible to flesh out what is meant by a nation state, simply by going back to first principles. A good starting point is Thomas Hobbes (1588–1679). In *Leviathan*, Hobbes asked not so much what citizens (or, given his enthusiasm for an all-powerful sovereign, subjects) wanted, but instead what they absolutely did not want.[13] In his view, no one wanted to suffer a violent death.[14] Yet this was precisely what people would be faced with in Hobbes' 'state of nature', in which there threatened to be a war of all against all.[15] In his words:

> In such condition, there is no place for industry, because the fruit thereof is uncertain; and, consequently, no culture of the earth; no navigation, nor the use of commodities that may be imported by sea; no commodious building; no instruments of moving and removing such things as requires much force; no knowledge of the face of the earth; no account of time; no arts, no letters; no society; and which is the worst of all, continual fear, and danger of violent death; and the life of man, solitary, poor, nasty, brutish and short.

In Hobbes' view, what we now think of as a social contract was an essential arrangement to avoid living in the barbaric 'state of nature'. It was appropriate for citizens to cede some of their rights in return for the state's protection. With a set of laws, rules, conventions and acceptable behaviours, citizens could live side by side in what Hobbes called a 'commonwealth', without an excessive fear of violent death. Failure to adhere to the commonwealth's rules and conventions, however, would lead to some form of punishment: without it, after all, any kind of social contract would be worthless.

Hobbes' *Leviathan* provides essential foundations for the modern nation state. At the very least, his views justify the case for having a well-functioning judicial system free of corruption. Without such a system after all, it would be all too easy to slip back into the 'state of nature'.[16] And *Leviathan* can also be used to justify a state's military spending: any social contract would be utterly useless if it could be torn apart following invasion by some foreign force and the subsequent toppling of the sovereign.

Hobbes was, however, no fan of democracy, arguing that a sovereign was less likely to be corrupt than those with vaunting political ambitions keen to gain the support of the people. Of modern-day political systems, he might have expressed a preference for, say, Lee Kuan Yew's Singapore, which enjoyed huge increases in living standards over a handful of decades thanks to a strong legal system (a legacy of British colonial rule), a benevolent leader who also happened to be a Cambridge-educated lawyer, and a high level of political stability (helped by restrictions on civil liberties of which Hobbes might well have approved). Hobbes certainly would not have favoured the separation of powers between legislature and executive incorporated within the US Constitution, an outcome that owed a great deal to the writings of John Locke (1632–1704), who, unlike Hobbes, thought a monarch should not be allowed to rule supreme when men (and, presumably, women) were by nature free and equal.

Others went further. Montesquieu (1689–1755) argued in *The Spirit of the Laws* that a democratic nation state would only survive if the citizens living within its borders thought their own interests were in accord with the interests of the state as a whole. If instead some of those citizens began to think their interests could more easily be pursued by taking advantage of other citizens – through the exertion of political power – the 'spirit of inequality' would begin to undermine the social contract. Alternatively, should citizens no longer be willing to place their faith in elected lawmakers and politicians, preferring instead to 'manage everything themselves, to debate for the senate, to execute for the magistrate, and to decide for the judges', a democracy would eventually collapse on account of an excessive 'spirit of equality'. All the while, Montesquieu worried that, irrespective of whether the system of government was democratic, aristocratic or monarchical, there was always the risk of a collapse into despotism. Despotism was to be avoided if at all possible, but creating better alternatives – whether monarchy or republic – was not easy: to do so required 'a masterpiece of legislation, rarely produced by hazard, and seldom attained by prudence'.[17]

Put another way, arguing in favour of the nation state says little about the nature of that state: is it to be ruled by a sovereign, a dictator (benevolent or otherwise), a group of powerful oligarchs, a chamber of elected politicians to represent the voters, or by the people themselves through continuous referendums? And even if there were a simple answer, how should nation states relate to each other, particularly if their systems of government appear to reveal fundamentally different core values and beliefs?

FROM THE NATIONAL TO THE INTERNATIONAL: CLUB THEORY

One way to bridge the gap between the national and the international is to make use of James Buchanan's 'Economic Theory of Clubs'.[18] Buchanan's analysis applies to clubs large and small – from those full of retired politicians and captains of industry that grace London's Pall Mall and St James's to this day, through to, for example, the IMF, the OECD and the European Union. All of these are clubs – to the extent that they are for members only. Buchanan's theory rests on three key requirements.

First, goods and services provided by the club are *excludable*. Non-members cannot enjoy the benefits associated with club membership. In a typical London club, only members enjoy access to the club's best vintage claret at a non-vintage price. Only members of the EU can easily be part of the single market or join the single currency.

Second, goods and services provided by the club are *congestible*. In other words, each club member imposes some kind of externality on other club members. Going to the gym at lunchtime might be convenient, but if all members turn up in their lunch breaks, there will be lengthy queues and, in some cases, raised levels of blood pressure, threatening to make at least some members' visits largely counterproductive. Similarly, increasing membership of the European Union reduces the chances of agreeing on common policies, threatening disgruntlement among the EU's members.

Finally, the goods and services provided are *divisible*. In other words, if one club ends up full to the brim, similar clubs can be formed along roughly the same principles. Thus, along London's Pall Mall and its surrounding streets, a captain of industry – having garnered the requisite nominations – can take his pick of the Athenaeum, the Reform or, if he prefers horses to women, the Turf. Likewise, the European Union is not the only possible free trade club (and nor is it only a free trade club – it also offers free movement across borders for its citizens, a factor that contributed to the UK's 2016 Brexit): the North Atlantic Free Trade Agreement provides much the same free trade product for the US, Canada and Mexico, while the Trans-Pacific Partnership – abandoned by the Americans towards the end of 2016 – in theory would have delivered similar benefits for a number of countries in the Americas and Asia.

Yet applying the 'club' concept to international institutions is not easy. The most obvious club problem is that of the 'free rider', the person or group that takes out more than he or she puts in: for the euro area, the inability of countries to stick to the fiscal rules contained within the Stability and Growth Pact is a classic example of the problem, leading to persistent budget deficit overshoots through both good times and bad. Then there's the issue of decision-making. For nation states – with varying living standards, differing domestic agendas and incompatible political systems – it is not at all obvious that a large international club will necessarily achieve very much (the December 2015 Paris climate deal promised a great deal – and its subsequent ratification by both the US and China was very encouraging; but whether countries really will be able to deliver on the pledges they appear to have made is another matter altogether). Not surprisingly, perhaps, Buchanan himself thought that clubs were more likely to succeed if they were small, largely homogeneous in terms of membership, and thus not easily able to create majorities that could dictate to vulnerable minorities. At both the national and the international level, that's an unhelpful conclusion. Rarely are those conditions met on such a large scale; and even when one or another country attempts to take the lead – the US globally, Germany within Europe – others are often reluctant followers.

A further problem lies with the delegation of decision-making to statesmen who supposedly represent the interests of the member countries. Hans Morgenthau (1904–80), an American political realist, drew a key distinction between the diplomatic skills required of a statesman and the views and moral standpoint of a typical citizen: 'The statesman must think in terms of the national interest, conceived as power among other powers. The popular mind, unaware of the fine distinctions of the statesman's thinking, reasons more often than not in the simple moralistic and legalistic terms of absolute good and evil.' For good measure, he added that 'Realism maintains that universal moral principles cannot be applied to the actions of states.'[19] This creates a seemingly paradoxical situation: a state has to look after the collective interests of its citizens, even if that means that those citizens, individually, might feel a grave injustice had been committed on their behalf.[20]

Yet the interests of the international statesman may not always align with the 'national interest', particularly if the statesman is now also a member of some international organization that provides him with a whole bunch of new incentives.[21] At that point, the statesman's role is in danger of becoming disturbingly ambiguous. Does the new international club provide a convenient scapegoat for the delivery of unpopular measures at home, as happened with the imposition of austerity measures in Southern European countries during the Eurozone crisis that began in 2010? Does the homogeneity of view associated with club membership – for example, adherence to the Washington Consensus or acceptance of inflation-targeting conventions – undermine otherwise legitimate protests at home? Does the new club limit the powers of domestic government through the growth of, for example, a supranational legal authority? And what happens if the views of the international statesman – and the new club he has now joined – are rejected by the nation he is supposed to represent?

None of these issues is new. The scale of the problem is, however, bigger than ever before. Even as markets – in trade, capital and labour – have become ever more globalized, the institutions able to govern those markets have become ever more fragmented. In 1945, when the United Nations was founded, there were 51 member nations. In 2011, the year in which South Sudan joined, there were 193. With the collapse of the Soviet Union, there is no longer a binary choice between what might loosely be described as US-style free-market capitalism and Moscow-inspired communism.

Managing an increasingly integrated global economy under these circumstances is incredibly difficult. For a while, it seemed as though the system might be self-regulating, through the wonders of the invisible hand. With the onset of the global financial crisis, that view was clearly wrong. And, in the absence of a self-regulating mechanism, it appears that our existing arrangements – based primarily on national self-interest and the occasional prod from various Washington-based institutions – may be inconsistent with an ever more integrated global economy. For globalization, we have reached a genuine fork in the road.

MONTESQUIEU REVISITED

If globalization is to succeed in a world of nation states, it either needs to retain the support of nation states, or the nation states themselves need to change. Yet if each nation state experiences an increase in Montesquieu's 'spirit of inequality' – thanks to unintended or unexpected effects stemming from globalization – a point may be reached where domestic support for closer integration inevitably falters. Establishment politicians and lawmakers who remain in favour of globalization – Morgenthau's 'enlightened statesmen' – may find themselves increasingly out of touch with the voters who, in turn, will either force the statesmen to change their ways or replace them with populist – and nationalist – politicians at either end of the political spectrum. This is one reason why Hillary Clinton, the Democrats' nominee in the 2016 US presidential election, made clear – reluctantly, no doubt – her rejection of the Trans-Pacific Partnership 'as drafted': she felt she had to bundle up the proposed trade deal with provisions regarding both currency manipulation and intellectual property, which only served to make any ultimate deal a lot less likely.

And the 'spirit of inequality' – in its broadest possible sense – is most certainly on the rise. Post-war international institutions worked well for a cosy club of like-minded industrialized democracies. Yet, thanks to the effects of globalization, their share of global economic activity has been persistently in decline. In 1980 – the year in which the West properly rediscovered free-market philosophies and China began to emerge from the economic deep-freeze – the world's 'advanced economies' accounted for 64 per cent of the world's national income. China, India,

Russia and the rest of what might be described as emerging and developing nations made up the other 36 per cent. In 2007, the two country groupings were of equal economic size. By 2015, the 'advanced economies' made up only 42 per cent of the world's national income, with the rest now accounting for 58 per cent. If the US was once 'first among equals', it cannot so easily claim to be so today. The consequences are profound. Whereas at the end of the Second World War the US could reasonably expect to be the ultimate architect of key international institutions, at the beginning of the twenty-first century that expectation is no longer realistic. Whether it is the creation of the European single currency, the Asian Infrastructure Investment Bank or the Shanghai Cooperation Organization (all to be discussed in more detail in Chapter 7), other countries have increasingly taken international initiatives – for good or ill – which have left the US watching from the sidelines.

Within nations, it is increasingly obvious that pre-financial crisis globalization was not a force for social cohesion. The idea that international free-market capitalism has delivered the best outcome for all is less than compelling. Take, for example, the US economy. On average, living standards appear to have risen a long way since President Reagan first took office in 1980. Gross domestic product per capita – an overall measure of living standards – almost doubled between 1980 and 2015. The distribution of the overall gain, however, has been heavily skewed in favour of those who were – for the most part – already well-off. The median weekly salary for full-time employees has barely budged in real, inflation-adjusted terms since 1979 – the year before Reagan came to power. For men, salaries in real terms have actually declined by over 7 per cent.[22] Admittedly, companies now pay a lot more of their employees' health costs than once was the case, so there have been compensations here and there. Nevertheless, this does little to alter the overall distributional story. The share of income going to the top 1 per cent of income earners rose from 8 per cent in 1979 to over 19 per cent in 2012, and much of that increase went to the top 0.1 per cent: their share went up from 2.2 per cent to 8.8 per cent over the same period.[23]

Thanks in part to these rapid income gains, very wealthy Americans have mostly done very well indeed. Since the early 1980s the top 1 per cent of income earners has received 41 per cent of the total increase in net worth (assets less liabilities), 43 per cent of the total increase in non-home wealth and 49 per cent of the total increase in income. Beyond the top 20 per cent of income earners, there have been no gains to speak of whatsoever. Middle-income earners in the US – those in the middle three income quintiles – got through much of this period only by upping their borrowing. Their average ratio of debt to income rose from 100 to 157 between 2001 and 2007, while their debt–equity ratio (mostly the level of their debt relative to the value of their house or apartment) rose from 46 to 61 per cent over the same period. Not surprisingly, they found themselves in an acutely vulnerable position when the US housing market thereafter came crashing down, as noted by Atif Mian and Amir Sufi in *House of Debt*.[24] And even as the recovery from the ensuing great recession began, many middle-income earners continued to suffer, having no choice but to dip into their – often meagre – savings to make ends meet.[25]

The very wealthy had a lot less to worry about. True, the value of their financial assets initially fell a long way: in the initial stages of the global financial crisis, equities fell much further than housing. Yet the rich had two advantages. First, relative to their assets, they had a lot less debt and so, even as their assets fell in value, they were under no threat of finding themselves financially under the water. Second, they proved to be major beneficiaries of quantitative easing – the supposedly magical monetary medicine where, in effect, a central bank purchases financial assets in a bid to drive their price higher, in the hope that households and companies will spend more. The S&P 500 index peaked before the global financial crisis at 1,557. It then plummeted to a low of 683. A handful of years later – partly a response to sustained pump-priming from the Federal Reserve – the index had jumped to a new high of 2,270.

Given that around 90 per cent of the total value of financial assets in the US is owned by the top 10 per cent of households, this was – particularly for the very well-off – a very pleasant windfall gain.

Yet despite this financial uplift for the wealthy, broader economic gains – those that might have benefited society more widely – proved few and far between. Quantitative easing may have been designed to kick-start economic growth, but the pace of recovery in the US – and elsewhere – was unusually weak. In particular, despite strong gains in equity markets, companies mostly remained unwilling to invest. In many cases, they didn't need to. Subdued labour incomes – thanks to a mixture of weak demand, technological change and competition from cheaper labour elsewhere in the world – meant that gains in sales revenues alone led to higher corporate profits; higher profits, in turn, fed through to further stock market gains, even in the absence of a recovery in investment. For both the owners and managers of companies, this appeared to be a case of 'heads I win, tails you lose', triggering much gnashing of teeth and, not surprisingly, a renewed interest in the causes of, and the cures for, rising income inequality. Not for nothing did Thomas Piketty's *Capital in the Twenty-First Century* become a *New York Times* bestseller. Piketty made the strong claim that the rate of return on capital was – in the absence of wars and revolutions – always likely to be higher than the rate of economic growth: the implication was simply that the already well-off – basically those with no shortage of capital – would steadily get richer, a conclusion that appeared very much to be playing out before our eyes.

Whether the evidence really supports Piketty's claims is debatable. In an IMF Working Paper,[26] Carlos Góes notes that there are several alternative – and equally robust – interpretations of Piketty's data, from higher skills premiums and lower union membership, through to the short-run benefits to entrepreneurs of technological innovation and the impact of inclusive versus extractive institutions (in effect, those that spread wealth through the population, as opposed to those that reward the ruling kleptomaniacs), consistent with the arguments of Acemoglu and Robinson.[27] Still, for many, the alternative explanations didn't matter: Piketty offered a view of the world that reinforced their priors, and they were not about to change their minds.

The UK's experience is less extreme, but the underlying trend appears at first sight to be heading in the same direction. In the immediate aftermath of the financial crisis, the share of income going to the top 1 per cent and above in the UK dropped from the pre-crisis peak of 15.4 per cent to 12.6 per cent – and for the top 0.1 per cent, from 6.5 per cent to 4.7 per cent. Yet the post-crisis lows were still considerably higher than at the end of the 1970s: back then, the share accruing to the top 1 per cent was only 5.9 per cent, while the top 0.1 per cent pocketed just 1.3 per cent of the total.

Timing, however, is much more awkward for the UK than for the US: much of the increase in inequality occurred in the 1990s, a time when enthusiasm for globalization was generally rising, not falling. In the UK, it is more difficult to link the growing opposition towards aspects of globalization – notably heightened immigration – to rising inequality alone.

Other countries – including Germany, France and Japan – have seen inequality widen to a much lesser extent. Yet they still have distributional challenges. For Germany and Japan in particular, population ageing threatens a growing divide between the interests of the mature (who will hope to see resources steered towards increased healthcare, pensions and old age homes) and the young (who will want to avoid facing a life of excessive tax payments and rising charges to fund their parents' and grandparents' public services). Globalization provides a potential solution to this problem – increasing the number of immigrants of working age to redress the demographic imbalance – but whilst the economics make sense, political realities are moving in the opposite direction.

THE EUROZONE'S PROBLEMS

As for France, it forms part of a single currency system that has only served to increase inequality between its member states. There has been a remarkable shift in relative economic fortunes among the 'Big Five' European nations – Germany, France, Italy, Spain and, outside the Eurozone, the UK – since the euro's formation. In the 20 years before the single currency came into being, Spain and the UK topped the 'increase in living standards' league table, Italy was mid-table, while Germany and France were in the economic equivalent of the relegation zone. Since the single currency was created, Germany and the UK have vied for the top spot, France and Spain have been mid-ranking, while Italy has been firmly at the bottom.

The change in the relative fortunes of Germany and Italy is nothing short of remarkable. In 1999, the year in which the euro was founded, Italian living standards were around 90 per cent of those in Germany. Fifteen years later – following a period during which the Italian economy totally stagnated – Italian living standards were only 75 per cent of those in Germany.

In itself, this is not a particularly big gap. Welsh living standards, for example, are only just over 40 per cent of those in London. Slovakia, which joined the single currency area in 2009, has living standards less than 40 per cent of those of some of its richer Western European cousins. What matters, however, is the extent to which the gap has opened up – and the degree to which the widening gap can be attributed to the arrangements governing the Eurozone. Far from converging – which is perhaps what Europe's economic and financial architects had in mind when they came up with both the single market and the single currency – Europe's economies are actually diverging. Put simply, the gap between North and South has steadily got bigger and bigger.

Within a nation state, there is a reasonable chance that a government will attempt – successfully or otherwise – to offer support to those in poorer regions. Even if the attempt ends in failure, it is important that the government is seen to be doing something. In the UK, for example, 28 per cent of employment in Northern Ireland and 24 per cent of employment in Wales is in the public sector, while in the much richer south-east only

15 per cent of workers are employed on the same basis.[28] The better-off – mostly in the south-east again – also pay a lot more income tax: according to the Institute for Fiscal Studies, the top 1 per cent of income earners paid around 30 per cent of all income tax in 2013/14, up from a mere 11 per cent in 1979/80. While the increase largely reflected spectacular gains in pre-tax income accruing to globalization's 'winners', the extent to which those extra revenues were subsequently used either to support employment elsewhere in the country or to remove people from the income tax system altogether demonstrates that there was at all times an implicit commitment to redistribution in the UK. Put another way, there was a politically acceptable burden-sharing arrangement.

Between the nation states of the Eurozone, that burden-sharing arrangement does not operate to anything like the same extent: the institutions that might deliver such a result either do not exist or lack democratic legitimacy. German driving licences are not processed in Athens in the same way as London driving licences are processed in Swansea. French social security contributions are not managed in Bilbao in the same way as Brighton's national insurance contributions are managed in Newcastle.

Before the formation of the euro, this was not a significant problem: underperforming countries would devalue against their stronger neighbours. The devaluation was an implicit burden-sharing arrangement. If, for example, Italy devalued against Germany – with the lira thereby falling in value against the Deutsche Mark (DM) – Italian exporters would become more competitive, but German exporters would lose out. Italian consumers, on the other hand, would be worse off – and German consumers better off – thanks to an increase in the lira price of Italian imports from Germany (and a reduction in the DM price of German imports from Italy). Meanwhile, Germans who had invested in, for example, the Italian government bond market would now be worse off (because, in DM terms, their bonds would now be worth less), while the Italian government, having devalued, would have to pay a higher-than-average interest rate to compensate its creditors for the risk of further 'bad' behaviour.

Within the euro, however, there is no equivalent burden-sharing arrangement. True, countries that once would have devalued can instead attempt to drive down domestic wages and prices to achieve roughly the same outcome. The process can, however, be very challenging politically. John Maynard Keynes made the point forcefully in response to Winston Churchill's decision in 1925 to allow the UK to rejoin the gold standard at the pre-war parity, thus locking in a massive competitive disadvantage vis-à-vis Britain's industrial rivals: 'Mr Churchill's policy of improving the exchange by 10 per cent was, sooner or later, a policy of reducing every one's wages by 2s. in the £.'[29] The consequences were, as Keynes had warned, very painful: a General Strike in 1926, persistent austerity through the remainder of the 1920s and, in 1931, a humiliating devaluation.

The lack of a foreign exchange 'safety valve' is particularly unfortunate in a world of high debt and ultra-low inflation – precisely the conditions facing many Southern European countries in the years following the 2008 financial crisis. Ultra-low inflation tends to be associated with ultra-low interest rates. If, under these circumstances, a country within a single currency area is still uncompetitive, it will have no choice but to push prices and wages lower. The outstanding nominal amount of debt, however, will not change. Nor, unhelpfully, will debt service costs, because, with interest rates at or close to zero, the cost of borrowing cannot fall much further.[30] As a result, the real level of debt actually goes up. The ratio of debt to national income persistently rises, more and more austerity is required, the risk of ultimate default rises and political populism takes root.

THE POPULIST BACKLASH

Populism is not just a knee-jerk reaction. It stems, in part, from a sense that policies delivered during difficult times have – sometimes unintentionally – unequal and unfair effects on different members of society. Bailing out banks in the aftermath of the financial crisis may have helped avoid a 1930s-style meltdown, but very few individuals in the banking industry were subsequently punished; the banking industry – at least in the US – ended up being even more concentrated (and hence oligopolistic) than it had been before the crisis; and regulations designed to keep banks in check were, in many people's eyes, watered down far too quickly. Offering quantitative easing might be better than nothing when interest rates have already fallen to zero, but since it puts more money into the pockets of the already wealthy, it is never going to be seen as the fairest way of stimulating the economy (particularly when households and companies are more interested in repaying debt than in opening their wallets and purses). Demanding that debtors repay their debts while creditors absolve themselves of blame might, by avoiding a messy default, reduce the risks of an extended financial meltdown, but as the Eurozone has discovered, it is likely to trigger a breakdown in trust between debtor and creditor nations in a rerun of the absurd Dickensian moralizing of the nineteenth century.

And populism is particularly likely to take hold in the aftermath of financial crises. Since the 1870s, there has been strong evidence to suggest that financial crises – as opposed to simple recessions – have boosted political populism, most obviously through a lurch to the extreme right. And the results are not just skewed by the rise of Mussolini and Hitler in the interwar period, years in which the extreme right made substantial gains in elections not just in Italy and Germany, but also – within Europe, at least – in Belgium, Denmark, Finland, Spain and Switzerland. Most obviously, there has been a return of populist right-wing politics – and a smattering of populist left-wing politics – in the aftermath of the 2008 financial crisis.[31]

Support for the two mainstream parties in the UK, for example, is lower than it once was: in the 2015 general election, the Tories and Labour together managed to win 67.3 per cent of the vote, whereas through the 1980s and 1990s their combined share was mostly well over 70 per cent. In 1979, when Margaret Thatcher came to power, their combined vote was over 80 per cent; and remarkably, Labour's *losing* share – 36.9 per cent – was a smidgeon higher than the Tories' *winning* share in 2015. The main populist winner in the 2015 election was the Scottish National Party, whose principal aim is for Scotland to gain its independence from the United Kingdom. Elsewhere, parties have either emerged from nowhere or chased electability from the political fringes – Podemos, Ciudadanos and the Junts pel Sí Catalonian separatists in Spain, Syriza and Golden Dawn in Greece, the Five Star Movement in Italy, the Finns Party, the Hungarian Jobbik party, the Dutch Party for Freedom and the French Front National. Meanwhile, in 2016, having won the Republican presidential nomination on an anti-Muslim and anti-Mexican platform, Donald Trump was eventually propelled, seemingly against the odds, all the way to the White House. And, for the Democrats, Bernie Sanders gave Hillary Clinton a run for her money by appealing to younger voters with an offer of free college places to be funded by heavy taxes on the rich, alongside considerable opposition to free trade.

In effect, the financial crisis uncovered an inherent paradox in the structure of late twentieth-century Western societies. Nation states, led by the US (and, in Europe, Germany), were the bedrock on which were built the institutions that governed globalization – the IMF, the World Trade Organization and the European Union. But with the huge increase in cross-border capital flows since the early 1980s, those institutions proved ineffective. And to the extent that the financial crisis revealed inherent inequities within globalization – either within or between nation states – there is an increasing retreat into the 'sanctuary' of the nation state and, by implication, a creeping rejection of globalization and the principle of a common humanity. Politicians are more than happy to tap into this nationalist sentiment. At the 2016 UK Conservative Party conference, Theresa May, Britain's new prime minister, noted that:

Today, too many people in positions of power behave as though they have more in common with international elites than with the people down the road, the people they employ, the people they pass on the street. But if you believe you are a citizen of the world, you are a citizen of nowhere. You don't understand what citizenship means.

She may have been right to criticize international elites, but she was wrong to imply that only elites see themselves as citizens of the world. In one survey, around 51 per cent of respondents across 18 countries agreed with the statement 'I see myself more as a global citizen than a citizen of my country'.[32] Do all these people really have no idea of what citizenship means?

Conflating elites with those who see themselves as global citizens is a dangerous game. It will only serve to encourage 'nativist' and xenophobic undercurrents. Still, Hans Morgenthau's suggestion (echoed by Theresa May) that our international representatives tend to be more comfortable in each other's company than they are with the citizens they are supposed to represent is, in itself, a serious challenge to globalization, particularly if they insist on looking down upon their fellow citizens from a great height.

Today, however, it is less jet set and more mountain retreat.

THE SPIRIT OF ELITISM

The gap between the very rich and the rest may be getting bigger, but the extent to which this growing gap in financial resources is leading to shifts in political power may ultimately prove to be more important. This shift threatens to undermine the democratic legitimacy of globalization. Put simply, the rich have more in common with each other – regardless of their respective national, racial or religious identities – than they have with everybody else. And, if money buys power, this creates an obvious problem.

LAKES AND MOUNTAINS

Consider, for example, the various international forums in which the rich and powerful tend to congregate. There's the ultra-secretive Bilderberg Club, named after the hotel in the Dutch town of Oosterbeek which hosted the first gathering of the transatlantic political elite in 1954. The original aim was to counter a growing anti-American mood in much of Europe. Today, Bilderberg – rightly or wrongly – has become a byword for elitism. Then there's the Forum Villa d'Este, held at the eponymous five-star hotel on the banks of Lake Como by the European House Ambrosetti. In the organization's own words, it is:

> An annual event of international scope and prestige. Heads of state and government, top representatives of European institutions, ministers, Nobel prize winners, businessmen [not women, apparently, although maybe something has been lost in translation], managers and experts from around the world have been meeting every year since 1975 to discuss current issues of major impact for the world economy and society as a whole.[1]

Moreover, although the Forum is 'a unique event held in a highly-prestigious venue . . . the secret of the event's success lies in its *exclusive nature*. Since its inception, its sessions have always taken place behind closed doors.'

Then there are the semi-annual meetings of the IMF and World Bank, mostly in Washington, DC, but from time to time in a 'guest' city: recent examples include Lima, Tokyo, Istanbul and Singapore. The 'public' events at these meetings are mostly for show: the real action typically takes place behind the scenes in countless bilateral meetings.

Of all these gatherings, however, perhaps the best-known – and possibly the most notorious – venue is Davos, the ski resort in Switzerland which, at the end of each January, hosts the World Economic Forum, a gathering of the great, the good and the not so good, with a handful of celebrities thrown in to spice up proceedings. Although it claims to address the big issues of the day, the all-encompassing 'theme' each year appears to be devoid of any real meaning: recent examples include 'Responsive and Responsible Leadership' (2017), 'Mastering the Fourth Industrial Revolution' (2016), 'The New Global Context' (2015), 'The Reshaping of the World' (2014), 'Resilient Dynamism' (2013) and 'The Great Transformation' (2012). At some 1,560 metres above sea level, it is tempting to believe that the world's economic and political problems can easily be solved. Certainly, enough people are willing to toast their collective 'success' each evening, encouraged by the large number of champagne receptions on offer. And, to top it all, there's an opportunity to sign up to a celebrity 'nightcap': in Angelina Jolie's case, the nightcap one year proved far more popular than all manner of discussions on, for example, terrorism, the environment, inequality and human rights. The 'Spirit of Davos' – as Klaus Schwab, its founder, often describes it – is truly a wonderful thing.

Davos originally found fame as a mountain retreat for sufferers of tuberculosis: they went there to benefit from the alleged restorative properties of fresh mountain air. Thomas Mann, the Nobel Prize-winning German author, set his masterpiece *The Magic Mountain* in this now-famous small Alpine town. Though it was published in the early 1920s, Mann began writing the novel in 1913, a year after his wife, Katja, had languished in a Davos sanatorium recovering from a suspected case of tuberculosis. While visiting her, Mann himself was diagnosed with the disease. The mountain in question is the Schatzalp. Most of the characters in Mann's book are patients at the Berghof sanatorium (now a hotel) in Davos Platz at the foot of the Schatzalp. They spend their time eating, philosophizing, sitting on their balconies having 'rest cures', lusting after their fellow sufferers, hearing through remarkably thin walls the sexual antics of their consumptive neighbours, having their chests X-rayed, whistling through their pneumothorax half-lungs (thanks to the pioneering treatments offered by Director Behrens) and, inevitably in many cases, waiting to die.

Mann's mockery of his pre-First World War characters is just as relevant today. Up the mountain, life for the sufferers is oddly pleasurable: 'Viewed from up here, life in the flatlands below seemed strange and perverse.' Few are willing to question the sanatorium's business model:

Director Behrens was neither the owner nor the proprietor of the sanatorium ... above and beyond him stood invisible forces, made manifest only to a certain degree in the management office: a board of directors, a joint-stock company – and the stock would not be a bad thing to have because . . . juicy dividends were distributed annually to the shareholders, despite the high salaries paid the doctors and some very liberal business practices.

And, in the guise of Ludovico Settembrini, an Italian who attempts to offer an optimistic voice of reason, Mann laughs at the Enlightenment values that persuaded many to believe that war in the twentieth century was impossible:

As technology brought nature increasingly under its control by creating new lines of communication – developing networks of roads and telegraph lines – and by triumphing over climatic conditions, it was also proving to be the most dependable means by which to bring nations closer together, furthering their knowledge of one another, paving the way for people-to-people exchanges, destroying prejudices, and leading at last to the universal brotherhood of nations. The human race had come out of darkness, fear and hate, but now it was moving forward and upward along a shining road toward a final state of understanding, inner illumination, goodness and happiness – and technology was the most useful vehicle for travelling that road.

It turns out that the spirit of Davos at the World Economic Forum today is remarkably similar to the spirit of Davos before the First World War.[2]

SUPPORTERS, BENEFICIARIES AND DOUBTERS

The problem with all these gatherings can be simply stated. Those who attend these forums are natural supporters of globalization for one simple reason: they are by far globalization's biggest beneficiaries. And this is a story that long pre-dates the financial crisis. Branko Milanović, one of the world's foremost authorities on global inequality, notes that since the late 1980s, globalization has created both big winners and – at least in relative terms – substantial losers. Simply put, the big winners include those in China, India, Vietnam and Indonesia who have seen sizeable income gains from a relatively low base, and those in the very highest income brackets in the industrialized world (not so much the top 1 per cent but, instead, the top 0.0001 per cent), who have seen monumental gains. The relative losers – those who have experienced hardly anything in the form of income gains over almost three decades – are largely to be found in the bottom half of the income distribution in North America, Western Europe and Japan. By global standards, they are well-off, but within their own nations, they have had a miserable experience. Globalization might work, but it hasn't worked for everyone.[3]

This, in turn, has led to a sense of exclusion, triggering a breakdown in trust between the elite and the rest within the Western world. One telling example comes from an opinion poll conducted a few days before the 23 June 2016 UK Brexit referendum. Those who intended to vote to leave the European Union were much more likely to take the view that 'it's wrong to rely too much on so-called experts who often make predictions and recommendations that turn out to be wrong: it's often better to reply on the wisdom of ordinary people and a bit of common sense'. Those who intended to vote to stay in were, by contrast, more likely to agree that 'the opinions of professional people with expertise, learning and experience on a subject are almost always better than relying on the opinions of the ordinary man on the street, or so-called common sense.'[4] The Brexiteers' enthusiasm for 'common sense' may simply have reflected their mistrust of those 'professionals' considered to have vested interests of one kind or another. Indeed, in another part of the poll, those intending to vote for Brexit had as little trust in the opinions of politicians, journalists, senior religious figures, think tanks and anyone from the United Nations or the IMF as they had in the views of famous actors, sportspeople and entertainers. Those voting to remain, by contrast, were willing to make a distinction between fashion and fame on the one hand, and expertise on the other. Those heading the Brexit campaign were happy to exploit this sense of mistrust. On the eve of the referendum, Michael Gove – chair of Vote Leave – suggested that experts arguing in favour of the UK remaining in the European Union were no better than scientists recruited by the Nazis in the 1930s for the purposes of proving Albert Einstein wrong. For an intelligent man, it was a particularly stupid thing to say – unless, of course, he fully intended to whip up levels of mistrust to an even higher level.

In the 2016 US presidential contest, the choice ultimately came down to an increasingly grudging supporter of globalization – Hillary Clinton – and those who had always favoured an isolationist approach. Donald Trump, channelling one version of isolationism, adopted a protectionist manifesto, whilst Bernie Sanders, Clinton's rival Democrat, was openly against globalization and its linkages with the 'elite'. Throughout the campaign – and doubtless a reason behind her eventual defeat – Clinton struggled to convince people that she understood their concerns. An email scandal didn't help, and nor did her many speeches to Wall Street bankers. And at her April 2016 victory speech at the New York primary – which covered topics ranging from job creation and inequality through to retirement prospects for America's boomers – she wore a $12,495 Giorgio Armani jacket. Hillary Clinton wanted to present herself as an ordinary woman with the common touch and in no way part of a privileged elite. She wasn't kidding anyone.

If the views of the elite – and the experts they hire – are increasingly seen to be representing vested interests, it is easier to see how political populism can take root. Globalization may well be a good thing in aggregate – by raising average living standards and creating economic opportunities for the previously dispossessed – but unless losers are compensated, protected or given the opportunity to retrain, it is difficult to see how the process can easily continue: popular revolts typically take place against those who are increasingly seen to be revolting.

THE IMPACT OF CAPITAL MOBILITY

Elites benefit from modern-day globalization in part because elites own a lot of capital, and capital is, in the modern era, highly mobile. That mobility has changed the bargaining power of Western labour relative to international capital. With manufacturing activity shifting away from the West to lower-cost areas of the world, Western workers have become more dependent on demand for services. Yet, thanks both to the dwindling importance of the 'factory floor' as a natural habitat for organized labour and hostile legislation to speed the process along, union membership has plummeted. And with it, the ability of workers to earn excess 'rents' has declined.

Elite workers, meanwhile, are increasingly compensated through both wages and capital, the latter in the form of shares and options. As a consequence, it is increasingly difficult to assess how much of their total compensation is based on merit and how much is, instead, a reflection of rent-seeking behaviour and, in some cases, their company's monopoly profits.

And elite workers increasingly have a habit of marrying each other. One consequence of the emancipation of women in the workplace is that status is determined not just by attendance at the debutantes' ball, the level of education or parental background, but instead by simple earning power. Rich would-be partners nowadays are more interested in merging their earnings and assets than in subsidizing each other. By cohabiting, co-working and asset-pooling, they can enjoy the fruits of their labours and employ large numbers of staff to manage their lifestyles. This merging of financial power, however, has an important consequence. It reduces social mobility.[5] The offspring of these families are born with the modern-day equivalent of a silver spoon in their mouths. They will attend the best schools, pass through the best universities and end up with the best jobs. And their careers will often receive a kick-start thanks to the influence of mummy's and daddy's friends and acquaintances.

110

MIXED EVIDENCE ON SOCIAL MOBILITY

To be fair, the evidence regarding social mobility – much of it concentrating on the US – offers mixed messages. One study suggested that, despite the public perception of a decline in intergenerational income mobility in the US, evidence gathered from tax returns suggested that there had been, if anything, a mild increase. A child born to parents in the bottom fifth of the income distribution in 1971 had an 8.4 per cent probability of ending up in the top fifth of the income distribution later in life, whereas a child born in 1986 had a 9.0 per cent probability of achieving the same thing.[6] Yet this does not quite capture what is going on at the very top end of the income distribution. Making it to the highest quintile may seem like a big achievement, but it's not quite the same as reaching the top 1 per cent, let alone the top 0.0001 per cent. Other studies have suggested that those who have money keep their money: it can take 10–15 generations for any initial advantage to be eroded. And it also, of course, works in reverse: those who come from families with low social competence in deprived neighbourhoods are themselves likely to remain stuck in the same position.[7] Only if they are able to move to neighbourhoods with – frankly – better neighbours are their opportunities likely to improve. Another study – based on the mid-1990s 'Moving to Opportunity' experiment (designed by the US Department of Housing and Urban Development to assist low-income families in moving to better neighbourhoods) – showed that 'every year spent in a better area during childhood increases a child's earning in adulthood, implying that the gains from moving to a better area are larger for children who are younger at the time of the move'.[8] Unfortunately, very few have the opportunity to do so.

Opportunities for social mobility in the UK are also limited. As Philip Collins, a *Times* columnist, wrote in September 2016:

This is a prosperous country and the existence of poverty on its present scale is shaming. A child born into a poor family will have a lower birth weight than a child born to a rich family. By the age of three, the cognitive development of a child born into a poor family is already well behind its richer peers. The gap opens during school and is confirmed in work. Life for so many people is constant anxiety. There are 2.3 million households, in which 1.5 million children live, that cannot afford to heat their homes. The duration of life itself has a price. The child from a poor family is likely to enjoy nine years less of life than his or her richer counterpart.[9]

It's not so surprising, then, that many people are distrustful of elites who appear to thrive whatever a country's economic circumstances.

THE LEWIS MODEL

Admittedly, this is not the first time that we have seen a big increase in inequality; nor is it the first time that we have seen a disproportionate benefit accruing to the owners of capital. The Lewis model – named after Arthur Lewis, who, in 1938, became the first black academic at the London School of Economics – describes the typical increase in income inequality in the early stages of a country's industrialization.[10] In Lewis's version of events, an impoverished country will likely have an excess supply of labour, much of which will be underemployed in rural poverty. Entrepreneurs set up shop in urban areas. Their efforts encourage an influx of underemployed rural workers into the cities. Yet because the supply of such workers is, initially, perfectly elastic (or seemingly infinite), wages – both rural and urban – remain depressed. The rewards for entrepreneurial risk and subsequent productivity gains go directly into the pockets of the entrepreneurs, in the form of higher profits. These 'capitalists' have the chance to become very rich, even if the majority of workers see little, if any, improvement in their lifestyles. Eventually, however, a Lewis 'turning point' is reached, when the excess supply of rural labour dries up, wages begin to rise and the benefits of industrialization spread to the masses: think, for example, of the transition from Dickensian squalor to urban comfort in London over the last 150 years (a process Karl Marx failed to anticipate) or, more recently, the extraordinary transformation of living standards in Beijing and Shanghai (thanks, in part, to the efforts of entrepreneurs who themselves became billionaires).

Once this stage of development is out of the way, the Lewis model implies that income inequality should fall: with labour no longer in excess supply, wages are likely to rise more swiftly, ensuring that labour's share of national income rises. Moreover, with the emergence of a middle class strongly incentivized to prevent the rich from lording it over them and equally determined to prevent the poor from stealing from them, society ends up appearing to be increasingly meritocratic. And it is also likely to end up with institutions designed to reduce post-tax inequality: most obviously a progressive tax system and a social security system designed to prevent society from being permanently divided between the 'have yachts' and the 'have nots'.

GLOBAL CITIZENS

All of these things have happened. Yet income and wealth inequality in some parts of the Western world are, once again, on the rise, both pre- and post-tax, and both pre- and post-benefits. The usual fiscal checks and balances no longer seem to be working. There's a simple explanation. If the two defining features of the modern era are, first, the increased concentration of capital ownership and, second, the greater cross-border mobility of capital, it is hardly surprising that a national system of taxation and benefits can often do little to prevent the continued rise of inequality. (The US is a notable exception: US citizens are taxed on their global – not local – income, although, despite the long arm of the Internal Revenue Service, US inequality has nevertheless risen.) Russian oligarchs prefer to invest their wealth in London or New York property rather than risk their gains falling into the hands of the Russian taxman. British billionaires choose to live in Monaco – or at least persuade their British spouses to become Monaco residents for tax purposes – to limit their tax burdens. The construction of new homes in major international cities appears increasingly to benefit those who wish to hedge their investment bets across the globe – even as they leave their property portfolios mostly empty – at the expense of local residents, who find themselves priced out of the market. Shareholders demand that mobile capital should be invested where labour costs are at their lowest, preferring companies to invest in Asia than in Europe or North America. The Western middle class becomes a 'squeezed middle': even with a good education, the lack of access to increasingly mobile capital leaves many 'professional people' relatively income poor, even if their productivity may, over time, be on the rise. As such, their political 'voice' slowly recedes. And evidence from the US strongly suggests, unsurprisingly, that money buys political influence: American senators are far more likely to take seriously the views of the rich than those of anybody else, and are far more likely to ignore the views of the poor altogether. Given that the rich are generally more willing to vote than the poor, perhaps that outcome is not so surprising – but it does suggest that success breeds success not only within the family, but also within the polity.[11]

For much of the post-war period, the biggest single determinant of a person's lifetime income was his or her nation of birth: someone born in wealthy Switzerland would most probably end up with much higher lifetime earnings than someone born in, for example, Indonesia. Yet the importance of a person's place of birth is slowly diminishing. On the – reasonable – assumption that average incomes in emerging nations slowly converge with average incomes in the developed world, it may be that the biggest single determinant of a person's purchasing power will, in future, be their status within the society in which they live. That status – or class – will increasingly be determined by a person's parents – and, by implication, the parents' capital. Some kids will have all the luck.

And those that do will be able to meet each other on their own magic mountains.

LIMITS TO ELITISM

Still, politics will eventually get in the way, placing limits on what elites can achieve. Whilst they may have been some of the greatest beneficiaries of globalization to date, elites need to remain close to those in power to enjoy their success. History suggests, however, that they should watch their backs. Even if individual governments are either unable or unwilling to intervene, international elites are vulnerable to the emergence of cross-border power struggles, signalling a move away from cooperation towards conflict.

At the beginning of the twenty-first century, that is exactly what we are beginning to see. The idea that nations are converging on a universal set of values – consistent with the end of history – is nonsense. There is no meaningful 'international community'. We are, instead, witnessing the re-emerging influence of history, geography and religious belief in shaping values in different parts of the world. And, to the extent that belief systems vary, the future of Western-led globalization is suddenly looking very fragile, threatening to undermine both economic progress and financial wealth.

7

COMPETING COMMUNITIES, COMPETING HISTORIES

Too often, the three words used by politicians and news organizations lazily seeking to establish some sense of moral superiority are 'the international community'. If the government of a particular nation acts in a way that 'draws condemnation from the international community' then it has apparently done something very bad indeed. If it has merely acted in a controversial way – perhaps impulsively, without spending enough time weighing up the evidence – its actions may be 'frowned upon by the international community'. If, alternatively, a government has done something that appears to be morally upstanding, its actions are 'applauded by the international community'.

MYTHICAL COMMUNITIES

What exactly is this mysterious, all-knowing 'international community'? Is there really a remarkable group of like-minded individuals or national governments who, collectively, are able to divine at all times the differences between decisions that are wise or foolish, actions that are right or wrong and consequences that are good or bad? It is, of course, a preposterous idea. And a close look at how this mythical 'international community' operates rather proves the point.

One way in which the 'international community' expresses its views is via the United Nations Security Council. Thanks, however, to the veto powers of the Council's permanent members, those views are a mass of contradictions. The Soviet Union was condemned in January 1980 by 52 countries for its invasion of Afghanistan the previous month, yet simply used its power of veto on the Security Council to avoid any further serious punishment. When the US later voiced its displeasure by boycotting the 1980 Moscow Olympics, others, including the UK, chose not to follow America's lead. Whitehall was presumably too busy salivating at the idea of a showdown between Sebastian Coe and Steve Ovett, British middle-distance runners who had been busily stealing world records off one another in the run-up to the Games, to spend too much time worrying about the rights and wrongs of a bust-up between Soviet troops and Afghan freedom fighters.

Another way in which the international community might express itself is via the collective views of Western democracies. Yet, on controversial matters, they often do not agree with one another. The second Gulf War was roundly condemned by Germany and France, even as George W. Bush and Tony Blair allegedly prayed together for a successful outcome. While the UK still talks in romantic terms about its 'special relationship' with the US, it's special largely because it is so unequal, as Anthony Eden discovered to his personal cost during the Suez Crisis. And Germany's relations with the US temporarily soured when Edward Snowden's WikiLeaks revealed that Chancellor Angela Merkel's mobile phone had been hacked by the US National Security Agency. Presumably, Barack Obama was hastily removed from her speed dial.

A third way might simply be a moral equivalent of the Washington Consensus. In this case, behaviours should somehow be judged relative to moral norms established by America's Founding Fathers and subsequently delivered to the world through the benevolent exercise of

American 'soft power'. Yet the US itself has never offered a vision of moral stability. Notably, it has been unable to show any consistent approach in its foreign policies, especially in the Middle East.

In 1983, Donald Rumsfeld, later to become George W. Bush's hawkish secretary of defense, was sent by Ronald Reagan to 'initiate a dialogue and establish a personal rapport' with Saddam Hussein. The aim was to reassure Saddam that Washington 'would regard any major reversal of Iraq's fortunes as a strategic defeat for the West'.[1] As this conversation came only a handful of years after the US had been selling its nuclear technologies to pre-revolutionary Iran and shortly before it broke its own embargo on selling arms to post-revolutionary Iran, it is no wonder that many in the Middle East struggled to form a positive – let alone consistent – view of US involvement in the region.

MYTHOLOGY AND HISTORY

In truth, there is no permanent 'international community'. For the most part, nations act in their self-interest – enlightened or otherwise – in an uncertain and sometimes chaotic world, creating temporary alliances that may last weeks, months, years or decades, but which are always in danger of eventually crumbling. Each country's self-interest, meanwhile, is determined by its own mythology and history – and how that mythology and history is reinterpreted over time. For someone born in the UK at the turn of the twentieth century, the British Empire was a source of wonder and pride. For someone born in the UK at the beginning of the twenty-first century, the British Empire is more likely to be regarded as a source of considerable embarrassment.[2]

Mythology and history go a long way to explain why the European and US views of the 'international community' are not fully aligned, even though the two sides of the North Atlantic are ostensibly close allies. The US may have been a big supporter – both politically and financially – of major international institutions since the end of the

Second World War, but on many occasions has opted not to be governed by those institutions. The fact of its own creation, after all, was an attempt to free its citizens from accepted international norms at the end of the eighteenth century. Since the mid-1980s, the US has vetoed more UN Security Council Resolutions than the other four permanent members of the Council put together.[3] Frankly, given that it has more teeth – economically and militarily – than anyone else, the US does not need to go in search of support from the 'international community' to reach decisions that, in many cases, the international community would be powerless to resist. A good example is the 1983 US-led invasion of Grenada which, at the time, led to huge condemnation from the General Assembly of the United Nations. On being asked about the 108 to 9 vote deploring the invasion – intriguingly, a much greater level of opposition than had been offered in response to the Soviet invasion of Afghanistan – Ronald Reagan pithily observed that 'it didn't upset my breakfast at all'.[4] Then there are the asymmetric extradition arrangements between the US and much of Europe. Even if, say, a UK citizen has broken no UK or European law, he or she can still be extradited to the US to face US justice which, as a UK citizen, might sound completely unjust.

Europe's position, meanwhile, is tainted by its own historical baggage. Most European countries would rather tie themselves in international knots than offer anything by way of leadership in the international arena. The European Union is designed to limit the freedoms of the individual member states even as it safeguards the individual freedoms of the states' citizens. And for much of its life, member states have mostly been happy to accept the resulting reduction in sovereignty (the UK is, of course, the glaring exception). Their joint history has taught them not to trust their own instincts: they'd rather have less sovereignty in exchange for more peace. And, aside from the murderous conflict in former Yugoslavia, most Europeans have got their wish: the French and Germans are no longer at war with each other, the British no longer have to embark reluctantly on continental military ventures and, from the 1990s onwards, Central and Eastern European countries were able to import prefabricated democratic arrangements from the European Union which, initially, kept political extremism at bay.

Yet as economic power heads towards Asia, so a whole series of competing communities are likely to be formed. Mythology and history will, in turn, begin to play an increasingly important role. It is worth spending a few moments considering – in admittedly the most concise fashion – how mythology and history elsewhere in the world differs from the Western model and how those differences will help shape attitudes towards globalization in the modern era.

THE WESTERN VERSION

The West's all-conquering version of globalization arguably began with two accidents. The first, courtesy of the fleas and rats that came in the aftermath of Genghis Khan and the Mongol hordes, was the Black Death. Populations in some cases more than halved. In north-western Europe, the ensuing severe shortage of young workers led to higher wages and – thanks to an excess of land – lower rents. The feudal arrangements of the early fourteenth century gradually fell apart. Workers were better fed, less likely to drop dead on the job and more willing to spend on the medieval equivalent of consumer fripperies. That, in turn, led to greater incentives for trade with the rest of the world.[5]

The second accident was a political response in Western Europe to the news in 1453 that Constantinople had fallen to the Ottomans. There was much gnashing of teeth about the possibility that Europe was about to be overrun by Islam. After all, Christians and Muslims had been at each other's throats for hundreds of years and the collapse of Byzantium provided evidence that Christianity might be on its last legs. For some, the answer lay to the east. Could European Christians somehow find a way to link arms with the Great Khan, effectively opening a new eastern front against the Muslim aggressors? It was an attractive idea, but it was not obvious how such an alliance could easily be arranged. Christopher Columbus offered a solution: he would head west, confident in the belief that, if he sailed far enough, he would end up in Asia.

With Columbus having accidentally discovered the New World, the need for an alliance with the Great Khan suddenly evaporated. Western Europeans quickly found new sources of economic – and military – strength to allow them to stamp their authority on the rest of the world: initially, they owed everything to silver, sugar and slaves, and the technologies they developed to exploit these 'resources'. Thanks to these new sources of wealth, the world's economic centre of gravity decisively shifted from Asia and the Middle East towards Europe and, in time, North America.

As incomes rose, so levels of education improved, democracy blossomed, free speech replaced religious dogma, and science and technology began to advance at a rate of knots. By the late nineteenth century, the Industrial Revolution was in full swing, creating the foundations for economic and political dominance that only at the beginning of the twenty-first century appears to be under threat.

THE CHINESE VERSION

At the other end of the Eurasian land mass, China's first serious attempts at globalization came 1,500 years before Columbus discovered the Americas. Faced with constant demands for tribute from Xiongnu warriors to their west, the Han Chinese eventually decided to fight back, in the process discovering an agricultural bounty, a path through the Gansu corridor and, via the Pamir Mountains, the beginnings of a trade route that later became known as the Silk Road. The ebb and flow of both trade and power thereafter meant that the magnetic appeal of the Silk Road – and, later, its maritime equivalents – became a dominant part of the pre-New World global economy. In the thirteenth century, China capitulated to the Mongol hordes, who promptly set up camp in what became known as Beijing. By the early fifteenth century, the whole world was keen to get its hands on Chinese products, from the finest silks (which had been admired in the West from Roman times onwards) to the most delicate porcelain.

Yet in a fifteenth-century version of the Global Financial Crisis, China's economy became unstuck – largely as a result of excess production at home and excess debts abroad. In the early 1400s, China was benefiting hugely from a successful export machine, the revenues from which were being channelled into the total renovation of the Grand Canal between Beijing and Hangzhou and the accumulation of a vast navy under the command of Admiral Zheng He, probably the most fearsome eunuch that ever lived. Unfortunately, however, foreigners were not always able to produce the kinds of goods that the Chinese themselves wanted. The result ultimately was non-payment of bills, a collapse in confidence, a hoarding of silver (the internationally traded currency of the era) and the beginnings of fifteenth-century austerity. The Chinese navy was scrapped, China itself became increasingly insular and, within the next 100 years, the Europeans had usurped China's dominance in the Indian Ocean. Where Columbus had sailed west, Vasco da Gama had sailed east, rounding the Cape of Good Hope and, in the process, discovering a maritime alternative to the Silk Road that would cut out layer upon layer of avaricious middlemen.

Thereafter, China's experience with globalization was increasingly negative. By the mid-nineteenth century, the British had worked out that the best produce to offer the Chinese in exchange for tea, silk and porcelain was opium. And when, in 1858, the Chinese understandably prevaricated, an Anglo-French expedition arrived, marched on Beijing, destroyed the emperor's Summer Palace and imposed on China the 'Convention of Peking', which led to the opening of more and more 'treaty ports' and allowed Europeans to roam at will through much of China's interior. Things went from bad to worse a few decades later when, in 1931, Japan invaded Manchuria.

Only with a new-found confidence under Mao and, later, a new-found openness under Deng, did China begin to re-establish its poise of old: confidence in the destiny of its people, a willingness to connect, on its own terms, with the rest of the world, and an acute and enduring mistrust of Western power.

THE OTTOMAN VERSION

The Roman and Persian Empires were too busy sparring with each other over the relative merits of Christianity and Zoroastrianism to notice the arrival of a new religious, political and military movement in the seventh century. Yet, thanks largely to the rapid unification of often nomadic Arab tribes, and helped along by their deep knowledge of existing trade routes, Islam spread extraordinarily rapidly: under the Umayyad Caliphate, established only three decades after the Prophet Mohammad's death, Islam reached through North Africa to the Iberian Peninsula and marched through the Middle East into India. For Arabs in particular, the Quran had both spiritual and practical attractions. Whereas existing religions had offered instruction only in alien languages – Aramaic, Latin, Persian – Islam's language was Arabic: God, it turned out, was communicating with his followers in their own language. And, initially, faced with severe economic hardship (the spread of bubonic plague hadn't helped), many were open to Islam's spiritual, as opposed to material, salvation.

Thereafter, it helped that the faithful who signed up early were typically richly rewarded when cities fell to the Islamic conquerors. Importantly, the Umayyad Caliphate allowed merchants free movement within its borders, in effect creating a pre-industrial version of the European single market. Within this market, there was a bustling trade in furs, silks, spices and slaves.

As Islam expanded – geographically, philosophically, culturally and scientifically – Western Europe was regarded, rightly, as no more than a backwater. Economic opportunities lay elsewhere. Global economic power began to be centred on Mesopotamia, notably in Mosul, Basra and, in particular, Baghdad. As Baghdad's citizens began to live increasingly opulent lives – under the Abbasid Caliphate, which had replaced its Umayyad forebear in 750 – new trade routes opened up. More and more people flocked to do business in what was probably the wealthiest city in the world. Even Vikings found their way there. Raping and pillaging on the east coast of England were mere sideshows compared with the opportunity to round up slaves (Slavs) and then transport them down Russian rivers in search of those with particularly deep pockets.

As Baghdad became richer, it also became a target for those intent on making their fortunes through the use of force. In 1258, Baghdad fell to the advancing Mongol warriors who – being enthusiasts for extreme violence – slaughtered most of its inhabitants and destroyed much of its infrastructure. Yet not all nomadic groups were interested in butchery alone. The Seljuk Turks (who had converted to Islam in around 950) were overrun by Mongol warriors in the thirteenth century. They, in turn, also converted to Islam. Together, the Turks and the newly assimilated Mongols divided Anatolia into a series of small emirates. Of these, the Ottomans – led initially by Osman I – proved to be first among equals. Over the next three hundred years, they went on to conquer many others, in the process building the infrastructure of empire.

Had railways existed in the late seventeenth century, an intrepid Ottoman student planning to spend his gap year exploring the empire might have hopped on a train in Budapest, headed down through Sofia and Constantinople, and then turned east towards Baku on the Caspian Sea. Had he chosen instead to head south, he might have passed through Damascus and Jerusalem before heading to Medina and Mecca. Or, had he double-backed in Jerusalem, he might have headed west across North Africa, passing through Cairo, Tripoli and Tunis before finishing up in Algiers.

Eventually, of course, the Ottoman Empire crumbled: effective Austrian resistance and Russian expansionism exposed the first fault lines; nineteenth-century nationalism undermined the concept of empire – Egypt, for example, became increasingly semi-detached; and the First World War administered the *coup de grâce*.

Thereafter, the Ottoman Empire was divided artificially into a series of nation states that, to this day, are in some cases barely functional.[6] Nationalism has never sat well with old ideas of empire or caliphate. Even in Turkey itself – which has often been regarded as a proper, rather than artificial, nation state – the attempt by Atatürk to create a predominantly secular Turkish society in the 1920s was always in danger of being undermined by the competing claims of the religious and, importantly, the Kurds. By the second decade of the twenty-first century, those contradictions were underlined by a surge in bloody violence, a fate that had already, tragically, become part of the daily routine in Iraq, Libya and Syria. These localized conflicts, in turn, increasingly reflected the proliferation of proxy wars as Sunni Saudi Arabia and Shi'ite Iran sparred with each other, both attempting to solidify their respective influences on Islamic thought across the Muslim world.

THE RUSSIAN VERSION

It took a few hundred years before a bunch of Viking bounty hunters – alongside their Slavs – had turned themselves into a proper nation state. In 1721, Peter the Great, a giant man with an unusually small head (and a peculiar fascination with dentistry!), established the Russian Empire – a vast land mass initially handicapped by terrible transportation linkages. Yet those linkages were already improving. By defeating the Swedes in the 1709 Battle of Poltava, Peter had managed to gain secure access to the Baltic Sea (given that St Petersburg had been established in 1703, this was vital). Later on, when she wasn't busy cavorting with her many lovers, Catherine the Great pushed back the Ottomans, establishing

Sevastopol, Russia's gateway to the Black Sea. By the beginning of the nineteenth century, Russians were beginning to spill over into Alaska and, from there, make their way down to northern California.[7] These were the beginnings of globalization, Russian-style.

As the nineteenth century progressed, Russia pushed south and east within Asia, upsetting the Persians, forming alliances with the Afghans, conquering the Caucasus and challenging the Chinese. Underneath all of this, however, Russia saw herself increasingly as a superpower able to rival the British Empire – something the British themselves were well aware of. Indeed, by the late nineteenth century, British foreign policy was increasingly focused on how to contain Russian expansionism. To Whitehall eyes, a rapidly growing Russian Empire seemed increasingly to threaten British commercial interests in China and the Raj.

That threat was made all the more relevant thanks to massive Russian investment in a railway system that criss-crossed the various parts of a now-extended empire. Railways were useful not only as a way of opening up trade across different regions, but also, of course, as a mechanism for transporting large numbers of troops from one part of a now-massive empire to another. That was necessary both defensively – Chechen rebels were a problem for the empire long before Vladimir Putin was born – and offensively: one reason why the British were so uneasy about Russia's ambitions.

Yet for all Russia's apparent might – and its rapid industrialization in the late nineteenth century in response to the opening up of trade and the emancipation of the serfs – it was still economically underdeveloped compared with its European rivals. As it turned out, it was also not quite as skilled in the art of war as it might have hoped: defeat at the hands of Japan in the 1904–05 Russo-Japanese War revealed not only hitherto unrecognized military weaknesses but also the fact that Japan, thanks to the Meiji Restoration, had become a serious industrial player in its own right.

The 1917 Bolshevik Revolution may have overthrown the Romanovs, but it did little to limit Russian imperial aspirations. In the aftermath of the

First World War, Russian Soviet ambition in the Baltics faltered, but the Red Army was ultimately able to make amends thanks to the 1939 Molotov–Ribbentrop Pact, which divided Eastern Europe into German and Soviet spheres of influence. Thereafter, even as the British and Ottoman Empires fell by the wayside, the Soviet Union – the Russian Empire in all but name – seemed to go from strength to strength. Now, however, the Kremlin was no longer interested in expanding to the south and east: it could happily march westwards, thanks in part to the vacuum created following Germany's implosion at the end of the Second World War.

The Soviet Union's collapse at the beginning of the 1990s was thus not just the end of communism. It was also, seemingly, the end of an empire that had created its own version of – communist – globalization. And, with the empire's collapse, many of Russia's carefully assembled strategic gains were lost: no easy access to the Black Sea, a much-reduced exposure to the Baltic Sea, a loss of control over the mineral-rich republics of Central Asia and a struggle to contain Islamic opposition on its southern borders. Under these circumstances, faced with a whole raft of strategic losses, perhaps it's not so surprising that Vladimir Putin's brand of nationalism has been a roaring success at home, even if it has led to increasing nervousness abroad, fuelled by a fear that Russia will one day attempt to re-establish its colonial ambitions.

THE PERSIAN VERSION

A Persian version would probably start in the sixth century BC: its empire thereafter spread from the Mediterranean and Egypt to its west, through to the Himalayas to its east. For hundreds of years it was the centre of world trade, helped along by its willingness to construct an extraordinary network of roads and its openness to the ideas of others. Its bureaucrats made sure that standards were adhered to in the market place, leading to a rapid expansion of commerce. A vast array of irrigation systems created an agricultural bounty that others could only dream of.

Following its retreat in the face of counter-attacking Roman forces and its ensuing collapse in the early seventh century AD, it proved an easy target for the spread of Islam.

Yet it wasn't long before Islam split. Islam's rapid spread into Egypt and through North Africa was inspired initially by Abu Bakr, Mohammad's close companion and the first of the caliphs. Persia, by contrast, was about to give birth to an alternative version of Islam, linked to the belief that not Abu Bakr but Ali, the prophet's cousin and son-in-law, was Mohammad's rightful heir. Following Ali's death and the Battle of Karbala (680), in which Ali's son Husayn and many of his followers were massacred, Islam divided between Sunnis (supporters of the caliphs) and Shi'as (supporters of Ali).

More than eight centuries after this momentous event, Shi'a Islam finally became Persia's official religion, thanks to the beginnings of the Safavid dynasty in 1501. Externally, Persia went from strength to strength, pushing back the rival Ottomans and, under Nader Shah in the eighteenth century, winning control over the Caucasus and, in a fit of military expansionism, sacking Delhi. Decline only set in in the nineteenth century, following defeat at the hands of imperial Russia. Those pursuing the Great Game increasingly treated Persia as not much more than a plaything, with trust between Iran and Britain proving to be a major casualty as it became increasingly clear that Britain's apparent support for constitutional revolution at the beginning of the twentieth century was only designed to weaken Russia (as opposed to strengthen Iran). Matters got worse in the 1950s when Iran threated to nationalize its oil industry. In 1953, the prime minister, Mohammad Mossadeq, was toppled, thanks in no small part to the activities of the British and the CIA. Thereafter, and with continuous Western support, Mohammad Reza Shah, a man initially lacking in confidence, became Iran's increasingly autocratic leader. It was not to last: the 1979 Revolution marked Iran's rejection of the West and an effective return to power of the *ulema*, the men of religion. They, in turn, vied with the Saudis for leadership of the Islamic world,[8] a rivalry that only added to political instability in

Yemen, Syria and Iraq. Still, even if they were unable to win that battle, the ayatollahs could at least claim to have re-established a strong sense of Persian identity that extended all the way back to Darius the Great, the leader of the Persian Empire when it sparred with ancient Greece.

THE AFRICAN VERSION

Trade drove Africa's early connections with the rest of the world. From what is now known as Mali, there was a steady flow of produce across the Sahara to the bustling Mediterranean ports of North Africa: as Islam spread west, so opportunities for traders in sub-Saharan Africa grew. The main commodities sent north were gold, slaves, ivory and ostrich feathers. Along the east coast of Africa, traders got their first taste of Islam not through armies but, instead, via merchants.

These trade flows created extraordinary riches: in 1324, the Sultan of Mali, Mansa Musa, made his pilgrimage to Mecca, allegedly accompanied by 60,000 people and 12 tons of gold. Meanwhile, on the east coast, Mogadishu and Mombasa became African outposts of the Silk Road.

Africa's later tragedy came about almost by accident. Following Vasco da Gama's adventures at the end of the fifteenth century, the European imperial powers – initially interested only in extracting spices from the Far East – began to construct trading posts along the African coast to take on supplies. A journey to the Spice Islands was, after all, long and arduous. Entrepreneurial Europeans quickly recognized, however, that there was money to be made from trade with Africans (or with Arabs, who themselves ran a lucrative slavery business). The idea was simple. Africans and Arabs would round up slaves inland, bring them to the coast and then sell them to Europeans who, for the most part, would ship them across the Atlantic. The Portuguese took theirs to Brazil. Later, the English took theirs to the Caribbean as part of a triangular trade: rum, weapons and cotton were typically sent from England to the west coast of Africa in exchange for slaves who were then sent across the

Atlantic. On arrival in the Caribbean, the slaves were exchanged for sugar that, in turn, was sent back to England to be turned into rum, some of which found its way back to Africa.

It wasn't until the second half of the nineteenth century, however, that Europeans made much headway inland (with the exception of the Boers in South Africa, the Europeans were well behind the Arabs). Thanks to the likes of Livingstone and Stanley, the Nile's source was identified, as were the routes for many other rivers. Suddenly, the heart of Africa had opened up and, thanks initially to the ambitions of King Leopold II of Belgium, the European empires engaged in a mad scramble to gain control. Each wanted to keep an eye on their imperial rivals. Each wanted to benefit from Africa's economic bounty. Each justified their actions in the name of civilization. None spent much time thinking about the consequences of their actions for the indigenous populations.

After the Second World War and the collapse of empires, Africa became a reluctant stage for Cold War politics. Americans and Russians were too often willing to extend excessive credit in exchange for what often proved to be unreliable political support. And when the Cold War ended and the Americans and Russians went home, too many African nations were faced with impossible debt burdens that might have condemned them to poverty in perpetuity. China's renaissance, however, pointed to new opportunities. With rising commodity prices and increasing demand from the East, suddenly African nations were able to grow quickly. How many of their citizens would benefit was another matter altogether. Still, it appeared that, for the first time in centuries, Africa's fate would be determined as much by developments in the East as in the West.

DIFFERENT PERSPECTIVES

Differing historical perspectives inevitably shape attitudes towards globalization and its sub-plots. The Western view of globalization has always been just that: a view based on the spread of Western values to the rest of the world. Other parts of the world, with their competing histories and mythologies, are not so immersed in Western values. And from their perspectives, Western values have, in any case, been anything but stable: the imperial attitudes of the nineteenth century, for example, are hardly aligned with the self-determination of the twentieth.

During the Cold War, these competing histories and mythologies were typically repressed, thanks to a persistent ideological battle between capitalism and communism. In the twenty-first century they have re-emerged, forcing upon nation states choices that, in an increasing number of cases, end up either restraining the forces of globalization or putting them into reverse. We are returning to a world of territorial disputes, competing ideologies and unstable alliances. It's as if we're still coping with Columbus's unfinished business.

THE PIVOT

Columbus only got to the Americas. Under Barack Obama, the US wanted to pivot to Asia. Given the shift in economic power there, the logic was obvious. It was the same logic as was used by the British Empire in the nineteenth century. However, whereas Britain wanted to contain the Russians, the US was more interested in containing the Chinese.

Yet doing so was not going to be easy, for the simple reason that the US economy was – and is – hugely dependent economically and financially on its relationship with China. In 2015, for example, China's exports of goods and services to the US amounted to a whopping $500 billion, whereas the US managed to export only $162 billion back to China, leaving the US bilateral deficit with China at $338 billion. That compares with US deficits of $114 billion and $57 billion with the European Union and Mexico, and surpluses of $63 billion and $24 billion with Central and South America and the combined might of

Hong Kong, Singapore, Taiwan and South Korea. Meanwhile, the US has become increasingly dependent on the deep pockets of its foreign creditors to, in effect, allow its citizens to live beyond their immediate means. And, of the more than $6 trillion in Treasury securities owned by foreigners at the end of 2015, over a third were owned (in equal proportion) by just two countries – China and Japan.

The US–China imbalance is, however, as much a worry for China as it is for the US. As the leaders of the Ming Dynasty discovered in the fifteenth century, there is no point in China producing vast amounts of goods and services to be purchased by others, if those others are either unable or unwilling to pay. Before the global financial crisis, Chinese exports were growing at a rate of between 20 and 30 per cent each and every year. Since the financial crisis – a period of persistent deleveraging – Chinese exports have been more or less flat. There are many reasons for China's remarkable economic progress in the late twentieth and early twenty-first centuries, but before the financial crisis one factor dominated all others: China's ability to increase its share of world trade was nothing short of remarkable. Post-crisis, progress on that particular metric has been a lot more muted.

ROUGH TRADE

Under Barack Obama's presidency, the US became a major sponsor of the Trans-Pacific Partnership (TPP), ostensibly a free-trade zone involving a large number of countries from both Asia and the Americas, but from the Obama administration's perspective a rather useful way of either bringing China into the international fold on American terms or, alternatively, isolating China as other parts of Asia become increasingly integrated with the US. In the early months of 2016, the Office of the United States Trade Representative happily extolled the virtues of the apparently 'made in America' TPP, asserting that it would 'level . . . the playing field for American workers and American businesses', claiming that it would 'write the rules for global trade – rules that will help increase Made-in-America exports, grow the American economy, support well-paying American jobs and strengthen the American middle class', and declaring that 'TPP will make it easier for American entrepreneurs, farmers, and small business owners to sell Made-in-America products abroad by eliminating more than 18,000 taxes and other trade barriers on American products across the 11 other countries in the TPP – barriers that put American products at an unfair disadvantage today'. It also offered a dark warning: 'The rules of the road are up for grabs in Asia. If we don't pass this agreement and write those rules, competitors will set weak rules of the road, threatening American jobs and workers while undermining US leadership in Asia.'[9] There are no prizes for guessing who those competitors with their weak rules were.

At best, these claims were tendentious. TPP was never going to rewrite the rules for global trade. Of the 193 member states of the United Nations, only 12 countries had signed up: aside from the US, they comprised Australia, Canada, Japan, Malaysia, Mexico, Peru, Vietnam, Chile, Brunei, Singapore and New Zealand (although others would be free to join at a later date). In 2015, their combined national income stood at around $27 trillion, around three-eighths of the global total. That sounds like a big number, but it's only because the US economy itself is so big. Excluding America, the remaining 11 countries' combined national income stood at around $9 trillion. In contrast, the EU's stood at $16 trillion. Perhaps more importantly, TPP did not include the $16.5 trillion of national income accounted for by China, India, South Korea, Indonesia, the Philippines and Thailand: of these, the two biggest economies were, in effect, the panda and the elephant in the room.

Moreover, if the claims made by the Office of the United States Trade Representative were really true, why would any country other than the US sign up to the deal? The Office's case appeared to be based on a levelling of the playing field, implying that the other signatories had, in some sense, been cheating: seen this way, TPP represented a chance for the US to get its own back. Yet the Office's interpretation was wide of the mark: like any meaningful trade agreement, TPP would have been disruptive for all concerned. Where David Ricardo's comparative advantage applied, countries would have ended up specializing in some areas and exiting from others.[10] In other words, there would have been both winners and losers in the US labour market, even if overall economic activity had ended up at a higher level (labour standards across the region would also have ended up higher, one reason why TPP's demise comes at considerable cost).[11] Where global supply chains were formed, specialist production would have been concentrated in some countries, and would have disappeared from others: again, there would have been labour market disruption even if the pie had increased in size. Meanwhile, countries integrated into Asian supply chains that had not signed up to TPP would have found themselves excluded from those supply chains in the future: for them, the playing field would not so much have been levelled, but rather tilted dramatically against them.

TPP should have been seen for what it was: a battle for economic leadership in the Pacific region, in which the US and China were the main protagonists. It was, in effect, a competition for hearts and minds. It was also a mis-sold competition, one of many reasons why, ultimately, US voters rejected the internationalism of the Obama administration and instead opted for what appeared to be the isolationism of Donald Trump. To claim, as the Office of the US Trade Representative had done, that the US would enjoy all the benefits and none of the costs was simply not true.

Indeed, the available evidence strongly suggests that the closer regions are to free trade, the smaller are the benefits stemming from a further dismantling of trade barriers, and the greater are the costs associated with a rise in income inequality. And those who are most vulnerable – the low skilled and the least educated – tend to be hit repeatedly: for them, the removal of trade barriers is a significant threat, particularly if policymakers fail to provide sufficient compensation through, for example, the tax and benefit system or generous retraining opportunities.[12] No one likes to be left on life's scrapheap.

PIVOTING TO THE HOTSPOTS

The battle for influence in the Pacific is not really about economics at all: it is instead about power in what is still, potentially, a very unstable region. From a domestic US or European perspective, it is all too easy to believe that the world's territorial disputes are over. Yet for many other parts of the world, that simply isn't true. In East Asia there is no shortage of hotspots. In the South China Sea, China, Taiwan, the Philippines, Malaysia, Vietnam and Brunei all make territorial claims over the Spratly Islands, which offer plenty of fish and potentially bountiful supplies of oil and gas. China has been in the process of establishing 'facts on the ground' – or, more accurately, 'facts on reclaimed reefs' – through the construction of airstrips, the provision of a mobile phone network and even the erection of a lighthouse. In July 2016, and following protests by the Philippines, the Permanent Court of Arbitration in The Hague declared much of this unlawful. In the Tribunal's words, there was 'no legal basis for China to claim historic rights to resources, in excess of the rights provided for by the Convention, within the sea areas falling within the "nine-dash line"'.[13] It went on to say that China had 'breached its obligations under the Convention on the International Regulations for Preventing Collisions at Sea' and had 'violated its obligations to refrain from aggravating or extending the Parties' disputes during the pendency of the settlement process'.[14] There were just two problems with the rulings: first, the Chinese simply refused to recognize the Court's authority, and, second, following the election of Rodrigo Duterte as the sixteenth president of the Philippines, the former American colony suddenly chose to realign itself with China. The icing on the cake – if that's the right phrase – was Duterte's decision to label Barack Obama the 'son of a whore', an accusation Duterte later stated 'wasn't personal'.

Heading north along the nine-dash line, both China and Vietnam claim the Paracel Islands. China and the Philippines are in dispute over the Scarborough Shoal, largely because of its plentiful supply of fish. Both China and Taiwan claim sovereignty over the Pratas Islands (and China, meanwhile, sees Taiwan itself as Chinese). The Senkaku Islands – currently occupied by Japan, but, as the Diaoyu, regarded as sovereign territory by China – are another 'hotspot': their sovereignty ultimately rests on whether they were *terra nullius* (unoccupied and unclaimed territories) when the Japanese got their hands on them in 1895, or whether the Japanese occupied them only as a result of the spoils stemming from China's submission following the First Sino-Japanese War of 1894–95. North of Japan, meanwhile, another historic claim continues to fester: the Southern Kurils are occupied by Russia, which opportunistically took over all of the Kurils at the end of the Second World War, even though, under the 1855 Treaty of Shimoda between Japan and Russia, they had for decades been Japanese sovereign territory. Still, given that later in the nineteenth century Japan claimed all the Kurils in a fit of imperial expansionism, some might argue that the country had forfeited its earlier rights.

The US Pacific Command – PACOM – has, for the most part, helped to keep these unruly disputes from turning into something nastier. Keeping the peace, however, is not the same as resolving underlying contradictory claims. And for the US, peacekeeping will become ever more costly. Keeping a poor and militarily backward China at bay in the past was not particularly difficult, but as China's economy expands and its military capabilities inevitably improve, the US will struggle to offer the same level of 'protection' to those in fear of rising Chinese influence. Policing the Pacific is a huge challenge at the best of times: it takes four days for US ships to sail at full steam from the west coast to Hawaii, and from Hawaii, a further six or seven days to reach Guam or Japan. The more China expands, therefore, the less credible US 'protection' will likely be: whilst American military power is deployed through much of

East Asia, replenishing bases in the event of an outbreak of hostilities would not be achieved so easily.

The 'pivot to Asia' under Barack Obama reflected these new realities. Yet there was – and is – an opportunity cost. With more resources devoted to Asia, fewer could be deployed elsewhere. Doubtless, US thinking was heavily influenced by the shale energy revolution. Thanks to new technologies associated with hydraulic fracturing – alongside horizontal drilling – the US was no longer so dependent on Middle Eastern oil and gas. Why, therefore, spend so much time and trouble investing in a region that for much of the post-war period had only been a thorn in America's side?

Given America's shrinking share of the global economy, however, it followed that the decision to devote more of its – limited – resources to the Pacific risked an increase in power 'vacuums' elsewhere in the world. Indeed, the Pacific pivot may inadvertently have reopened both opportunities and fault lines associated with earlier, more Eurasian, versions of globalization. It is no surprise, then, that concomitant with the US pivot, Vladimir Putin felt more confident in asserting his claims over Crimea while playing a bigger diplomatic and military role in Syria; that Saudi Arabia and Israel became increasingly uneasy about the olive branch apparently being offered to Iran from the US and Europe; that ISIS had been able to muster its forces and fill a void left following the decision – by George W. Bush – to withdraw all US troops from Iraq by 2011; and that China became increasingly willing to spell out its own strategic plans for economic expansion westwards and southwards.

Donald Trump's victory in the 2016 presidential election may, inadvertently, have further clarified the sense of American retreat from international affairs. Relative to Obama's equivocation on foreign policy decisions – most obviously his failure to meet his 'red line' threat on the Assad regime's use of chemical weapons in Syria – voters could either opt for the 'universalist' stance of Hillary Clinton or the isolationist stance of Trump. Clinton's instincts would have been to enforce the Syrian 'red line': having won the presidency, Trump was more inclined to completely erase it, in effect placing Syria within Russia's sphere of influence. And his announcement shortly after his January 2017 inauguration that he would walk away from the Trans-Pacific Partnership created an Asian vacuum that the Chinese were happy to fill.

CHINA HEADING WEST

China's ambitions represent an intriguing combination of Silk Road nostalgia and Marshall Plan vision. They also reflect a desire to reduce the risk of internal instability within China itself. China's economic success has come at a price. Regionally, it is now a very unequal society. Its most prosperous eastern provinces and municipalities – Tianjin, Beijing, Shanghai and Jiangsu – are three or four times richer than its poorest, mostly western, provinces – Guizhou, Gansu and Yunnan. In effect, China is more like an empire than a single nation state, even if it is an ethnically singular empire.[15] Its income disparities are far bigger than those that exist between the states of the US, the prefectures of Japan, the countries within the Eurozone and the regions of the UK.

Part of this income disparity reflects the peculiarities of the *hukou* household registration system, which imposes a distinction between urban and rural workers in much the same way as the German *Gastarbeiter* system treated German and Turkish workers differently in the 1960s and early 1970s: in China, rural workers can move to urban centres, but when they get there, they are typically treated as second-class citizens. The result is a bifurcated labour market where millions upon millions of people are denied the opportunity to fulfil their potential. While there may originally have been good reasons for limiting movements of workers from one Chinese region to another – in much the same way that border controls limit movements of workers between countries – the *hukou* system may ultimately have been a major contributor to growing regional imbalances and missed opportunities for boosting productivity via the accumulation of skills.

Abolishing the *hukou* system – which, at the time of writing, was Beijing's intention – would help to spread Chinese economic success westwards: 'learning by doing' is only going to work if people are allowed to 'do'. Yet Beijing ultimately has its eyes on a much bigger prize. Recognizing that its pre-financial-crisis export model is now spluttering, and wary of pouring too much money into domestic investment projects with dubious prospects, Beijing is looking beyond its borders for new opportunities. And it is putting in place the institutions that might eventually lead to a redrawing of the global economic map. They reflect its 'Belt and Road' strategy, first articulated by President Xi Jinping in 2013. The strategy reflects an obvious, but important, point: the further inland Chinese manufacturing goes, the more difficult it is for products to be shipped abroad. Far better, therefore, for China to find ways of linking its western provinces directly with the rest of the world. And that means, most obviously, rebuilding the old land-based links through to Europe (the 'Belt') and the old sea-based links through to the Middle East and East Africa via the Indian Ocean (curiously, the 'Road').

A NEW ASIAN BANK

The Asian Infrastructure Investment Bank, an institution first mooted by the Chinese in October 2013, is designed to support Beijing's Belt and Road ambitions. It is headquartered in Beijing, and perhaps the best way of illustrating the scale of its vision is to list the cities in which the bank's Articles of Agreement were negotiated and agreed upon: Kunming, Mumbai, Almaty, Beijing and Singapore. The bank is designed to complement existing multilateral development banks, most obviously the World Bank and the Asian Development Bank. But it also challenges those institutions.

The World Bank was created out of the ashes of the Second World War and is headquartered in Washington. Its presidents have always been American. The Asian Development Bank, established in 1966 as an Asian version of the World Bank, is headquartered in Manila. Its presidents, however, have always come from Japan.[16]

Both institutions are a reflection of a world economic order that no longer seems quite so relevant: a world in which Japan was encouraged by the Americans in the aftermath of the Second World War to reject militarism, to accept that its future defence depended on the support of Washington, to look to North America and Western Europe for its economic development and to help keep a lid on Asian communism, whether of the Soviet, Chinese, Vietnamese or North Korean variety. The Asian Development Bank's voting structure – determined primarily by each country's subscribed capital – to this day reflects that post-war economic order. The US and Japan have almost 13 per cent of available votes each, while the European Union as a whole has almost 16 per cent. China – with a population of well over 1 billion – has only 5.5 per cent of the votes, marginally ahead of Australia (population 23 million) and Canada (population 35 million).

The Asian Infrastructure Investment Bank potentially marks a dramatic shift away from the immediate post-war world, largely because neither the US nor Japan is currently involved. China pulls the strings, with a 26 per cent share of the vote, followed by India (7.5 per cent), Russia (5.9 per cent), Germany (4.2 per cent), South Korea (3.5 per cent), Australia (3.5 per cent), France and Indonesia (3.2 per cent), Brazil (3.0 per cent) and the UK (2.9 per cent). And even though Washington allegedly attempted to dissuade its allies from joining – Australia and South Korea had their arms twisted to no avail, while the UK's decision to sign up in 2015 left the Obama administration more than a little irritated – the US has ended up impotently observing from the sidelines as other nations have effectively voted with their feet, seemingly dismissing Washington's concerns regarding governance, social justice and environmental risks.[17] It is as if the rest of the world has suddenly recognized that the future lies in the past. The Silk Road, it turns out, wasn't dead. It may only have been resting.

HAPPY EURASIAN FAMILIES?

The Asian Infrastructure Investment Bank is only one part of China's push for economic advantage and political influence across Eurasia. The Shanghai Cooperation Organization (SCO), originally known as the Shanghai Five when first assembled in 1996, is a true Silk Road organization, made up of China, Russia, Kazakhstan, Kyrgyzstan, Tajikistan and Uzbekistan.[18] Its headquarters are split between Beijing, where the secretariat resides, and Tashkent, home of the Regional Anti-Terrorist Structure (RATS). It is, therefore, more than just a regional trade arrangement. Originally formed to reduce military tensions across common borders – given their history, it should come as no surprise that the founding nations were more than a little suspicious of each other – the aim increasingly is to cooperate on military and anti-terrorist matters. Heightened cross-border security should, in turn, foster shared economic development: Beijing sees the SCO as a way of supporting China's 'Belt and Road' ambitions, while Moscow hopes that it will encourage the development of the Russian-sponsored Eurasian Economic Union.

Whether, ultimately, the members of the SCO will be sufficiently cooperative is a matter of considerable debate: to put it mildly, Sino-Russian relationships have not always been ideal, even if they were improving in the early years of the twenty-first century; the former Soviet republics in Central Asia are understandably wary of Russia's flattering embrace, particularly given its recent track record with Georgia and Ukraine; both India and Pakistan hope to join, yet are hardly the best of friends; and while Iran has applied for membership, its enthusiasm for such an arrangement might fade should its relations with the West continue to improve.

Still, with a newly confident Russia already looking to take advantage of a potential vacuum created by America's pivot to Asia (demonstrated most obviously by Moscow's military and diplomatic efforts in Syria), and with China recognizing that it needs to find new sources of economic growth (thanks, in part, to the persistent weakness of Western economies since the onset of the global financial crisis), it is not impossible to imagine that the two main Eurasian protagonists will ensure that the Shanghai Cooperation Organization ends up being more than a simple sum of its parts. After all, Germany and France managed much the same thing with the formation of the European Coal and Steel Community, even though their mutual history hardly inspired optimism.

Meanwhile, with TPP consigned to the rubbish heap, the Chinese can fill the vacuum with the Regional Comprehensive Economic Partnership (RCEP) which, at the time of writing, was in late-stage negotiations, ready to become the leading free trade actor on the Asia stage. RCEP is a proposed free trade zone between the ten members of the Association of Southeast Asian Nations (ASEAN)[19] and individual Asia-Pacific countries with which ASEAN already has free trade agreements: Australia, India, China, Japan, South Korea and New Zealand. Importantly, RCEP excludes the US: with the failure of TPP, China may end up being the biggest player on the Asian free trade stage.

LET THE TRAIN TAKE THE STRAIN

Already there are modest signs that these new institutions are reshaping opportunities within the region. No longer are Chinese goods transported to Europe by container ships and aircraft alone. The train can now take the strain. From Yiwu, a (by Chinese standards) modestly sized coastal city, it is now possible to send goods all the way to Madrid thanks to a railway line that snakes its way through the steppe of Central Asia. From Chongqing, a far larger Chinese urban centre, goods can be sent by train to Duisburg in Germany, cutting through Kazakhstan, Russia, Belarus and Poland along the way.

Admittedly, train travel is not without its complications: most obviously, the various national railways do not share a common gauge, and so containers have to be transferred from one train to another at border crossings (although sophisticated versions of this seemingly cumbersome process can complete the task in less than an hour). Other complications have, however, largely been removed: a combination of cross-border customs agreements and bonded containers means that the whole journey should be completed without a customs hitch (or bribe).

Relative to air freight, the train is cheap. Relative to ocean freight, the train is quick. It can take around 60 days to shift goods from inland Chinese cities to the coast and then take them by ship to European markets. For high-street fashion and consumer electronics, that simply isn't fast enough. The train takes a quarter of the time. And, rather than Europeans paying for their Chinese goods with opium – as the British did in the nineteenth century – it is more likely that, on the return leg to Chongqing, the train is full of Spanish ham, German beer, French wine and a variety of upmarket European automobiles. Even if the new Silk Road remains a shadow of its former self, there is every chance that the ocean-going trade between Europe and Asia that was established in the seventeenth century, and which drove imperial expansion thereafter, may finally be faced with some serious competition – one reason why, starting in 2014, the Suez Canal is being widened to allow bigger ships to pass in both directions.

Admittedly, connecting different parts of Asia together by rail is not in itself a guarantee of economic success. Work on the Trans-Siberian Railway began in 1891. On its completion in 1916, a passenger could hop on board at the Yaroslavsky station in Moscow and, 5,772 miles later, end up in Vladivostok on the Pacific coast. It may have been a marvel of the modern world, but it wasn't marvellous enough to transform the lives of the majority of Russians, a fact that doubtless contributed to Tsar Nicholas II's subsequent downfall. Ultimately, however, the Trans-Siberian Railway was an internal Russian route, designed as much as anything else to allow troops to shuttle between Russia's European and Pacific interests. The twenty-first-century versions – crossing from one country to the next – are more a reflection of economic opportunity. As such, they more closely follow the spirit – and indeed the path – of the original Silk Road.

FREEDOM, DEMOCRACY AND EDUCATION

Still, much of Eurasia faces the same authoritarian systems of government that, arguably, held back Russia's economic development over the last 100 years. According to Freedom House, Eurasia has the lowest level of 'freedom' of any region in the world. Put another way, Eurasian nations and democracy do not make happy bedfellows. The figures are striking: by Freedom House's calculations, 79 per cent of Eurasians are 'not free', 21 per cent are 'partly free' and none are 'free'. Only countries in the Middle East and North Africa score more poorly: within that region, 85 per cent are 'not free' and only 5 per cent – those living in Israel, the only enduring democracy in the region – are 'free'. Contrast these numbers with other parts of the world: in Asia-Pacific, 42 per cent are 'not free', in the Americas, 1 per cent are 'not free' and, in Europe, no one is 'not free'.

Conventional Western thinking suggests that the failure to rid themselves of their authoritarian regimes will prevent sustained economic development across the nations of Eurasia. Yet the argument can only be taken so far. First, the world's rich democracies no longer appear so easily able to do the economic equivalent of turning base metal into gold. Decade by decade, economic growth has been slowing down in the world's major industrial nations.

Second, given this broad-based economic slowdown, Western democracies appear no longer so committed to globalization: the rise of populist protectionist movements in the US and much of Europe suggests that, even as Eurasian nations have the opportunity to become more closely linked, Western nations may be heading in the opposite direction.

Third, the world's most populous non-democracy – China – has already been through an epic transformation: since the 1980s, its average living standards have risen from a level equivalent to those in the US circa 1790 to a level to be found in the US in about 1940. If China's 'know-how' spreads westwards – funded by the Asian Infrastructure Investment Bank, for example – then anything is possible.

Fourth, that 'know-how' is on the rise. Educational attainment for the vast majority in East Asia is remarkably high, eclipsing the West's efforts. Standardized tests[20] reveal that the top ten countries ranked by their 15-year-olds' mathematical ability are mostly Asian: Singapore comes first, followed by Hong Kong, Macao, Taiwan, Japan, China (urban centres) and South Korea. The UK comes 27th, while the US flounders in 40th position. Admittedly, American and British 15-year-olds perform relatively better in science and literacy,[21] but this is only a small crumb of comfort: Asian teenagers may not be as rich as their Western cousins, but the evidence suggests that they work harder, that they achieve better overall results and that they – and their parents – are ambitious. Whether or not Asian regimes are authoritarian, the quality of the human capital is very high indeed. And, with a high level of human capital, even authoritarian regimes can sometimes make considerable progress. After all, Western nations themselves did so in the nineteenth century: they may have been democracies of one kind or another at home, but their colonial adventures farther afield too often put democracy to shame.

THE INTERNATIONAL COMMUNITY REVISITED

Economic and political power is heading east: China and India are the new economic heavyweights, while Japan, South Korea and Taiwan have living standards which, on average, are at least as good as those typically on offer in Europe. By resurrecting the ancient Silk Road, China is reaching across to Europe and Africa. In the process, it is re-energizing hitherto dormant Central Asian economies. Under President Obama, the US was responding by reaching out across the Pacific, chasing both political influence and economic opportunity; with TPP now shelved, it may be that President Trump will adopt a more isolationist approach.

Europe, meanwhile, sits passively, seemingly waiting for the best offer to come its way: it is not sure whether its future still lies with the US, the late twentieth-century imperium, or with the countries and regions to its east. Given America's Asian pivot under President Obama, Europe's prevarication is unsurprising. And given the pivot, perhaps Washington shouldn't have been so surprised that so many European countries were quick to sign up to the China-led Asian Infrastructure Investment Bank. Europe, after all, finds itself at the other end of a twenty-first-century Silk Road. Perhaps European policymakers with a sense of nostalgia gaze at Venice and Florence, hoping that a new Silk Road could once again be a source of bountiful wealth.

There are plenty of obstacles standing in the way of this vision – not least the Islamic world that, in effect, separates much of Europe from Asia, and where, through violence or otherwise, many still harbour dreams of a unified caliphate. Nevertheless, countries and regions in the twenty-first century will doubtless continue to do what they have always done, whatever their religion or creed. They will follow economic opportunity. Forget the international community. The US and China are scrabbling for power in the Pacific. Russia is rethinking its relationships with its many neighbours. And Europe is in danger of being stuck in no-man's land, not sure about the on-going commitment of the world's most successful democracy to its future, yet uneasy about falling into bed with the authoritarian regimes that lie to its east.

DISRUPTIVE ELEMENTS

Still, whatever the changing relationship between countries – and whatever the changing relationship between elites and the rest within countries – the challenges to globalization in the twenty-first century are not just about politics and power. They are also about people, technology and money. These might be regarded as the 'disruptive' elements, beyond the control of any one nation or region, but hugely influential regarding the political and economic choices we will make in the decades to come. And, as we shall see in Part Three, those choices, in turn, will help determine whether globalization advances or retreats.

Part Three

TWENTY-FIRST-CENTURY
CHALLENGES

8

PEOPLE AND PLACES

Through much of the late twentieth century, globalization was dominated by cross-border capital flows. Yet, as the century drew to a close, a
partially dormant force of globalization became active again. As it did,
attitudes towards globalization began to sour. Immigration, it seems, is
once again a political hot potato.

PEOPLE ON THE MOVE: THE NINETEENTH-CENTURY
GLOBALIZATION STORY

During the nineteenth century, the single biggest driver of globalization
was neither trade nor capital flows. It was people. Before the onset of the
Industrial Revolution, most of those people were slaves: of the 11.3
million who went to the New World before 1820, 8.7 million came –
involuntarily – from Africa. With the advent of the Industrial Revolution
and an associated decline in transportation costs, voluntary (as opposed
to coercive) migration accelerated rapidly. Entrepreneurial European
workers – mostly young men – were suddenly given a chance to buy a

lottery ticket. No longer did they have to be continuously held back economically by their place of birth. The New World beckoned.

In the mid-nineteenth century, roughly 300,000 emigrants left Europe each year, mostly to head across the Atlantic. In those early years, a good proportion of migrants came from richer countries, most obviously England and Germany: they were just about able to scrape together the money for the – one-way – fare. And they were – by definition, in most cases – willing to take a risk: as such, they added to the entrepreneurial stock of the 'receiving' nation.[1] Often, their wages were higher than those of their new-found countrymen – they enjoyed the benefits of being in a 'sellers' market' for skilled labour. And the more money they earned, the easier it became for them to fund the crossings of friends and family. In this way, immigrants begat immigrants.

Yet this was not the case for everyone. Environmental shocks sometimes forced even the poorest to move in search of a better outcome. While many of the migrants to the US in the mid-nineteenth century were relatively skilled and well-paid young men, there was one major exception, thanks largely to *Phytophthora infestans* – more commonly known as potato blight.

The Irish potato famine began in 1845. For the poorest of Irish tenant farmers – and there were plenty of them – potatoes had become the main source of nutrition. Much of the potato crop was of a single variety, the Irish Lumper. This lack of diversity meant that the entire crop was at greater risk in the event of disease. And so it came to pass. In 1845 alone, almost half the crop was lost to the fungus. In 1846, three-quarters of the crop was lost. In 1847, a lack of seed potatoes – a consequence of the earlier failures – led to further severe shortages. Meanwhile, the ruling British government appeared, at best, ambivalent. In the face of mass starvation, soup kitchens were provided, but for a limited time only. While plenty of grain arrived in Ireland to help make up the shortfall, there were serious distributional failures: those in greatest need in the west and south of Ireland continued to suffer. Vast numbers of tenants, unable to pay the rent to absentee landlords, faced eviction: some esti-mates suggest that around 500,000 were forced out of their homes in the decade after the famine began.

These broader failures – which went far beyond the destruction of the potato crop alone – reflected a number of beliefs held by the British. These, in turn, encouraged the development of Irish Republicanism. Committed to free-market capitalism, Westminster was ideologically ill-disposed to any kind of government intervention. Many in Britain thought the Irish had only themselves to blame: their agrarian economic system had been a persistent source of failure over many decades and, in the eyes of some, the famine was an act of divine providence. As Sir Charles Trevelyan, a British civil servant, wrote in 1848, the famine was 'a direct stroke of an all-wise and all-merciful Providence'. It was 'the sharp but effectual remedy by which the cure is likely to be effected.' [2]

And there were plenty in Britain whose attitudes towards Irish Catholics were – to be frank – brutally racist.

Estimates vary but it is now thought that around 1 million Irish citi-zens died of either starvation or disease in the years of the potato famine. In addition, 1–2 million emigrated. Of those, many headed across the Atlantic to the promise of a better life in the New World. It was a perilous journey – the nineteenth-century equivalent of modern-day Africans crossing the Mediterranean in tiny overcrowded boats. So-called 'coffin ships', mostly unregulated, sailed from the west coast of Ireland to North America. Of the 100,000 who headed to Canada in 1847, around 20,000 perished, typically killed off by the starvation and disease they had hoped to escape from. Nevertheless, the majority survived. As a conse-quence, cities on either side of the Atlantic became increasingly 'Irish'. In 1851, roughly a quarter of Liverpool's population and half of Toronto's had come directly from Ireland. The Irish also established large commu-nities in Boston, New York and Philadelphia.

Meanwhile, the population of Ireland itself shrank rapidly – a reflec-tion of both death and emigration. In 1841, the Irish population stood at around 8.2 million. Ten years later, it had dropped to just 6.6 million, an astonishing figure given that much of Europe was enjoying a demographic boom. Ireland's population shrinkage continued through to the end of the nineteenth century. Many of its youngest and potentially most fertile workers had gone elsewhere, leading to a sharp contraction in the fertility rate. By 1900, the Irish population had halved, compared with the 1841 peak. The Irish diaspora, meanwhile, was going from strength to strength. By the beginning of the twenty-first century, around 80 million people worldwide could claim to have Irish roots. Yet, of those, fewer than 4 million lived in Ireland.

Later in the nineteenth century, there was an acceleration in flows to the New World from poorer parts of Southern and Eastern Europe, reflecting both a further sustained decline in transportation costs and, particularly for Eastern European and Russian Jews, an entirely understandable desire to escape the pogroms that were under way by then. In the first decade of the twentieth century, emigration from Europe was running at an annual rate of around 1.4 million. Most emigrants headed to the United States, which at the peak was receiving over a million immigrants each year[3] – four times the number of Syrian refugees seeking asylum in Europe in 2015 (although, to be fair, refugees were also coming to Europe from elsewhere).

In total, around 60 million Europeans – the equivalent of the entire population of Italy in the early twenty-first century – sailed to the New World. This, in turn, meant that New World populations were expanding rapidly, in effect turning into European 'offshoots'. In 1910–11, the foreign-born share of New World populations was particularly large: 17.1 per cent for Australia, 30.3 per cent for New Zealand, 14.7 per cent for the US and 29.9 per cent for Argentina.

THE INTERWAR COLLAPSE IN MIGRATION

During the First World War, however, everything changed. Attitudes from the 'receiving' countries hardened, in part because lower transportation costs had led to what might be impolitely described as a 'lower quality of immigrant'. With immigrants increasingly coming from poorer parts of Europe (and, to a more limited degree, Asia), their educational attainment was typically lower and they arrived with fewer skills. By the beginning of the twentieth century, immigrant wages were already well below those enjoyed by the 'indigenous' US population, thanks in part to the shift in emigration from Northern Europe to Southern and Eastern Europe. Immigrants were increasingly perceived to be undercutting the wages of those already performing low-skilled work.

The political consequences were profound. Congress pushed through the 1917 Immigration Act, popularly known as the 'Literacy Act' because it barred all would-be immigrants over the age of 16 who were unable to read and write. In addition, however, the act imposed a blanket ban on Asians from a defined – and very large – geographical area: it thus also became known as the Asiatic Barred Zone Act. And, for good measure, the act further banned homosexuals, idiots, feeble-minded persons, criminals, epileptics, insane persons, alcoholics, professional beggars, those who were in any way 'mentally or physically defective', polygamists and anarchists. If the US had an 'open doors' policy in the late nineteenth century, the door had suddenly been slammed shut. It wasn't quite Donald Trump's wall along the Mexican border, but the message was clear enough.

Immigration collapsed, thanks both to the new 'closed door' policy and to a further narrowing of the wage differential between workers in the 'Old' and the 'New' worlds which inevitably reduced the economic incentive for Europeans to head west. In the 1920s, around 400,000 immigrants per year made it to the US. In the 1930s, that number had fallen to around 50,000 per year. After the Second World War, immigration quickly returned to the 1920s average, but it was not really until the very end of the twentieth century – and the first decade of the twenty-first – that immigration rose to its pre-First World War highs. By then, the US population – at over 300 million – was three times bigger than it had been at the beginning of the twentieth century. So, in other words, despite the renewed acceleration, immigrants made up a much smaller proportion of the overall US population than had been the case at the beginning of the twentieth century.[4]

THE DEMOGRAPHIC BOOST AND THE ETHNIC SHIFT IN THE US

The late twentieth-century acceleration in US immigration owes something to the 1965 Immigration and Naturalization Act and to the re-establishment of some of the economic incentives that had been at work before the First World War. This time, however, immigrants came not so much from Europe as from Latin America and Asia. By the beginning of the twenty-first century, immigrants to the US were arriving mostly from China, India, the Philippines, Vietnam, Mexico, Cuba, the Dominican Republic, Haiti, Jamaica, South America and Africa. Ellis Island – the New York entry point for early twentieth-century European immigrants – had reopened, but only as a tourist attraction.

The gradual opening up of its borders from the mid-1960s gave the US a rather useful demographic boost. Given that fertility rates for first- and second-generation immigrant families tend to be higher than for the population as a whole, the US ended up with a 'Benjamin Button' population profile, steadily becoming more youthful even as, for example, the ageing process was stifling Japan's economic advance. Yet the US population was also changing in other ways. By 2015, there were more Spanish speakers in the US (41 million native speakers and another 11.6 million bilingual speakers) than in Spain. The US Census estimates that, by 2050, there will be 138 million Spanish-speaking US citizens,[5] almost half of the total population.

This Hispanic concentration may create new challenges. The 'melting pot' that so attracted immigrants to the US over the centuries may no longer work quite so well. In the first decade of the twenty-first century, almost a fifth of legal immigrants – 1.7 million out of a total of just over 10 million – came from Mexico alone. Such bulk immigration may be more difficult to integrate into American society. Large numbers of immigrants from a common country may choose to stick together. In doing so, they may not be incentivized to develop the language and other skills that might offer both themselves and their children the widest of opportunities in the 'land of the free'.[6] And in time, the US could end up split between predominantly English-speaking and mostly Spanish-speaking parts. Whether such a bifurcation matters is an issue for debate: German-speaking Zurich and French-speaking Geneva happily coexist within Switzerland, after all. Nevertheless, during the 2016 presidential election campaign, it was abundantly clear that, for many Americans, immigration had become a major political and emotional issue, whatever the economic rights and wrongs. And, to the extent that this debate threatens a return to US attitudes seen in the interwar period, it points to the return of American isolationism.

BEYOND *WINDRUSH*

Across Europe, different approaches to immigration were adopted after the Second World War. But for the most part, they had a common aim: with millions of working-age men and women dead as a result of battle, bombs or concentration camps, there weren't enough left to support the process of post-war reconstruction. With persistently low unemployment rates, immigration was an obvious answer. In many cases, the process was a reverse of the nineteenth-century story. Back then, Europeans emigrated to the rest of the world. Now, the rest of the world was emigrating to Europe – and Europeans themselves were increasingly hopping across their common borders.

For the UK, many immigrants in the 1950s and 1960s came from its remaining and former colonies. In response to the British Nationality Act of 1948, which gave Commonwealth citizens free entry into the UK, the first batch of West Indian workers arrived on the SS *Empire Windrush*. Over the next two decades, large numbers also arrived from the Indian subcontinent, a mixture of Hindus from Gujarat, Sikhs from the East Punjab and Muslims from both Pakistan and modern-day Bangladesh (not that the indigenous British population was very interested in the distinctions between these various groups). And in 1972, thanks to Idi Amin's brutal racism, over 27,000 East African Asians, whose forebears had arrived in East Africa under nineteenth-century British colonial rule, found sanctuary in the UK. In Amin's own words, 'Our deliberate policy is to transfer the economic control of Uganda into the hands of Ugandans, for the first time in our country's history'.

Still, Amin was not the only politician suspicious of the 'foreigner' in his midst. Enoch Powell, in his notorious April 1968 'Rivers of Blood' speech, argued:

> For reasons they could not comprehend [the existing UK popula-tion] found themselves made strangers in their own country ... The Race Relations Bill ... is the means of showing that the immigrant communities can organise to consolidate their members, to agitate and campaign against their fellow citizens, and to overawe and domi-nate the rest with the legal weapons which the ignorant and the ill-informed have provided. As I look ahead, I am filled with foreboding: like the Roman, I seem to see 'the River Tiber foaming with much blood'.

Powell was also happy to quote a constituent who suggested that, 'In this country in 15 or 20 years' time the black man will have the whip hand over the white man'.[7] Powell's whole speech is littered with references to Negroes, Sikhs and differences 'of colour', with no mention whatsoever of any 'perils' associated with white immigration. Plenty at the time thought he was a man of brilliant insight, but in truth he was no more than a ghastly racist who happily pandered to others' fears and insecurities. To his credit, Edward Heath, later to become prime minister but at the time leader of the opposition, sacked Powell from his shadow front-bench team the day after the speech.[8]

Fears and insecurities tend, irrationally, to change over time. In the early 1960s, the people of Bedford in England were more bothered about Italians than they were about Sikhs or West Indians. In 1960, the Marston Valley Brick Company applied to the local Conservative council to employ an additional 200 Italians. The manager of the business, one Robert Miller, said, 'They are first class workers. We simply can't get Englishmen to work in the brickfields. It's a difficult and hard job. And the Italians do it well.' The council, however, simply stated, 'We want no more foreigners.' The local mayor, Alan Randall, noted that 'Bedford is proud of its Italians . . . But there are complex problems. They pack into houses like sardines. Our Public Health Department has had to be augmented to cope with the problem. And we still have 1,100 on our housing list. In our schools, the language problem is acute. English children are being held back.'[9] Today, British people complain less about Italians and more about Poles, Romanians and Syrians: why pick on Italians when it turns out that among the most popular foreign dishes consumed in the UK are spaghetti Bolognese, lasagne and spaghetti carbonara?[10]

Labour shortages also appeared in other parts of Western Europe, particularly during the 'golden years' of rapid economic expansion in the 1950s and 1960s. West Germany responded by launching its *Gastarbeiter* programme. Workers were invited to Germany as 'guests': they were treated as second-class citizens, didn't enjoy the rights bestowed upon Germans themselves and, for the most part, were expected to return to their country of origin within a couple of years or so. Of all the nationalities that took up the offer, Turks were the most enthusiastic, in part a reflection of dismal economic prospects at home.

By the beginning of the 1970s, over 1 million Turks were living in Germany. Many of them performed menial tasks that did little to further their own economic prospects (although they were probably still better off in Germany than they would have been had they stayed in Turkey). Those who subsequently returned home seemingly made little difference to the performance of the Turkish economy, which continued to languish in agricultural poverty. And as soon as Germany's *Wirtschaftswunder*[11] came to a sudden end in the aftermath of the 1973 global oil price shock, the *Gastarbeiter* programme was shut down. Guest workers, it turns out, were no more than a means to an end. For the remainder of the 1970s – and for much of the 1980s – immigration flows subsided. Then the Berlin Wall came down and everything changed.

THE KEY DRIVERS OF MIGRATION

The past two hundred years show that waves of immigration are not driven by one factor alone, and nor can they be completely suppressed by trigger-happy border guards. A big income gap between those thinking about emigrating and the citizens of the country they are planning to immigrate to provides a useful incentive: otherwise, from an economic perspective, there is little point in making the journey. A dramatic demographic shift that is associated with the fact that infant mortality is falling more rapidly than fertility will eventually trigger a substantial increase in the number of young people of working age: unencumbered by family commitments, some of them will be keen to spread their wings. A large fall in transportation costs, and a reduction in the dangers associated with transportation, will encourage more people to emigrate: too high an initial price for an uncertain future is a price simply not worth paying. Along the same lines, a sustained increase in incomes at home, thanks to the impact of industrialization on productivity, will allow more people to afford the journey (in other words – and seemingly counter-intuitively – rising incomes at home initially make it more likely that people will head elsewhere). And destination countries need to be either willing to accept the immigrants or, failing that, unable to prevent their arrival.

Within the Western developed world, the influence of these factors has diminished as the gap in living standards between rich and poor countries has narrowed: there simply aren't enough poor Italians still dreaming of an exciting and enriching life in the US. The gap now lies not so much between Europeans and their offshoots, as between the OECD nations – with their high incomes – and the rest. Yet the huge increase in state provision of goods and services through the twentieth century and beyond has made immigration more controversial politically. Should newly arrived immigrants be allowed to enjoy the fruits of a social benefits 'club' when, by definition, they cannot possibly have made any kind of financial contribution? Heightened immigration controls – very much a feature of the twentieth century and beyond – have prevented market forces from operating to their fullest extent: in the absence of those controls, the flow of immigrants from poorer parts of the world into developed markets would almost certainly have been far greater and the allocation of resources more efficient. The end of colonialism, meanwhile, has meant that white, mostly European settlers can no longer travel the world in search of a new home with the confidence associated with nineteenth-century missionary zeal. Instead, it is people from the former colonies who are more likely to be heading to the developed West.

SCHENGEN: A JOURNEY BACK TO THE NINETEENTH CENTURY

Despite the increase in border controls, history suggests that at least some determined migrants eventually do find a way of moving from one country to the next. And in the first half of the twenty-first century, there is likely to be a very large number of such migrants.

Change was already under way within Europe thanks both to the European Union's dramatic eastward expansion and (apart from the UK and Ireland, which both opted out) to the Schengen Agreement.[12] Schengen was first signed in 1985, but was not truly a European Union arrangement until it was formalized within the 1997 Amsterdam Treaty. In the Schengen area, there are no border controls: in other words, no passport checks, no vehicle checks, no customs checks – nothing that would give the impression that someone was leaving one country and entering another. Schengen guarantees that, within its borders, people are free to come and go as they please. It is, in that sense, very much a nineteenth-century libertarian model. The only borders relevant in Schengen are its external borders with the rest of the world.

From an economic point of view, Schengen appears to make a lot of sense. Border controls inhibit economic relationships. Opportunities for exchange are denied. Resources are allocated inefficiently. In the same way as canal tolls were a barrier to trade in the eighteenth and nineteenth centuries, so border controls became a barrier to trade in the twentieth century. By creating a properly European labour market, Schengen should – at least in theory – lead to a better allocation of labour resources and a better flow of information regarding economic opportunities across borders (indeed, during the Eurozone crisis, many Spaniards headed north, finding work in other, less crisis-prone European nations).

To a degree, the evidence points in that direction. Notwithstanding language differences, wider EU and Schengen membership has triggered substantial movement of both people and capital and, in the process, cross-border trade flows have expanded.[13] German companies happily invest in Eastern Europe; Eastern Europeans happily live and work all over Western Europe. This process, however, is not just about efficiency gains: cross-border movement of both labour and capital is also, in part, a process that reduces inequalities of income and opportunity by levelling a previously very steeply inclined playing field.

The failures of Soviet-style communism prevented Eastern European countries from making significant economic progress in the decades following the Second World War: their living standards slowly fell

behind those in the West. While there has been some renewed convergence since the fall of the Berlin Wall in 1989, a large gap in living standards remains: in 2014, per capita incomes in Hungary, Romania and
Bulgaria were less than half those in the Netherlands, Germany, France
and the UK.

Merging these labour markets should ultimately mean higher levels
of output and more investment, in theory making everyone better off.
But, as with moves towards free trade, there will also be distributional
winners and losers. Thanks to an increased pool of cheap labour, owners
of capital will tend to do rather well. Within the richer nations, suppliers
of labour – particularly of the unskilled variety – may suddenly discover
that life is no longer quite so comfortable: more competition in Western
European labour markets will tend to exert downward pressure on the
wages of French, German and British workers, even as the process of
convergence places upward pressure on the wages of their Hungarian,
Bulgarian and Romanian rivals.

It is precisely this effect – even if its size is indeterminate[14] – that
populist political parties in Western Europe have seized upon. In the
aftermath of the global financial crisis, and with the iniquities of the
Eurozone crisis like a festering wound, there are plenty of people willing
to sign up to the populist message.

SYRIA: A RETURN TO THE TWENTIETH CENTURY?

More than most, economists tend to suffer from the idea that people are
all the same: that the labour market is homogeneous; that people have
similar values; that rational man is, well, rational. The idea is a useful
assumption: economic models work better as a result. Sometimes,
however, it can be an unhelpful simplification. When it comes to migration, the idea of the 'common man' masks some of the key issues pertinent to the debate. Whether we like it or not, economic 'clubs' are not
always about the nation state: they can also be defined by cultural, ethnic

or religious differences. The melting pot doesn't always work. And when it doesn't, economic outcomes can be hugely disappointing.

Initial work in this area focused on Africa. High levels of ethnic diversity within African nation states were associated with poor schooling, rudimentary financial systems, corrupt dictators and a lack of decent infrastructure: too many competing interest groups – each with its own agenda, each unwilling or unable to agree with the others, each looking to maximize its economic rents, and each in effect disrupting the provision of public goods – collectively gave rise to persistent economic underperformance.[15] But this is not a uniquely African problem. The prevalence of religious schools in the UK – whether Christian, Muslim or Jewish – has the potential to create competing interest groups at a very young age (and, in some cases, pits the schools and their governors against the educational authorities). Similar issues apply in France: the decision in 2010 to ban the niqab and burqa in public spaces furthered a debate on the relative power of state and religion which, in the early twentieth century, had created a schism between the Catholic Church and the Third Republic.

The welfare state can be swiftly undermined in the absence of shared cultural norms. Why would people choose to be members of a club in which other members have a different conception of – and perhaps lower levels of adherence to – the club rules?[16] Social protection is, more or less by definition, provided at the local or national level: defining who is to be protected is, in effect, defining who is *not* to be protected.

This, in turn, creates a fundamental problem. Welfare states were mostly created behind closed doors. Thanks to the increase in border controls in the interwar period – bizarrely helped along by a series of proclamations by the League of Nations in the late 1920s – countries were more easily able to choose their own desired mix of tax, benefits and state provision. Borders thus provided nations with considerable fiscal sovereignty: in doing so, they allowed nations more easily to become economic clubs.

Within the European Union, the creation of the aforementioned four freedoms (free movement of goods, services, capital and people) alongside a common border via Schengen suggested the best of both worlds: a more efficient allocation of resources, thanks to greater mobility of both labour and capital, alongside EU-wide support – shared norms – for a social market model, including generous welfare payments for those facing economic disadvantage.

Syria may undermine all of this.

In 2010, on the eve of the Syrian civil war, its population stood at 22 million. Five years later, 12 million of those had been displaced – either within Syria itself (8 million) or, increasingly, beyond Syria's borders. Initially, most refugees ended up in Turkey (well over 2 million), Lebanon (over 1 million) or Jordan (over half a million). For Turkey, a country already facing economic challenges and an upsurge in political violence, the fiscal costs were large, amounting to US$8 billion, or roughly 1 per cent of national income in 2015.

For many Syrian refugees, however, neither Turkey nor Lebanon marked the end of the road: they were merely the first base on a journey that some hoped would eventually lead to a better life within the European Union. As a consequence, 2015 saw more than twice as many people seeking asylum in the European Union as in the previous year. Of these, roughly a quarter were Syrian; others came from the Balkans (15 per cent), Afghanistan (13 per cent), Iraq (9 per cent) and Pakistan (4 per cent). The numbers were larger than immediately after the fall of the Berlin Wall and larger, too, than in the various crises of the 1990s associated with the break-up of Yugoslavia.

One result was a massive backlog in the processing of asylum applications: towards the end of 2015, around 850,000 asylum seekers still formed what was fast becoming a tragically disorderly queue. Many were waiting within those EU countries closest to Syria, most obviously Greece and Italy.[17] Another result was a very unequal dispersion within the EU of those granted asylum: once in the EU, the majority headed to Germany and Sweden, both wealthy countries with (initially, at least) a more welcoming attitude towards migrants than others.

Whatever the humanitarian needs of the refugees themselves, the numbers arriving in the EU created a serious challenge to Schengen and, by implication, to the EU's very existence. The problem can best be described in terms of incentives. The Schengen 'border' that surrounded the signatories to the Treaty of Amsterdam was not controlled by a single EU force. Each country was responsible for its own part of the common border.

Yet the authorities within those EU countries that first received the asylum seekers rightly concluded that, once in the EU, the migrants would head elsewhere. So, whether the asylum seekers were genuine or bogus, whether they came from Syria or other countries, whether they were political refugees or economic migrants, whether they were likely to be upstanding citizens or, in a tiny minority of cases, terrorists planning death and destruction, the processing countries might simply wave them through. If there was a problem, it would go somewhere else. And that meant, in turn, that Schengen could no longer be viable.

Ultimately, Germany was relying on Greece to control a European border that, if leaky, had a bigger impact on Germany than on Greece. Greece, faced with its own huge economic problems, lacked the resources – and perhaps the will – to provide the necessary controls. Leaky borders, however, created an obvious challenge. If Thomas Hobbes was right to argue that the central role of a nation state was to protect its citizens, Schengen increasingly looked like a failure: nation states themselves increasingly had to reclaim the initiative, thereby undermining one of the four freedoms on which the European Union rested. Whatever its economic advantages, Schengen was in danger of perishing, thanks to a migratory movement entirely beyond Europe's control. Border controls at national borders were making a comeback.

TWENTY-FIRST-CENTURY MIGRATORY PATTERNS: A REVERSAL OF NINETEENTH-CENTURY TRENDS?

The unexpectedly large flows of asylum seekers into the Schengen area in 2015 might, however, prove to have been a mere dress rehearsal for what may eventually be coming Europe's way. If the nineteenth century was characterized by an exodus of Europeans to the New World, the twenty-first century may be defined by an exodus of Africans to the Old World.

Africa may be at the dawn of a demographic surge considerably larger than anything that happened in Europe in the nineteenth century. The surge is happening for all the usual reasons: infant mortality is declining, thanks to improvements in sanitation and healthcare; the fertility rate is also declining, but not as quickly as the infant mortality rate, so that a larger proportion of children will survive into young adulthood; and those in young adulthood have a better chance of reaching retirement age, thanks to more effective treatments for malaria and HIV, for example.

Nigeria provides one of the clearest illustrations of the revolution now taking place. In 1950, Nigeria's population was a mere 38 million, 1.5 per cent of a global population which, at the time, amounted to 2.5 billion. By 2015, Nigeria's population had risen to 182 million, 2.5 per cent of a global population now up to 7.3 billion. According to the United Nations, Nigeria's population is set to rise a lot further: to 263 million by 2030, 399 million by 2050 (more than ten times larger than in 1950) and to an extraordinary 752 million by 2100.

Admittedly, the UN's numbers are no more than projections, based on some fairly crude assumptions. Nevertheless, they are consistent with what typically happens in the decades after infant mortality starts to decline. If the numbers prove to be anywhere near right, by the turn of the next century Nigeria will account for 6.7 per cent of the world's population – more than North America (4.5 per cent), Europe (5.8 per cent) and the combined forces of Latin America and the Caribbean (6.4 per cent).[18]

While Nigeria is in the process of delivering a demographic surge, much of Europe will be undergoing a demographic retreat. In 1950, Italy's population stood at around 47 million, 1.9 per cent of the global total and larger than Nigeria's. By 2015, its population had risen to 60 million. Its share of the global total, however, had fallen dramatically, down to just 0.8 per cent. Again using the UN's projections, Italy's population may hold steady through to 2050, but could drop to around 50 million by 2100, a mere 0.4 per cent of the global total.

Italy's story goes beyond mere shrinkage: its population is also ageing. Whereas Nigeria's old-age dependency ratio will remain very low for much of the twenty-first century (thanks to a rapidly swelling population of working age), Italy's will be heading a lot higher. In 2015, there were already 35 Italians above the age of 65 for every 100 Italians of working age.[19] By 2050, there may be close to 70 Italians in their dotage for every 100 of working age. Put another way, as Italy progresses through the twenty-first century, there will be a growing shortage of Italians engaged in productive activities. And those so engaged may be faced with a huge tax burden to fund their parents' and grandparents' lifestyles – unless, that is, Italy is willing to accept immigration from elsewhere in the world.

Nigeria and Italy offer only a flavour of what will ultimately prove to be a new demographic epoch. By 2100, Africa as a whole may account for almost 40 per cent of the world's population, up from 16 per cent in 2015 and a mere 9 per cent in 1950. All other regions – including an ageing Asia, thanks largely to demographic change in China, Japan and South Korea – will be in relative decline. And, like Japan, Europe will increasingly be a mere shadow of its former self.

A moment's thought, however, reveals that our global governance arrangements will look increasingly anachronistic in the light of this demographic revolution. Take, for example, the permanent members of the United Nations Security Council: China, France, the Russian Federation, the UK and the US. In 1950, their combined populations added up to 898 million people, over 35 per cent of the global total. By 2015, even though their combined populations had risen to over 2 billion, their share of the global total had dropped to 27 per cent. By 2100, the UN's projections suggest that their combined populations will have fallen to 1.7 billion, a mere 15 per cent of the global total.

Alternatively, consider the G7, a self-appointed collection of rich industrialized nations made up of Canada, France, Italy, Germany, Japan, the UK and the US. The G7's combined population rose from 464 million in 1950 to 755 million in 2015. Thanks to country-specific strongly positive demographic trends – in part a consequence of large waves of immigration into the US, the UK and France – the G7's population may increase further, perhaps reaching 850 million by 2100. Yet, relative to the global total, the citizens of the G7 will have a rapidly diminishing voice. Whilst they accounted for over 18 per cent of the world's population in 1950, their share may have dropped to a rather insignificant 7.7 per cent by 2100.

TWENTY-FIRST-CENTURY MIGRATION TRIGGERS

Knowing that populations are likely to wax and wane is not in itself enough to demonstrate that there will be large migratory movements. There needs also to be a catalyst. There are likely to be at least three in the twenty-first century: rising living standards in poor countries; persistence of conflict where government and institutions are ineffective or where there are failed states; and climate change, the effects of which will impact some nations more than others.

Take Nigeria again. Its per capita incomes fell rapidly in the early 1980s: between 1981 and 1987, living standards dropped on average by 6 per cent per year, a truly catastrophic outcome. Given Nigeria's status as a major oil producer, the early 1980s collapse in oil prices didn't help. Thereafter, however, living standards rose steadily, albeit from a very low base, thanks in part to sustained increases in oil prices and considerable debt forgiveness. From the trough in 1987 through to 2015, per capita incomes increased at an annual rate of 3.7 per cent, leaving the average Nigerian with roughly double the income level seen in 1980: around $5,700, compared with less than $3,000. This modest rise in living standards was associated with an increase in net emigration: whereas in 1990 there was net emigration of 91,000, by 2015 the figure had risen to 300,000.[20] If – and with the huge uncertainty over both the outlook for oil prices and the distribution of income in Nigeria, it is a very big 'if' – Nigerian incomes rise further, the nineteenth-century model of migration suggests that more and more Nigerians will plan to take their life chances elsewhere in the world. In 2015, Italian per capita incomes, for example, were around $35,000. For those Nigerians who can afford – or are prepared to risk – the journey, that's a rather attractive incentive.

Then consider the results of the Institute for Economics and Peace's Global Peace Index 2015.[21] Many of those countries from which people have migrated are among the most war-torn and conflict-prone in the world. According to the institute, Syria, Iraq and Afghanistan were the three least peaceful countries in the world in 2015: in that year, they also happened to be three of the biggest sources of asylum seekers hoping to find a new life in the European Union. Pakistan, another source of asylum seekers, was also ranked poorly. Other low-ranking countries included six in Africa: South Sudan, the Central African Republic, Somalia, Sudan, the Democratic Republic of the Congo and, of course, Nigeria.

Some of these nations are incredibly poor: annual per capita incomes in the Central African Republic and the Democratic Republic of the Congo averaged between $600 and $700 in 2015, a truly dismal outcome that was sufficiently low to prevent the citizens of these two impoverished nations from heading elsewhere. For Nigeria, however, things are rather different: if they so wished, some of its citizens could afford to move.

Since 2000, waves of serious civil unrest have blighted Nigeria. In part, they reflect the increasing schism between a number of northern, predominantly Muslim regions which, in 2000, adopted Sharia law, and the mostly Christian south: 100 people were killed in Lagos in February 2002 in clashes between the largely Muslim Hausa and the Christian Yoruba, while more than 200 people died in November of that year in protests against a planned 'Miss World' contest in Kaduna (the event finally took place in the UK). These clashes marked the beginnings of increasingly sectarian violence: more than 200 Muslims killed by Christians in May 2004; 500 protesters killed by Nigerian troops in Port Harcourt later that year; attacks on gas pipelines in 2006; kidnapping of foreign oil workers; and, in 2009, the emergence of Boko Haram, the Islamist movement intent on imposing Sharia law on the entire country, whatever the cost in terms of bloodshed.[22] Should this violence escalate further (with luck, the risk may be less than before, following the peaceful democratic transition of 2015), Nigeria would eventually be in danger of becoming Africa's Syria. In the event, Syria's refugee crisis – appalling as it is – might end up being a mere footnote in a new epoch of mass migration.

Ultimately, the African migration story will be driven by population, modest gains in per capita incomes, improved transportation linkages with the rest of the world and, in some cases, the emergence of ethnic and religious violence: precisely the conditions, in fact, that led to the exodus from Southern and Eastern Europe in the late nineteenth century. In total, the population of the six 'least-peaceful' sub-Saharan African countries in 2015 was 327 million – compared with Syria's pre-war 22 million. On the UN's projections, the collective population of these African countries is set to rise to 741 million by 2050, before reaching 1.4 billion in 2100. Should the citizens of these countries eventually reach the stage where they could both afford and want to move, they would surely try to do so: they would then no longer have to spend their lives holding the losing economic and political lottery ticket handed to them at birth.

In an increasing number of cases, the losing lottery ticket will also reflect changes in the environment. The science of climate change can hardly provide precise predictions, but it is still possible to reach some broad-brush distributional conclusions. Glacial melt will have a large negative impact on people living in northern China, the Indian sub-continent and the Andean nations of South America. Declining crop yields will be a key challenge for much of Africa. Rising sea levels will have a disproportionately large impact on Bangladesh and Vietnam and, at the same time, will threaten livelihoods in some of the world's major coastal cities, including Tokyo, Shanghai, Hong Kong, Mumbai, Kolkata, Karachi, St Petersburg, New York and London. Malaria may decline in West Africa as its climate becomes drier, but could become a bigger problem in the east and south of the continent. Water shortages will likely become a more frequent occurrence in Southern Europe, Africa and the Middle East, even as Southeast Asia has to cope with a greater risk of flooding. In response to these rising climate challenges, there is likely to be a growing number of so-called 'environmental refugees' – people who will have to move if they are to have any chance of survival.

Estimating the likely number of environmental refugees is no easy task. Knowing where they will go is even more difficult. Will they move to other parts of their own country? Will they be forced to live off so-called 'marginal lands' – a process that itself is likely to contribute to further environmental damage – or will they instead head towards the developed world, which, for the most part, appears less vulnerable to climate change than the world's poorer regions? Wherever they go, the numbers could be very large indeed. One estimate suggests that as many as 200 million people could be on the move by the middle of the twenty-first century for environmental reasons alone.[23]

MIGRATION FLOWS AND GLOBALIZATION THREATS

More than anything, the last 200 years have demonstrated that waves of migration are driven by factors well beyond the control of any one nation state. Yet, given that nation states typically define themselves as political and economic 'clubs' – with the decision on whom to exclude as important as that on whom to include – it's hardly surprising that, whatever the driving factors, immigrants are not always welcome. On occasion, the imbalance between the supply of, and demand for, immigrants can encourage precisely the isolationist attitudes inimical to globalization. This is likely to be particularly true during prolonged periods of economic setback, during which people seek narratives for their own personal disappointments.

Such was the case in the UK at the beginning of 2016. An Ipsos MORI poll tracking the key issues worrying the British public revealed that immigration was more bothersome than any other major topic, ahead of health, the economy, terrorism, poverty, inequality, housing and schools. Admittedly, many of the issues tracked by Ipsos MORI have proved to be very cyclical: the economy and unemployment topped the list in the years shortly after the global financial crisis, but as a modest economic recovery came through, their importance faded. Interestingly, however, worries about both immigration and the National Health Service tend to be closely correlated. Following the global financial crisis, these two concerns increasingly became uppermost in people's minds – and, although those on the right of the political spectrum were more concerned about immigration than those on the left, those on the left still regarded immigration as a key issue. Other areas of rising angst included housing, low pay, poverty and inequality. For many, rightly or wrongly, these issues are related: immigration, in effect, is regarded as a threat to the benefits which come from membership of an economic and political club that's supposed to be 'members only'. We are back to the worries associated with the Marston Valley Brick Company in the 1960s.[24]

In the nineteenth century, those who opted to migrate elsewhere did so either because of opportunity or out of desperation. The same is likely to be true in the twenty-first century. In the nineteenth century, however, institutional arrangements were broadly supportive of migration. One reason why so many Irish headed to Canada was simply that both Ireland and Canada were parts of the British Empire. For all its advantages, the nation state – thanks in part to Woodrow Wilson's principle of self-determination – has increased the distinction between 'them and us'. Having done so, we may discover that we are poorly placed to cope with the possibility of very large waves of migration in the decades ahead.

And thanks to new technologies, those opposed to immigration will more easily be able to garner support for their barriers and barricades, even as those who wish to emigrate will be able to make more informed decisions on where to go. Technology is typically regarded as 'pro-globalization'. It is no such thing. It's time to look at technology in a new – more sceptical – light.

9

THE DARK SIDE OF TECHNOLOGY

THE INCREDIBLE SHRINKING WORLD

Technology supposedly shrinks the world. The falling cost of telecommunications has linked citizens, countries and continents together in ways that previously would have been unimaginable. Search engines have provided us with information at the press of a button or the swipe of a screen. With the advent of web-based systems such as Skype and FaceTime, we can talk to each other (and, if we really have to, look at each other) wherever we happen to be in the world. And we are not being directly billed for the privilege.

These extraordinary connections suggest that technology and globalization are fellow travellers. And they appear increasingly to be travelling at the economic equivalent of the speed of light. Using Moore's Law – which suggests that computing power doubles once every 18–24 months – it is not difficult to imagine a virtual world in which geographical separation is no longer important.[1] Distance will be no barrier to intimacy of whatever kind. Globalization will have triumphed. Sovereign borders will have melted away in the face of a digital onslaught.

DISRUPTIVE TECHNOLOGY CAN CREATE BOTH
WINNERS AND LOSERS

Technology, however, is unpredictably disruptive. The nineteenth-century model of globalization, for example, worked for some countries and societies better than for others. Steam power – the radical new technology of the age – changed everything. It introduced the seemingly alien concept of significant distance between production and consumption. The ability to transport goods by rail or ship paved the way for massive economies of scale. Using early mass production techniques, goods could be produced cheaply in a single location and thereafter easily sent all over the world.[2]

Yet while the new technologies hugely benefited the northern industrial superpowers, they led to massive de-industrialization elsewhere: for example, a nascent Indian steel industry was wiped out, as was much of India's textile industry. Thanks to the need for close coordination of industrial processes – this, after all, was more than a hundred years before the information technology revolution – skills and knowledge increasingly clustered in the cities and ports of the soon-to-be superpowers. As their fledgling industrial efforts could no longer compete, other parts of the world became overly dependent on subsistence agricultural income alone. As a consequence, the gap in living standards between the industrial nations and others widened enormously. Inevitably, their relative military capabilities followed suit.

THE LATE TWENTIETH-CENTURY REVOLUTION

Late twentieth-century globalization changed all that. Political upheavals helped. The collapse of the Soviet Empire and its satellites allowed a large number of Eastern European countries to join the European Union: their citizens headed west, while capital from Western European countries headed east. Deng Xiaoping's decision to open China for business was, in economic terms, even more momentous.

Economic reforms also did their bit: as we saw in Chapter 4, the gradual abolition of capital controls in the 1980s and beyond meant that capital previously 'trapped' within national boundaries was suddenly free to go in search of the best combination of low wages, long hours and high productivity. The emerging-market revolution owes a great deal to this new-found cross-border movement of capital.

Innovations in transportation also made a big difference. The container shipping revolution hugely reduced the costs of sea transport. Larger and more efficient aeroplanes able to travel vast distances led not only to a dramatic increase in the number of holidaymakers prepared to travel to far-flung places, but also allowed produce from all over the world to appear on our plates, whatever the season.

Yet without the information technology revolution, it is difficult to imagine that the world would have experienced anything like the degree of globalization witnessed since the 1980s. At a stroke, the nineteenth-century coordination problem – which led to a concentration of industrial activities in a limited number of areas – was removed. Global supply chains took over. Apple could design its iPhone in California, yet make it in China, courtesy of FoxConn. BMW could build its Minis in Oxford, yet have the engines made in Brazil. JP Morgan could package up US sub-prime mortgages, knowing that the bundles it had assembled could then be distributed to Norwegian pension funds. Distances hadn't changed, of course, but technology gave the impression that the world was shrinking.

The consequences were staggering. If nineteenth-century globalization was ultimately a story about divergence, the late twentieth-century story was, it seemed, all about convergence. Good-quality Western capital went in search of cheap emerging-market labour. Thanks to information technology, supply chains began to expand at a rate of knots. Asia was the main beneficiary. Until the 1970s, most supply chains were limited to connections between companies often operating in close proximity to one another either in North America or in Western Europe.

By the late 1990s, Asia had become the dominant region. Much of the new activity – not surprisingly – was associated with electronics.

Yet this wasn't simply a story about an extended daisy-chain of manufacturing processes across countries and continents. For the supply chains to work, there had to be new factories, closer business relationships, upgraded cross-border financial arrangements, better logistics, protection of intellectual property rights and effective training programmes. In other words, the supply-chain story went well beyond the nineteenth-century Ricardian concept of comparative advantage, in which Portugal and England would specialize, respectively, in the production of port and cloth. A new global economic ecosystem was being constructed. And its foundations were underpinned by information technology.

The combination of enhanced capital mobility and faster – and cheaper – information flows changed the nature of international economic connections. The new global economic ecosystem no longer depended on trade alone. New forms of exchange became increasingly important. A multinational company would only invest in a particular country – even if its labour was inexpensive – under certain specified conditions. Typically, to secure the capital inflow, the recipient country would need to provide better infrastructure, improved corporate governance and higher levels of legal protection to make the prospective investment 'safe'.[3]

In time, this 'exchange' – between investment and governance, rather than between exports and imports – created a virtuous circle, leading to an emerging-market revolution associated with rapidly rising living standards for the many, not the few. In China, for example, the first stirrings of economic convergence with the West appeared in the early 1980s. By 2010, Chinese per capita incomes had risen to 25 per cent of those in the US, by which time US incomes themselves were considerably higher than they had been in the 1950s. If nineteenth-century technology had been the great divider (thanks to industrial concentration), late twentieth-century technology was the great unifier (thanks to global supply chains). For the first time since the advent of the Industrial

Revolution, poorer parts of the world had the chance to catch up with the richer parts.

TECHNOLOGY AS A THREAT TO GLOBALIZATION

It might seem odd, then, to think that technology could threaten globalization. Yet it can – and it does. Information may be travelling around the world at an incredible speed, but a lot depends on what people then do with that information. Watching cat videos may be the twenty-first-century equivalent of Marx's opium of the people, and is probably not the most economically productive use of people's time. Learning how to construct suicide vests may, for some, be a noble cause; but for most of us, the information provided by jihadists over the internet is too often used for destructive intent. Replacing cheap labour with robots may provide us with even cheaper goods and services, but it may also lead to a collapse of global supply chains and, with it, a reversal of late twentieth-century globalization. 'Reshoring' – thanks to increased automation and robotics – may lead to the rebuilding of economic and financial barriers: nations might then be able to turn themselves into the economic equivalent of 'gated communities'. Substituting twentieth-century mass warfare for cyber-attacks and cybercrime may, thankfully, hugely reduce the number of battlefield casualties, but it nevertheless leads to heightened mistrust between the world's superpowers and, via WikiLeaks and other data dumps, threatens personal privacy, intellectual property and ultimately national security. Technology may have helped remove borders, but it could equally well enable those borders to be rebuilt.

Part of the problem with technology lies in what might loosely be described as the lack of an 'editor' for the information that comes our way. We are increasingly able to self-edit the views expressed on the internet; and by doing so, we are in danger of delivering what might loosely be described as 'self-censorship'. We can follow whomever we wish to on Twitter and either ignore or troll those with whom we disagree. We can watch one of hundreds of TV channels, to the extent that there is no 'shared experience' to be discussed around the coffee machine on a Monday morning (even *Breaking Bad* didn't quite do it, largely because people could watch the activities of Walter White at their leisure, using DVDs or Netflix). We can focus on self-gratification at the expense of traditional social discourse, whether it's online shopping, conducting virtual conversations at the dinner table or – still one of the most popular activities on the internet – watching pornography. For those like the UN- and UNESCO-backed Broadband Commission for Digital Development who argue that rolling out broadband across all nations will lead to ever-greater riches for both developed and emerging nations, the ability to 'self-edit' is a major challenge.

MONOCHROME MINSTRELS

To demonstrate why this is so, it is worth going back to an earlier era, before the advent of cable, satellite and broadband, when the main way in which we could view the world was via an aerial sticking out of the roof. It was the era of television.

For UK viewers, there was great excitement on 20 April 1964 when, for those lucky enough to have the latest technology, a third television channel was to be broadcast for the first time. Unfortunately, a huge power failure in west London meant that BBC Two didn't really properly get going until the following day. Still, the number of available channels had increased by 50 per cent overnight. And given that an increasing number of homes had a television, this was a sure-fire way of introducing quality educational programming into the typical living room. For the disciples of Lord Reith (the first director general of the BBC who, more than anyone else, had regarded broadcasting first and foremost as an educational tool), this was an opportunity to civilize the masses.[4]

A handful of years later, the BBC began to transmit Open University programmes. These mostly monochrome broadcasts represented the height of Reithian values: if they woke up early enough or went to bed late enough, viewers who wanted to improve their minds could turn on, tune in and swot up. Yet, other than for those on night shifts or looking for a cure for insomnia, Open University programmes were hardly the most popular broadcasts. Audiences in the 1970s preferred to opt for the lowest common denominator: given the choice between Reithian high-mindedness and basic entertainment, the latter was always going to win. Moreover, it turned out that viewers preferred programmes that were likely to reinforce racial and cultural prejudices. The most popular programmes across all channels in the 1960s and 1970s included *The Black and White Minstrel Show*, in which white male singers 'blacked up', and *Love Thy Neighbour*, in which the comedy (if that's the right word) was entirely dependent on racial stereotypes.

These programmes hail from another age. Yet the ability of technology to reinforce – rather than reduce – prejudice has, in many ways, come on in leaps and bounds. If you happen to be a white supremacist, you can easily find like-minded people on Facebook or Twitter and become their friends and followers. If you have anti-Semitic tendencies, you'll find no shortage of people inhabiting the digital realm who are more than happy to share your views. If you oppose immigration in all its incarnations, you'll find plenty of fellow travellers on the World Wide Web. If you wish to recruit for ISIS, you can reach out to inhabitants of countries all over the world. And each time you join forces with like-minded people, your own prejudices will be reinforced. You will no longer have to question your views because, however unpleasant they might be, you will always be able to find those who will happily tell you that you are right. It may be called 'social media' but it can all too easily support anti-social behaviour. And that behaviour increasingly transcends borders.

BLAND CAREER POLITICIANS AND DISRUPTIVE POPULISTS

Moreover, social media may have contributed to greater public cynicism about mainstream politicians and policymakers. Politics may be seen by cynics – and anarchists – as merely the exercise of power by governments over everybody else; but in reality, it's also about making deals, building alliances, coming up with compromises and finding ways of making peace with opponents and enemies. The process of doing so must inevitably imply that a career politician's position on specific issues will have to change over time.

Before the advent of social media, this was not a huge problem. Searching through a career politician's statements and evolving views required the painstaking work of biographers, archivists and historians. The process was slow and laborious, and the results were unlikely to make the front pages of popular newspapers unless there was a whiff of scandal involved.[5] The combination of Google and social media, however, allows a career politician's indiscretions and inconsistencies to be hunted down in a matter of seconds. And that leaves the career politician open to charges of hypocrisy.

This threat, however, incentivizes career politicians – keen to minimize those charges – to pursue the blandest of policies and offer the blandest of pronouncements. The idea is to limit controversy, in the hope that the would-be political leader might routinely be regarded by his or her party as a 'safe pair of hands', a person unlikely to upset the applecart, a person blessed more with managerial competence than political vision, a person with a steady hand on the tiller. And that's absolutely fine in a world in which there are few challenges to people's livelihoods, where the political narrative appears to make sense and where the politicians themselves can pretend to take credit for transforming people's living standards. It is not so fine in a world in which living standards are under threat, where there are competing narratives to explain increasingly uncertain outcomes and where dormant national, ethnic and religious rivalries are reawakening.

That, however, is the world we now inhabit.

Social media does not just leave mainstream politicians hamstrung. It also provides a platform by means of which (let us call them) 'disruptive' politicians can quickly establish a meaningful voice, and are easily able to recruit the support of like-minded people who may in no way reflect the views of the political mainstream. No longer does the aspiring disruptor have to go to Speakers' Corner in London's Hyde Park to air his or her views before an audience of people hoping to be amused rather than inspired. Instead, the disruptor can take to social media, in the process by-passing the established party systems that have traditionally acted as filters to limit the success of populists. This leads, in turn, to the success of previously fringe movements – Syriza in Greece, the Five Star Movement in Italy – and to the hijacking of mainstream parties. Think of Donald Trump's success in securing the Republican nomination for the 2016 US presidential election against the wishes of the party establishment, or Jeremy Corbyn's Labour Party leadership victory in 2015, much to the discomfort of many sitting Labour MPs. It may also lead to the increased influence of fringe movements on mainstream political choices. It is difficult to imagine, for example, that David Cameron and his fellow Conservatives would have held a vote on the UK's EU membership in June 2016 had it not been for the earlier rise of the UK Independence Party, its success based on its anti-EU and anti-immigration stance. Meanwhile, thanks in part to the success of Alternative für Deutschland (AfD), a right-wing anti-immigration and Eurosceptic political party founded in 2013, Angela Merkel's legacy was, by 2016, in danger of collapsing, as an increasing number of Germans objected to her accommodating approach to the Syrian refugee crisis.

The common feature of the majority of disruptors is their opposition to globalization. Whether they hail from the left or the right, they are deeply suspicious of closer international ties, often blaming other nations or conspiratorial international cabals for their woes. Syriza's victory in the 2015 Greek general election depended critically on its pledge to demand debt forgiveness from Greece's Eurozone partners (who, it turned out, were not in a forgiving mood). Italy's Five Star Movement is influenced by North America's cyber-utopians, gaining support largely online in a bid to overthrow or undermine Italy's – and the world's – political elites. Donald Trump's manifesto was, in many ways, inconsistent with received Republican wisdom: he spoke out against free trade, promised a wall between the US and Mexico, vowed to stop more Muslims coming to the country, and adopted a blatantly protectionist approach towards trade with China.

As disruptors gain power, so they are less likely than their predecessors to support the institutions of globalization – or, indeed, to worry too much if globalization is in danger of disintegrating. Their support depends on opposition to the established order – and they nurture that support through the use of technologies that, at one point, seemed to make globalization inevitable. Globalization ultimately depends on decisions made by people, not the linkages established by technologies. And if people choose to re-establish the primacy of the nation state – or the dominance of, say, a caliphate – then technology will increasingly be commandeered for that purpose.

TAILORED INFORMATION AND 'CREEPINESS'

Meanwhile, our self-editing allows others to further edit the materials we have access to: we are in danger of becoming narrow-minded without even realizing it. It's bad enough knowing that newspapers may choose a particular editorial line to appease their advertisers, even if it leads to biased reporting.[6] It's perhaps even more worrying to realize that a person's individual browsing habits on the internet – alongside her credit card history, her loyalty cards, her frequent flyer cards and the places she visits, typically tracked by her mobile phone – are meticulously recorded, so that the messages she receives digitally are, to use an increasingly tiresome vernacular, individually 'curated'. No longer does she have a view of the world in which she is able to pick and choose: some of her choices are, in effect, made by an infernal algorithm conjured up by an odd mixture of political lobbyists, advertisers and computer geeks.

In an illuminating experiment ahead of the 2016 US presidential election, the *Wall Street Journal* demonstrated precisely this problem. It created two separate Facebook accounts, one representing a Liberal (a so-called Blue Feed) and the other a Conservative (a so-called Red Feed). It then allowed readers to compare the items 'fed' to each account regarding specific topics: Trump, Clinton, Obama, guns, abortion and ISIS. The Blue Feed received items that served only to reinforce a typical Democrat's preconceived views, while the Red Feed did exactly the same for a typical Republican. In other words, the Blue Feed and the Red Feed provided alternative views of reality that, in essence, fundamentally contradicted each other: pre-existing differences of view were simply reinforced hour by hour, day by day.[7]

Admittedly, not all internet-based algorithms work terribly well. The British satirical newspaper *Private Eye* provides its own 'occasional column devoted to excellence in contextual advertising'. Examples of the *Eye*'s 'malgorithms' in 2015 included a headline announcing 'UN Cancels Holocaust Memorial Event' alongside an accompanying advertisement for walk-in showers; and a headline suggesting 'Weatherman Fred Taught Stone Roses Frontman How to Masturbate' alongside a video entitled 'The Stone Roses – The Hardest Thing in the World'. Nevertheless, there is no doubt that advertisers increasingly recognize the importance of tailored advertising. In 2014, Heineken USA conducted an experiment based on two advertising campaigns in its bid to launch a new tequila-flavoured beer by the name of 'Desperados'. The campaign concentrated on the south-eastern US. In some states, Heineken went down the traditional avenue of TV commercials. In others, it advertised through mobile phones, typically targeting millennials as they were preparing to go out for the evening. In raising awareness about the new brand, the mobile phone campaign proved far more successful.[8]

By targeting likely consumers more precisely, digital advertising can be both effective and cheaper. Consumers, however, are increasingly aware that they are being bombarded with 'personal marketing' that may be effective, but also leads to a sense of 'creepiness': many feel uncomfortable with the idea that their behaviour is being monitored by a 'big data' Big Brother, particularly if Big Brother then acts to reinforce that behaviour.[9]

Meanwhile, to win an election, it makes sense for party strategists to identify and focus on the floating voters – in the same way that Heineken was able to aim its mobile phone advertising campaign at millennials and not the population at large. The consequence of this 'tailored polling' is that the vast majority of voters – those who traditionally have had strong party loyalties – end up being ignored. It is not so surprising, then, that some of them may abandon ship in the event that a populist party or a charismatic politician comes along promising them something that the mainstream parties had simply not bothered with. No one likes to be ignored forever.

Social media cuts both ways. It allows advertisers – and mainstream political parties – to target specific audiences to maximize their goals, whether they happen to be profit or power. Yet it also brings down 'barriers to entry', allowing challenger businesses, charismatic political personalities and newly formed political groupings to enter the fray. These new entrants necessarily threaten the existing order not just locally, but also globally. And their quest is likely to be aided by the impact of technology on global supply chains.

DIGI-STASIS

The more costly the information, the less likely trade will take place. If you wish to buy something from a Chinese company but you are unable to see its products on the web, cannot find a common language in which to communicate, are unsure about the likely delivery time and are uncertain about your legal rights, you might decide to give the opportunity a miss, even if the price appears to be competitive. By reducing the cost of information – and by creating global online 'hubs' like Alibaba and Amazon, where buyers and sellers can 'virtually' meet one another – the global marketplace should expand, competition should intensify and pricing should become more transparent. All in all, the allocation of resources should improve, leaving output higher, prices lower and everyone – other than inefficient rent-seeking companies – happier.

Yet this argument assumes that technology only works by reducing barriers to entry, limiting information asymmetries and encouraging price discovery. That's much too narrow a view. Technology also fundamentally alters production techniques and hugely skews the distribution of income and wealth. In both cases, technology can be enormously damaging to globalization.

The decision on where to locate production facilities ultimately depends on a trade-off between the forces of dispersion and agglomeration. Supply chains are likely to be dispersed, either because there are big differences in labour costs between the more and the less skilled (which is why iPhones are designed in California but assembled in China), or because certain products are made by only one or two manufacturers globally. Following the Fukushima nuclear disaster in Japan in March 2011, for example, automobile manufacturers all over the world realized how dependent they had become on specialist suppliers: Renesas Electronics produced approaching 40 per cent of the world's automotive microcontrollers at a plant which completely shut down because of its proximity to the disaster. In contrast, production is likely to be agglomerated – or clustered – if, as in the nineteenth century, local demand for products is disproportionately high, or else if the local supply of workers with appropriate levels of education and skills is disproportionately high.

Thanks to new technologies, it may just be that the nineteenth-century model of agglomeration – with clustered production facilities – is making a return. Chinese labour may be cheaper than US labour, but the increase in computational power since the 1980s means that an increasing number of tasks that once could only have been performed by human beings can now be carried out by machines, which are capable of working 24 hours a day, seven days a week.[10]

To date, this is primarily true of tasks with a considerable degree of repetition – typically those in factories or involving a high volume of clerical work. In the process of automating many of these tasks, some workers gain even as others lose. People blessed with high levels of creativity, intuition, social skills and problem-solving techniques may well flourish: computerization allows them to concentrate on the tasks in which they have a comparative advantage. Others may fall by the wayside, discovering that even a decent high-school education might not be enough to guarantee them the opportunities they aspire to. At the same time, given that computers have yet to (inexpensively) replicate common manual tasks – a human is more adept than a robot at cleaning a bathroom or waiting tables – those who fall by the wayside may find themselves in competition for manual jobs with others who have fewer educational qualifications. The result is 'job polarization': the middle of the labour market is hollowed out, even as both high- and low-wage jobs expand.[11]

This process of polarization is obviously a problem within countries – and indeed goes some way to explaining the rise of income inequality within, for example, the US. Yet it also, potentially, has profound implications for globalization. If repetitive tasks can easily be carried out by robots and computers, there is little point in companies heading abroad in search of cheap labour. They can instead replace their cheap foreign labour with potentially even cheaper home-based machines. Because those machines can be programmed in seconds, training costs will crumble. And to the extent that machines can easily be repaired remotely – either by humans or by other machines via the 'internet of things' – there will be far fewer working days lost to sickness. Factories could be devoid of human life – with the exception of the man whose job it is to feed the guard dogs.[12]

The implications of such a model would be profound. Production would increasingly be reshored. The nineteenth-century agglomeration model would be given a new lease of life. The need for global supply chains would rapidly fade. Countries would no longer be mutually dependent on one another, other than for the basics of human life – most obviously commodities and raw materials. Those countries unable to invest in new technologies – including superfast broadband and advanced robots – might find many of their citizens still trapped in poverty.

Those with the most advanced military technologies could increasingly hope to exert their influence on the rest of the world with the use of remotely piloted drones, raising significant questions about the morality of war in which one protagonist's soldiers are seldom in the firing line. And nationalist politicians would no longer be so easily criticized for their protectionist attitudes. They could simply claim that the economic arguments of the nineteenth and twentieth centuries were no longer relevant: comparative advantage would be less important in a world in which robots could produce the same product virtually anywhere, while, if reshoring took hold, the exchange of capital for governance – the key characteristic of later twentieth-century globalization – would no longer need to take place.

Technology may allow us to view the rest of the world more easily, but there is no guarantee that the world becomes more joined up as a result. It might, instead, end up more divided: between the 'haves' in their gated communities and the 'have nots' elsewhere. The 'have nots', in turn, will have a powerful incentive to climb over the walls of the gated communities in a bid to grab their own share of the economic pie: in other words, technology and migration end up as two sides of the same coin. And, as greater division becomes a more worrying political problem, so policymakers will be looking out for solutions that work for individual nation states at the expense of the global economy. Some will involve robbing Peter to pay Paul. One, in particular, will involve debasing the coinage.

10

DEBASING THE COINAGE

Imagine a world in which globalization is more or less complete. In that world, there would only need to be a single global currency to support a single global market: more than one currency would only lead to costly speculative complications, reducing the number of transactions and, as a result, reducing living standards.

Remarkably, the real world has occasionally appeared to be heading in exactly the 'single currency' direction. Under the gold standard – which most nation states had subscribed to by the late nineteenth century – many currencies were, both in theory and in practice, exchangeable for gold at a fixed price. Indirectly, therefore, they were fixed in price against each other. Under Bretton Woods, currencies were exchangeable for US dollars at a mostly fixed price, even if prices could occasionally fluctuate, subject (in theory) to the IMF's approval. The US dollar, in turn, was supposedly fixed in value against gold: it wasn't quite the gold standard, but it meant there was at least one paper currency in circulation that, until the Nixon Shock, had the attributes commonly associated with currencies in the gold standard era. For a while, the US dollar was 'as good as gold'.

Following the Nixon Shock, and thereafter the gradual abolition of exchange and capital controls, there was a danger that currency markets would become a 'free for all'. European nations, however, had no enthusiasm for such an outcome: from the 'currency snake' of the European Exchange Rate Arrangement in the 1970s to the Exchange Rate Mechanism of the European Monetary System in the 1980s and 1990s and then, of course, the single currency, the majority of European nations have rejected the idea of currency chaos, preferring instead to limit their currency options to a greater or lesser extent.

For many years, emerging nations were also unwilling to have purely 'floating' currencies. To be taken seriously by international investors, policymakers in the emerging nations often chose to tie their currencies to US dollars, DM or, more recently, euros: by doing so, they hoped to demonstrate their commitment to monetary stability, even if their domestic financial arrangements appeared to be, at times, rather opaque. Unfortunately, this approach often didn't work: the apparent guarantee of stability typically encouraged excessive capital inflows, domestic credit booms, unproductive investments and a subsequent rush for the exit. Think, for example, of the Mexican tequila crisis in the mid-1990s, the Asian crisis shortly thereafter, the 1998 Russian debt default, the collapse of Argentina's currency board at the turn of the century and, most obviously, the global financial crisis.

Given these experiences, an increasing number of emerging nations began to reject currency peg arrangements as a way of advertising their financial probity. Many shifted to floating currency arrangements, aware that attempts to fix foreign exchange rates in a world of free-flowing cross-border capital had only given rise to repeated booms and busts.

And it is not only emerging nations that have had this problem. All countries are faced with what is known as the 'impossible trinity', an ultimate financial limit on economic sovereignty.

A country can choose both its inflation rate and its exchange rate only if it prevents capital from flowing across its borders. Otherwise an attempt to keep inflation at bay by raising interest rates, for example, will only encourage greater capital inflows, placing upward pressure on the exchange rate. A country can commit to unrestrained cross-border capital flows and a stable exchange rate, but only if it relinquishes control of its inflation rate: if the currency is under upward pressure thanks to strong capital inflows, interest rates will have to come down to prevent the currency from rising. By cutting interest rates, however, inflation will in all likelihood end up higher. Finally, and for the sake of completeness, a country can choose its own inflation rate and welcome cross-border capital flows, but only if it is prepared to accept a floating exchange rate.

In other words, a policymaker can commit to only two out of three key policy objectives, even if it might seem desirable to embrace them all. It is impossible to commit to free-flowing capital across borders and, at the same time, deliver both a stable exchange rate and a stable inflation rate. The three simply cannot be achieved simultaneously.

THE 1980S POLICY COORDINATION EXPERIMENT

In the 1980s, attempts were made to deal with this dilemma – or, more accurately, trilemma – through so-called international policy coordination. The free-market mantra of Ronald Reagan's first presidential term was toned down following his re-election at the end of 1984. In January 1985, Reagan made James Baker III his Treasury secretary. Baker had already recognized that economic policy was dangerously skewed in the US, with both large budget deficits and unusually high borrowing costs leading to an unusual combination of a rapidly widening trade deficit and a swiftly appreciating US dollar. These developments threatened not just the US itself, but also the rest of the world: high borrowing costs and a strong dollar had already triggered destabilizing debt crises elsewhere, notably in Latin America (many of these countries had built up large dollar liabilities on the back of local currency assets). Yet little was likely to be achieved by changing US policy alone: if, for example, Congress made strenuous efforts to reduce the US budget deficit, the US economy might slow without any compensating acceleration in other countries, leaving the world as a whole facing an increasingly severe demand shortfall. In turn, that threatened an outbreak of protectionism. Indeed, at the time, many in Congress were itching to impose tough sanctions on Japan, which, thanks to its remarkably successful export machine, was seen to be undermining American jobs.

Baker's appointment provided a signal to the foreign exchange markets that the US was no longer happy with an ever-strengthening US dollar. The markets could not be left to their own devices anymore. And the markets did Baker's implicit bidding. Anticipating some kind of international deal later in the year, the US dollar began to fall.

The anticipation was well placed. In September 1985, the G5 nations (the US, Japan, Germany, France and the UK) signed the Plaza Accord, a deal struck in the rooms of the eponymous hotel on the corner of Central Park South and Fifth Avenue. The home of *Eloise* suddenly had a more serious international role to play. The New York deal consisted of broad commitments on all sides. The Americans would endeavour to reduce the scale of their government borrowing, a process enshrined in what became known as the Gramm–Rudman–Hollings Act. Lower government borrowing, in turn, would limit America's insatiable appetite for imports and temper its borrowing costs: lower interest rates would then encourage the US dollar to fall further. Japan, meanwhile, hoped to offset the impact of yen appreciation on its export performance by boosting domestic demand via much lower interest rates, a process made easier thanks to a considerable reduction in inflationary pressures as a result of the mid-1980s collapse in oil prices. Japanese investment promptly boomed, its trade surplus collapsed – a mirror image of the decline in America's trade deficit – and the world economy seemed a lot better balanced.

Seventeen months later, the dollar's decline had turned into something of a rout. The world's leading finance ministers had to meet again.

This time, they gathered at the Louvre, parts of which were no more than a building site due to the on-going construction of I.M. Pei's now-iconic glass pyramid. There was growing nervousness among the finance ministers regarding their ability to put on a united front: in particular, an uptick in inflationary pressures suggested that it would not be easy for Germany and Japan to keep interest rates low enough to encourage investors to move out of yen and DM into US dollars. Nevertheless, a deal was struck, and for a while the dollar stabilized.

It wasn't to last. Over the summer, as the effects on inflation of the earlier collapse in oil prices began to fade, the German Bundesbank became increasingly trigger-happy. Eventually, the high priests of German price stability decided to tweak interest rates a little higher. Madness then ensued. Baker had a public row with the German minister of finance, Gerhard Stoltenberg. With the US trade deficit still widening, the US dollar plunged. Within a few weeks, the US stock market had collapsed.

For a short while, it appeared the game was up for international policy coordination. Yet markets had been too impatient. Over the next few months, the US trade deficit finally started to shrink, the Japanese and German economies continued to expand, and although inflation was on the rise, it seemed as though the imbalances that had struck such fear into the hearts of policymakers in the mid-1980s were finally in retreat.

The late 1980s, however, really marked the end of the experiment. With the 1990 Iraqi invasion of Kuwait, Washington's focus was now else-where, not least because Baker was now George H.W. Bush's secretary of state. Germany, meanwhile, was devoting its resources to the small matter of reunification. And the Bank of Japan was wondering precisely how to tame what had become a rather unwieldy financial bubble.

In the years that followed, the US suffered a mild credit crunch, but thereafter enjoyed a late 1990s technology-led boom. Newly reunified Germany re-established itself as the key power in Europe. Japan, mean-while, was left to lick its wounds. Its late 1980s financial bubble was ultimately a reflection of its desire to play the role of 'good global citizen'.

Yet, while Tokyo's actions may have helped resolve the world's economic imbalances, they only added to Japan's domestic difficulties. Ever since, Japan's experience has provided a salutary lesson to those other nations who, from time to time, have been placed under tremendous pressure to adjust their own policies in pursuit of the 'greater good'.

THE POST-GLOBAL FINANCIAL CRISIS ABSENCE OF COORDINATION

The enormous changes that have taken place in the world economy since the 1980s have turned the G5 – and, with Italy and Canada, the G7 – into ancient relics. Worse, attempts to bring Russia back into the fold – in an attempt to create a late twentieth-century G8 version of the Congress of Vienna – backfired when in 2014 Vladimir Putin began to show an unusually high level of interest in the Crimea. Instead, and reflecting the huge increase in the relative size of emerging economies in the intervening period, the world now has to cope with the G20, a ragtag collection of countries that are never likely to have a shared collective vision: China and Japan aren't the best of friends; Turkey and Russia have history (and, in Presidents Putin and Erdoğan, scope for frequent clashes of ego – even if, at the time of writing, an *entente cordiale* appears to have been established); Saudi Arabia feels left behind as the West makes friendly overtures to (non-G20) Iran; and, as Europe stares at problems to its east and internally, the US no longer looks across the Atlantic with the enthusiasm of old.

Under these circumstances, currency deals of the kind seen in the 1980s are much less likely. Instead, we are in danger of living in a world of endless currency wars.[1]

To be fair, in the immediate aftermath of the global financial crisis there were hopes that things could be very different. Alongside emergency monetary measures launched by the Federal Reserve and the Bank of England, the 2009 G20 summit in London offered a mix of Keynesian homilies and financial bailouts designed to limit the chances of a second Great Depression. The communiqué published at the end of the summit was full of confidence:

> We are undertaking an unprecedented and concerted fiscal expansion . . . We are committed to deliver the scale of sustained fiscal effort necessary to restore growth . . . Interest rates have been cut aggressively in most countries, and our central banks have pledged to maintain expansionary policies for as long as needed and to use the full range of monetary policy instruments, including unconventional instruments, consistent with price stability . . . We have provided significant and comprehensive support to our banking systems . . . We are committed to take all necessary actions to restore the normal flow of credit through the financial system . . . Taken together, these actions will constitute the largest fiscal and monetary stimulus . . . in modern times . . . We are confident that the actions we have agreed today, and our unshakeable commitment to work together to restore growth and jobs, while preserving long-term fiscal sustainability, will accelerate the return to trend growth. We commit today to taking whatever action is necessary to secure that outcome.

Their collective confidence was misplaced. True, the G20 members collectively managed to avoid another Great Depression. They did not, however, return their economies to the growth rates of old. The recovery in economic activity in the Western developed world was, by historical standards, unusually limp. China initially boomed, thanks to a switch from export-led growth – the prospects for which had inevitably deteriorated in the light of the financial crisis – towards spending on domestic infrastructure investment. In turn, China's infrastructure surge raised commodity prices, supporting the export earnings of many emerging nations which, in previous economic downswings, would have faced instant penury. Yet China's debt-fuelled expansion was never likely to be sustainable. From 2012 onwards, China delivered a series of unexpectedly weak economic outcomes associated with diminishing marginal returns on investment (which, by that stage, had risen to a remarkable 50 per cent of national income).

China's slowdown dragged commodity prices lower and, alongside the impact of the shale energy revolution, contributed to a major decline in oil prices. Suddenly, emerging-market commodity producers saw their main source of income dwindling rapidly. As their trade revenues fell back and their balance of payments positions deteriorated, they needed access to a higher volume of capital inflows to fund the growing gap between exports and imports. With the US threatening to raise interest rates in response to a (modest) domestic economic recovery, this was easier said than done. For a while, the love affair investors had with emerging nations – never wholly reliable – was in trouble. Some emerging nations, notably Brazil, were faced with collapsing currencies and deep domestic recessions, neither of which was helpful for political stability.

Elsewhere, countries and regions operated independently in pursuit of their economic goals. These actions, however, only served to pass the buck to somebody else. No one would admit such a thing – no one, apparently, was in the business of pursuing 1930s-style 'beggar-thy-neighbour' currency devaluations – yet as one central bank after another fired up its printing presses, it became increasingly difficult to think of quantitative easing in any other way. Admittedly, central banks tried their hardest to explain the domestic channels through which quantitative easing was supposed to work – the central bank would purchase existing government debt from investors using newly printed money with the aim of lowering yields, encouraging investors to switch into riskier assets like equities, which would then rise in value, signalling to companies that they should raise funds via the capital markets in order to increase capital spending – but the evidence was mostly unconvincing. In particular, although stock markets made impressive gains in the years after the financial crisis, capital spending in the developed world remained largely moribund. Instead, the most important channel of influence became the exchange rate.

In a world in which most economies are weak simultaneously, however, printing money to drive the exchange rate lower risks becoming a zero-sum game: one country's competitive gain is another's competitive loss; one country's inflationary increase is another's deflationary problem. And so it has proved. The dramatic drop in sterling in 2008 temporarily raised UK inflation, but only because the Eurozone ended up importing the UK's deflation. The huge fall in the yen from 2012 through to 2014 may have prevented total economic collapse in Japan, but the corollary of the yen's decline was a dramatic increase in the value of the Chinese renminbi, thereby placing unwanted downward pressure on Chinese inflation and creating a much tougher climate for Chinese exporters. The subsequent big fall in the euro's value – helped along by both quantitative easing and negative nominal interest rates – only led to a much stronger dollar, squeezing American growth and forcing the Federal Reserve to delay its planned increases in interest rates.

Put another way, monetary policy has – unwittingly – become a mechanism by which countries end up waging financial warfare.

It could have been different. It might, for example, have been possible to come up with another Plaza- or Louvre-type deal. Admittedly, the cast list would have changed. Japan would have had to make way for China. Germany, France and Italy would have had to set aside any differences and pursue a common European policy. The British would have had to join the Canadians on the sidelines. Nevertheless, it is possible to think of a deal that might – just might – have led to a better economic outcome, a pact that would have recognized the interdependence of the various parties.

One way to think about the post-crisis world is to recognize that, with high levels of debt, it makes sense for households, companies and governments individually to tackle those debts. If everyone repays debt at the same time, however, the result is likely to be a severe demand shortage. It is a reflection of John Maynard Keynes' 'paradox of thrift': if there is an increase in savings (or repayment of debt) with no corresponding increase in investment, there is likely to be a downward economic multiplier that will leave resources unemployed and growth below par. To combat this, those countries that can more easily sustain their debts or reduce their savings should be encouraged to maintain – or even increase – their spending, even as others take a more austere path.

In the post-financial crisis world, three countries were in a good position to do so: the US, China and Germany. The US was in the fortunate position of having the world's reserve currency and the world's most liquid government bond market. As such, it could easily raise funds from abroad and, in theory, could have added to its debts even as others were reducing theirs. China's huge balance of payments surplus – a whopping 10 per cent of national income in 2007 – meant that it could spend more without ever having to tap international capital markets for funds: there was no shortage of home-grown savings to plunder. Germany, also with a large current account surplus, could have played a similar role within the Eurozone: increased German spending could have offset the need for austerity in other parts of the Eurozone which, unlike Germany, were running large balance of payments deficits.

For a new 'Plaza deal' to succeed, the focus needed to be more on fiscal than on monetary policy: in the aftermath of the financial crisis, interest rates rapidly fell to zero, leaving central banks without much in the way of conventional 'wiggle room'. To their credit, both the US and Germany allowed their structural budget balances to widen considerably in 2009 and 2010. By 2011, however, both nations were looking to consolidate their fiscal positions. In other words, the spirit of the London G20 summit didn't last very long. Only the Chinese stuck to the task in hand. They, however, had assumed that, so long as the others kept their side of the deal, the world economy would quickly recover, allowing Chinese exporters to pick up where they had left off in 2008. Yet, in the event, world trade growth weakened further. By 2015, it was actually contracting – and China's economy was still slowing.

Had they successfully performed their respective roles, the protagonists' balance of payments positions would have changed considerably. Lower domestic savings (or, put another way, higher domestic expenditures) would have led to higher imports. Other things being equal, those higher imports would have led to either smaller balance of payments surpluses or larger deficits. Of the three key players, however, only China delivered this outcome. The Middle Kingdom's balance of payments surplus dropped from its 2007 peak to a mere 1.6 per cent of national income by 2013, rising modestly thereafter.[2] Germany's surplus, by contrast, rose relentlessly: up from 6.8 per cent to 8.5 per cent of national income between 2007 and 2015. The US, meanwhile, was either unable or unwilling to return to its pre-crisis habits: having run deficits of between 4 and 6 per cent of national income in the years preceding the financial crisis, the US thereafter ran deficits closer to 2 per cent of national income.

Why was it so difficult to summon up the spirit of Plaza? Why were policymakers seemingly unable to coordinate their policies? Why was there no easy recognition of the interdependencies that ultimately would determine whether the global economy would sink or swim?

The most obvious reason was politics. It was bad enough trying to get Congress to do deals with the Japanese in the 1980s. Trying to get any kind of binding agreement with communist China – no matter how far Beijing had changed since the days of Chairman Mao – was a completely different ball game. At least Japan was a democracy and, importantly, provided bases for Washington's military presence in Asia. China was – and is – seen much more as a threat.

Even if politics could be put to one side, however, there were other major challenges. Those with – theoretically – short-run fiscal flexibility were not willing to use it. Partly this was a simple numbers game: on the eve of the financial crisis, government debt levels were, in many cases, already relatively high. In both the US and Germany, public debt stood at

64 per cent of national income, enough to prevent a would-be member from joining the euro, at least according to a strict interpretation of the Maastricht convergence criteria. In the years following the financial crisis, government debt rose still further, soaring to 95 per cent of national income in the US and 81 per cent in Germany. For the US, this was by far the highest peacetime level of government debt. Both countries, meanwhile, understood that short-term increases in government debt might create longer-term problems: the costs associated with population ageing – revenue shortfalls and increases in pension and healthcare spending – were already threatening to send government debt into the stratosphere by 2030, even in the absence of renewed discretionary fiscal stimulus.

And there were also, importantly, institutional failures. Even if there was agreement in principle to deliver a series of stimulus packages, who within the European single currency area would the US and China negotiate with? The European Union as a whole eventually came up with the Juncker Plan for infrastructure spending, but that was not part of any international policy coordination.[3] Meanwhile, the Germans appeared unwilling to act for the good of Europe as a whole. They were more interested in demanding that those in Southern Europe who had been the 'beneficiaries' of German lenders' earlier largesse should repay their debts. As a result, the Eurozone as a whole had a depressing impact on the rest of the world, moving into steadily larger balance of payments surplus in the years following the financial crisis: it was the antithesis of successful international policy coordination.

A NEW ROLE FOR MONEY

In the absence of international policy coordination – and with ministries of finance unwilling to use fiscal policy in any meaningful way – it is hardly surprising that, even at zero interest rates, monetary policy is still being pressed into service in an attempt to solve all economic problems. Yet it's a bit like fighting a war with the Home Guard alone: the intention may be admirable, but the effectiveness is questionable – unless, that is, the burden of economic pain can be passed on to someone else.

Prior to the global financial crisis, many economists used to argue that money was somehow 'neutral' over the long run: in other words, printing more of the stuff would only lead to higher inflation with no sustained impact on real economic activity – one reason why central banks mostly ended up adopting inflation targets.[4] Post-crisis, it was no longer politically possible for central banks to focus simply on keeping inflation under control: they also had to worry about unemployment, growth, the exchange rate and financial stability (to be fair, the Fed had always had a so-called 'dual mandate', although operationally, it began to focus much more on inflation than on unemployment). Put another way, they were being asked to achieve both nominal and real goals, a collection of objectives totally inconsistent with the idea of neutrality.

Abandoning the belief in neutrality, however, offers scope for all sorts of dishonesties. The case for neutrality was based on the idea that the underlying drivers of rising prosperity – technological advance, market deregulation, education, free trade, free movement of capital – could not really be influenced positively by monetary policy. It was a view that stemmed in large part from experiences in the 1970s, when attempts to boost growth through monetary stimulus led only to higher inflation, in the process penalizing those with cash savings (mostly pensioners) and those with fixed cash incomes, while rewarding those with large debts (mostly homebuyers and governments).

With both inflation and growth now seemingly much lower than before – and much lower than expected – it comes as no great surprise that neutrality is slowly being abandoned. Yet monetary policy can offer distortions that go far beyond the mere creation of inflation. In a bid by individual nation states to grab a bigger share of a stagnant global economic pie, monetary policy is increasingly in danger of being deployed for 'beggar-thy-neighbour' purposes. Unlike the 1930s, however, this new 'protectionist' approach targets capital markets, not markets in goods and services. It's an attempt to turn back the clock to a world of currency dominance and debasement. In the process, we are in danger of losing the yardsticks with which we measure economic success and failure.

A HISTORY OF CHEATING

Long before the printing press was invented, money was being used either to demonstrate the power of empire or to defraud those who were, for whatever reason, easily open to abuse financially. Roman coins often contained imagery designed to reinforce the idea that, like the Death Star, Rome itself was very much the power behind the empire. In the year 690, the ruling caliph issued Islamic coins stating, unsurprisingly, that 'There is no God but God alone' and that 'Mohammad is the messenger of God'. Constantinople retaliated, issuing coins with the emperor relegated to the reverse and Jesus Christ on the front. Of the three surviving gold coins from the reign of Offa, king of Mercia from 757 to 796, one is a copy of an Abbasid dinar of 774, with Latin on one side and Arabic on the other, perhaps an early attempt at a currency peg arrangement: at the time, England was, at best, an emerging market and, for many, not to be trusted.

Meanwhile, there were plenty of opportunities for currency debasement. Before the advent of fiat money, coins themselves were made of precious metal, mostly gold and silver. Some coins were 'clipped', thereby reducing the precious metal content (one reason why, even today, many coins have ridged edges). Others were 'sweated', shaken together in a bag to extract precious metal 'dust'. And those who had a monopoly of issuance were too often tempted to debase the coinage by deliberately reducing the precious metal content: in the Great Debasement during the reigns of Henry VIII and Edward VI, the value of the silver content within each coin's face value collapsed. The money raised (or saved) by the monarchs was used to fund the construction of palaces and, inevitably, expensive military ventures across the English Channel.

Henry's behaviour led to the formulation of Gresham's Law: stated simply, bad money drives out good. If a currency is being debased, the bad stuff remains in circulation, while the good stuff is hoarded, reflecting a loss of confidence in the issuing institutions. The modern-day equivalents of such debasing behaviour are for the private sector, counterfeiting, and for central banks and governments, the printing press.

In the post-financial crisis world, the printing press has, for the most part, failed to deliver significantly higher inflation. In other words, central banks have struggled to debase their currencies at home. However, the printing press has helped in changing the value of one currency against another. And in that sense, central banks have succeeded, at least temporarily, in debasing their currencies abroad. For international capital markets, this matters. Movements in currencies can have a profound impact on the financial position of international creditors and debtors. In the modern age, it's a way for nations and regions to export their problems somewhere else.

The problem is most acute when interest rates drop to zero. If growth and inflation also remain excessively low, high levels of debt become an almost permanent burden. Attempts to repay debt lead only to even lower rates of growth and inflation, which in turn make the debt burden even more indigestible. A mechanism has to be found either to boost growth and inflation or to pass the burden of debt on to someone else.

Under certain conditions, devaluation – triggered by zero interest rates, negative interest rates or quantitative easing – can help. A fall in the exchange rate may, in time, increase the demand for exports to the rest of the world sufficiently to outweigh the increased cost of imports.[5] To the extent that an economy can then enjoy an export-led recovery, its growth and inflation rates might then rise, helping to stabilize or even reduce the burden of debt. This effect, however, appears to have diminished over time. The 2008 fall in sterling had a much more limited impact on British export performance and on the UK's balance of payments position than did the more or less equivalent decline in sterling when the

UK came off the gold standard in 1931. And while inflation rose temporarily in the latter period, it became apparent relatively quickly that there was little the Bank of England could do permanently to escape from a broader deflationary trend globally.[6]

A second – and increasingly important – effect comes via the capital markets. If a country has raised funds from the rest of the world in its own currency, a subsequent devaluation is likely to make foreign investors worse off in their currencies. Admittedly, the less trustworthy a country's financial institutions and the smaller its economy (and hence its tax base), the less likely it is to be able to raise funds in its own currency. The US, however, has had no such problem: since the 1970s, it has happily run a balance of payments current account deficit, thanks primarily to the US dollar's status as the world's premier reserve currency. In other words, it is a trustworthy international medium of exchange and store of value. And since the 1970s, the dollar has steadily declined in value. Against a basket of other major internationally traded currencies it fell 19 per cent between January 1973 and April 2016. Investing in the US stock market or bond market over that period might have been a very good bet, but for German or Japanese savers holding their funds in dollar cash, they would have had the same experience as those who lived during the reign of Henry VIII: over time, those funds would have been clipped or sweated.

This modern-day version of clipping reflects the so-called Triffin Dilemma.[7] With cross-border capital flows having expanded rapidly since the 1980s, the demand for reserve currency has skyrocketed. Whilst the dollar has traditionally played that role, the more dollars the rest of the world holds the greater is the incentive for the US to devalue, to 'go it alone', to focus on internal rather than global stability. Moreover, as America's share of the global economic pie has slowly diminished over time, the ability of US taxpayers to back the liabilities associated with foreign dollar holdings has declined. Put another way, the smaller the US economy relative to the rest of the world, the less reliable the US dollar is likely to be as the world's premier reserve currency. The Nixon Shock may only be a foretaste of future currency upheavals.

Those upheavals, in turn, may reflect an increase in competitive currency clipping. With the formation of the euro and the rise of the Chinese renminbi, the world appears to be entering a new phase in which the US dollar faces competition for reserve currency status. Yet if reserve currency status enables the issuing country to more easily escape from a debt trap, the number of countries and regions attempting to engineer reserve currency status will only increase. Meanwhile, those already with reserve currency status will more easily lose the trust of everyone else. As reserve currencies proliferate, so more countries will want to claim that it's 'our currency, your problem'.

Under those circumstances, however, it is difficult to see how globalization can easily progress. At best, we may end up with a series of regional currency blocs dominated by the US dollar, the euro and the renminbi. At worst, we could end up with a chaotic ever-changing constellation of currencies challenging globalization on three separate fronts: first, the desire for individual countries to deflect their debt problem somewhere else; second, the American economy's diminishing status on the world stage; and third, the absence of a global financial imperium to replace the US. It's no great surprise that, given this prospect, interest in new currency algorithms – most obviously the Blockchain that underlies Bitcoin – is on the increase.

'CONSPANSIONARY' MONETARY POLICY

Monetary policy's redistributional qualities are not, however, confined to cross-border effects alone. Within countries, it increasingly appears that monetary stimulus has both expansionary and contractionary effects – a combination that might best be termed 'conspansionary'.[8] Before the global financial crisis, these effects tended to even out over time. Periods of rising interest rates penalized debtors even as they rewarded savers:

and as debtors tended to be more spendthrift than savers, periods of rising rates typically led to weaker aggregate demand. In contrast, periods of falling interest rates had the reverse effect, triggering stronger aggregate demand. Over time, and reflecting the ups and downs of the business cycle, these effects tended to cancel each other out.

Since the global financial crisis, however, interest rates have been either at or, increasingly, below zero. The 'symmetry' associated with past economic cycles is no longer valid: interest rates have fallen a long way, but subsequently have scarcely risen at all. For the Western world at least, this is an experience remarkably similar to that of Japan in the 1990s and beyond. Even with interest rates at rock bottom, there has been an absence of robust economic recovery. Under these circumstances, 'stimulative' monetary policy can have perverse effects. While not all people's coins are being clipped simultaneously, some people's coins are being clipped repeatedly. The economic and political consequences have not been fully thought through.

Among the 'winners' in a world of negative interest rates and quantitative easing are, most obviously, governments themselves. Lower borrowing costs enable governments more easily to meet their fiscal ambitions without having to make painful political decisions regarding spending programmes or tax rates. Other winners include those who have large holdings of financial wealth in the form of equities, government bonds or corporate debt. Quantitative easing is designed to increase the value of such assets, making the world's financial plutocrats even more plutocratic. Then there are the providers of high-yield products who are likely to do well selling (or perhaps mis-selling) their products to a public too often unwilling or unable to recognize the risks involved. Companies and households with mortgages should also benefit, but if debts are very high and growth prospects appear not very good, the ability to generate a significant recovery in either investment or consumption may be unusually low – as, indeed, it has proved. Exporters, too, should benefit if a single central bank's actions drive down the exchange rate.

As for the losers, the most obvious are those with limited savings, mostly in the form of cash: in other words, many – particularly elderly – Western citizens. Worse, with returns on cash collapsing, people have to save more to meet their retirement objectives – one reason why consumer spending has failed to pick up strongly, despite the apparent offer of cheap credit. And financial go-betweens are faced with serious difficulties. Most obviously, many pension schemes may be faced with bankruptcy. Traditional banking businesses also lose out. Banks make their money partly through so-called 'maturity transformation', raising funds through short-term deposits which are then bundled together and lent out for longer-term investment purposes. With both short- and long-term interest rates very low simultaneously, the transformation process has become a lot less profitable. As a result, funds sit idly inside the banking sector, serving little or no purpose.

Negative nominal interest rates add to the problems facing banks. While the aim is to encourage banks to cut their lending rates, in order to encourage a pick-up in loan demand within the non-bank private sector, negative nominal interest rates are a perversity in a world in which notes and coin exist: in the absence of clipping, notes and coin by definition offer a zero nominal interest rate. Given this, negative interest rates are decidedly odd. To work, commercial banks would ultimately have to offer negative interest rates on bank deposits, a decision that would doubtless attract huge amounts of opprobrium. Depositors, meanwhile, would have to be persuaded to leave their money in banks – with guaranteed losses – as opposed to holding cash under the proverbial mattress: at a 0.5 per cent negative interest rate, that might just about be credible, but with a 20 per cent negative interest rate, say, there is every chance that there would be huge deposit flight, a surge in demand for both shotguns and safety deposit boxes, and an implosion of the entire banking system. Some have suggested that the best solution to this problem may be to abolish notes and coin altogether, thereby removing the effective 'floor' underneath the level of interest rates.[9] There would, of course, be certain advantages –

most obviously criminal acts currently financed or laundered through the transfer of suitcases full of $100 bills might be reduced. But there is an obvious disadvantage: governments and central banks would be free to dip into people's bank accounts at will, using negative interest rates as a technical – and largely non-democratic – alternative to a wealth tax to penalize those who have held onto their savings for a rainy day.

The biggest loser from central banks' experimental activities is, however, international capitalism itself. As central banks choose to purchase an ever-wider range of assets in a bid to stabilize the system as a whole, the allocation of capital is likely to deteriorate: Adam Smith's invisible hand is slowly being dismembered, one digit at a time. Mario Draghi's commitment to 'do whatever it takes' to preserve the euro has forced the European Central Bank to become a 'lender of last resort' to sovereign governments, effectively freeing them from the market discipline that might have encouraged some of them to deliver more in the way of fiscal consolidation or structural reform. In the event of another recession, central banks will have no option but to do more in the way of quantitative easing: knowing this, financial asset values will remain inflated, regardless of underlying economic performance. Under these circumstances, listed companies will continue to gain access to financial capital on favourable terms, whether or not that capital is deployed wisely. The danger is that large inefficient firms will remain large and inefficient, while start-ups and those with serious growth potential – dependent on a (shrinking) banking system – will be starved of funds. Overall, the result is likely to be persistent misallocation of capital and thus a sustained period of productivity underperformance. Put another way, economic opportunities will be left begging.[10]

THE BUCK STOPS WHERE?

Before the global financial crisis, money and capital flowed across borders with ease. After the crisis, even with the international effects of quantitative easing, the flows dried up.[11] The crisis had revealed an enormous gulf between the interests of financiers and those of taxpayers. To save the global financial system, national taxpayers – who, for the most part, had done nothing wrong – had to dig deep into their pockets to bail out what were, in some cases, global institutions. With much higher levels of government debt as a consequence of the financial crisis, they will continue to do so for many years to come. They and their political masters discovered that the costs of global finance could, at times, be painfully high: not surprisingly, they wanted to regain control.

This, in turn, created an obvious dilemma: to deliver a lasting economic recovery, it was imperative that bank lending should pick up; but to safeguard the financial system, and hence protect the interests of taxpayers, it was vital that banks take fewer risks than they had before. One way to square the circle was for banks to limit lending to borrowers closer to home. Part of this reflects a retreat by banks themselves, keen to refocus their efforts in a world in which bank profitability appears to be on the wane. But it also reflects the central banks' new powers. They may not easily be able to prevent capital inflows from abroad, but via macro-prudential policies they can stop those inflows from being lent out to what the central banks themselves might deem as excessively risky ventures. Equally, they should in theory be able to prevent the banks they are responsible for regulating from messing up the financial system again. In the UK, following the 2011 Vickers Report, ring-fencing is one such mechanism: banks have until 2019 to completely separate their UK retail operations – what might best be described as standard utility banking – from their international corporate and investment banking activities. The Vickers Report also recommended, however, that UK banks should have higher capital and loss-absorbing reserves than their international peers. In looking after the interests of taxpayers, that makes sense. The UK banks themselves may, however, end up competitively disadvantaged compared with their rivals. It's a small example of a broader trend in the aftermath of the financial crisis: with the regulatory pendulum swinging towards national interests, the global credit system is in retreat.

GIVING UP ON NEUTRALITY

Throughout history, money has never been 'neutral': it has been used and abused, clipped and sweated, counterfeited and printed. It has been a symbol of power, a sign of influence, an emblem of nationhood. For some, money has been a device to gain economic advantage; for others, it has led only to misery. Sometimes we overstate its value: how many people on the *Sunday Times* Rich List are genuinely happy? On other occasions, we don't take it seriously enough: on hearing the price of a Picasso painting, Stravinsky allegedly complained that the purchaser had shown flagrant disrespect for the value of money.

Most importantly, though, our current monetary arrangements are a halfway house between a fully globalized world and a series of nation states. And, in the light of the financial crisis, policymakers have discovered that money can rather usefully be used to shift the burden of economic adjustment from one country to another. The more they do so, however, the greater the degree of twenty-first-century 'clipping', creating a divisive world in which it is increasingly a case of 'heads I win, tails you lose'. And, to the extent that this 'winner takes all' approach is recognized, it will become a rallying call for all those who wish to push back on globalization. Our central banks may be independent, but their actions can no longer be regarded seriously as being totally 'neutral'.

THE ART OF THE IMPOSSIBLE

The three twenty-first-century challenges – migration, technology and money – suggest that globalization will come under increasing pressure from disruptive forces. Political narratives will dominate conventional economic narratives. The spirit of Bretton Woods will be replaced by mutual suspicion. Cooperative arrangements between nation states will be increasingly hard to come by. Conflict – at least in the economic sphere – will become ever more frequent. While there are solutions aplenty, how many of them are plausible – let alone likely? That is the subject of the final section of this book.

Part Four

GLOBALIZATION IN CRISIS

OBLIGATIONS AND IMPOSSIBLE SOLUTIONS

BEATING THE RETREAT

The international institutions created at the end of the Second World War and in the years following were ultimately institutions of the Cold War. Western economies and societies became ever more closely integrated, thanks in part to the machinations of the IMF, NATO and what eventually became the European Union. A world largely free of conflict, in which capital was unlikely to go up in smoke and where the financial rules of the game were mostly well understood, was also likely to be a world in which entrepreneurial capitalism was likely to flourish.

Following the collapse of Soviet communism, it was all too easy to believe that the West's model of liberal democracy and free-market capitalism, supported by a clear set of US-sponsored international rules, would spread to the four corners of the Earth. Yet, in the event, this proved to be nonsense. In the years following the fall of the Iron Curtain, there may have been economic, financial and, to a degree, technological globalization, but there was globalization of neither institutions nor ideas.

Both politically and economically, the West's version of globalization was reaching its limits, reflecting mounting opposition from other nascent superpowers, increasing resistance to globalization from emerging political movements within the Western nations and, piece by piece, the US economy's relative decline. Prior to the financial crisis, many Western policymakers and economists had simply been too complacent. Whilst, as many had predicted, the global economic pie had increased in size, too little attention had been paid to its distribution.[1] And what in hindsight proved to be an inevitable conflict between an integrated world economy and the sovereignty of the nation state appeared to go largely unnoticed. Many citizens wanted protection from the vicissitudes of globalization, yet amongst the international elites protectionism was a dirty word not to be uttered in polite company.

International economic arrangements that, once upon a time, would have been seen as perfectly enlightened and mostly uncontroversial were increasingly regarded, at the beginning of the twenty-first century, with both suspicion and fear. The Trans-Pacific Partnership died a death. The Transatlantic Trade and Investment Partnership faced severe resistance, notably in continental Europe. The European Union was blamed by many voters – not just in the UK, but also in increasing numbers elsewhere in Europe – for all manner of problems, ranging from austerity and unemployment to excessive immigration and an inability to deal with terrorism. Many countries in Asia looked upon the IMF with considerable scepticism given its controversial handling of the Asian financial crisis.

All of this raises a critical question. Can globalization be healed or, instead, are we facing a world in which our international relationships – political, economic, financial – are beating a disorderly retreat?

POPULISTS AND RENEGADES

Some argue that the problem represents no more than a growing divide between the traditional right and left. Yet a simple 'right/left' narrative does not work terribly well. Those on the left argue that the right thrives by exploiting divisions in society, yet the left itself is divided between those who support globalization (Hillary Clinton, Tony Blair) and those who do not (Bernie Sanders, Jeremy Corbyn).[2] Meanwhile, those on the right too often misinterpret economic arguments in order to push their 'free-market' agendas. Ricardian comparative advantage, for example, works a lot less well in the modern era: contemporary globalization is driven more by the heightened cross-border movement of capital and labour than by trade flows. By failing to recognize this distinction, the right too often ends up inadvertently supporting the interests of oligopolistic multinationals – what might loosely be described as 'big business' – at the expense of the population at large. By hijacking a perfectly good economic theory and applying it inappropriately, it becomes a twenty-first-century version of the nineteenth-century treaty ports in China.

In truth, the views of traditional left and right are in danger of being usurped by populists, keen to blame the rest of the world for their own countries' difficulties. Voters can no longer be so easily categorized as being on one or other side of the political spectrum. It's a result exploited by, among others, Donald Trump, Bernie Sanders, the UK Independence Party, Greece's Syriza party and France's Marine Le Pen. That's hardly surprising: the distributional consequences of globalization and technology have left many voters who might traditionally have voted for centrist parties opting instead to support populists who claim to be more in touch with voters' concerns. For many people, the institutions and ideas of globalization are part of the problem, not part of the solution. As such, 'fixing' globalization is hardly straightforward: if people increasingly crave the 'sanctity' of their nation state – and populists promise to satisfy those cravings – globalization is in danger of totally unravelling.

Still, there has been no shortage of – mostly technical – proposals to make the world a better place. It's not clear, however, whether any of them really deals with the underlying sense of discontent expressed with increasing frequency at the ballot box.

ANOTHER BRETTON WOODS?

Yanis Varoufakis, the former Greek finance minister and scourge of 'conventional' European politics, advocates what he calls a new, technologically advanced, green Bretton Woods.[3] In a bid to kill off financial speculation and limit cross-border capital flows, he proposes the creation of an international clearing system based loosely on Keynes' 1944 *bancor*. Unlike Keynes, however, he thinks currencies should be able to float against one another and that capital controls should be kept to a minimum.

Nevertheless, the Varoufakis system is closely modelled on the Keynes plan. A new global currency – *Kosmos* – would be issued by the IMF, its volume linked to the size of world trade. Individual central banks would have *Kosmos* accounts in addition to their foreign exchange reserves. Those accounts would be subject to a varying levy depending on the size of their nation's balance of payments surplus or deficit: the bigger the imbalance, the bigger the fine. Separately, private sector financial institutions would also be subject to a levy, depending on the pace with which capital flows were exiting (but curiously, not entering) any particular country: the idea would be to make speculative exuberance a lot more expensive.

The Varoufakis scheme ultimately relies on a judgement that the bigger the balance of payments surplus or deficit, the greater the risk of instability. It also assumes – reasonably – that imbalances are just as much the fault of surplus countries as deficit countries: all sides are thus required to adjust. Yet it has some important drawbacks.

Imagine a world of just two countries whose respective governments neither borrowed nor lent. Imagine, in this world, that one country – let's call it the Wrinkly Kingdom – had a relatively mature population, while the other – the Adolescent Republic – was full of young people. Savers in the Wrinkly Kingdom might sensibly take the view that their savings should be invested not with their fellow Wrinklies, but instead with the Adolescents: after all, the Wrinklies need to get access to a young workforce to produce things for them to consume during their retirement. All things being equal, the flow of savings from the Wrinkly Kingdom to the Adolescent Republic would leave the Wrinklies with a balance of payments current account surplus (and hence a capital outflow), while the Adolescents would end up with a deficit (and hence an inflow): the imbalances would be the mirror image of one another, while their overall size would ultimately depend on the age structures of the two populations and their retirement preferences. The size of these imbalances could be anything from the very small to the extraordinarily large. Varoufakis, however, effectively takes the view that small is better, regardless of differing demographic circumstances.

THE LOGICAL CHALLENGE FROM NATION STATES

Others have pursued similar arguments. Joseph Stiglitz, the Nobel Prize-winning economist, notes that:

> in the current global system, we rely on central banks to set interest rates, hoping somehow that the resulting trade balance, investment, and consumption, will be 'right'. They typically aren't. The alternative approach focuses on the quantities of, say, investment and trade balance, that we need, and lets the market set the price to achieve this.[4]

Like Varoufakis, Stiglitz thinks the appropriate volume of capital flowing from one country to another should somehow be determined not by the market, but by the collective wisdom of policymakers.

Consider, however, two nations that, for one reason or another, become one. It's not so difficult to do. The various states of the Italian peninsula, for example, were united between 1815 and 1871. Prior to Italian unification, Varoufakis and Stiglitz would presumably have wanted to judge whether capital flows from, say, Lombardy to Calabria were excessive or otherwise. After unification, they would presumably have had no opinion either way. Within countries, balance of payments data simply do not exist. Admittedly, fiscal policies at the national level can help ease the regional imbalances associated with internal capital flows. But they do not eradicate them. Per capita incomes in prosperous northern Italy, at around €32,000, are on a par with Germany, France and the UK. Per capita incomes in southern Italy – the so-called *mezzogiorno* – are only around €17,000, on a par with Slovenia, Greece and Portugal. In other words, the gaps that exist within Italy are just as big as those that exist across much of Europe. Yet, while Varoufakis and Stiglitz have strong views about the appropriate level of capital flows across countries, they struggle to explain what should happen within countries, even when a country's borders may result more from historical accident than from economic good sense.

Stiglitz argues that the euro should be split into two currencies, one for the north of Europe and one for the south. He then suggests that all Southern European debt – a large chunk of which is held by Northern Europeans – should be redenominated into the new Southern European currency. Given the likely decline of the Southern European currency against its northern counterpart, this would effectively be a default (Northern European creditors would get their money back in devalued Southern European euros). If so, the logic of the Stiglitz approach suggests not only that Southern Europe should devalue against Northern Europe, but, in addition, that southern Italy should devalue against northern Italy. Yet no one is advocating the introduction of a new southern Italian lira. The apparent sanctity of nation states, it turns out, has a pesky habit of interfering with economic logic: what appears to be so obviously true between nations is often unthinkable within nations.

Perhaps the biggest challenge, however, is that the original Bretton Woods system ultimately depended on the sponsorship of the US. A new version would almost certainly require similar support: the global foreign exchange market is totally dominated by US dollars, and even if the US is a diminished economic superpower, it is unlikely to sign up to an international monetary arrangement in which it would be compelled to pay fines for running an excessively large balance of payments deficit. Indeed, as the issuer of the world's reserve currency, the US is virtually obliged to run a deficit: its persistent borrowing from foreigners stems at least as much from the rest of the world's desire to hold dollars as it does from America's own economic gluttony. It remains 'our dollar, your problem'.

SMOKIN'

Others, meanwhile, fear that global institutions too often undermine the degree to which individual nation states can make their own political and social choices. International rules-based systems might seem fair, but they are simply unable to cope with nation states' varying preferences. A good example is Australia's legislation in favour of plain paper packaging for cigarettes. Tobacco companies are unable officially to object through the World Trade Organization: it exists for countries, not companies. Nevertheless, a group of tobacco companies have sponsored Ukraine and Honduras – both of whom produce modest amounts of tobacco – in challenging Australia's decision via the WTO on the grounds that the plain packaging is an anti-competitive measure that unfairly damages the brand value of, say, a pack of 20 Marlboro.

Some regard examples such as this as legitimate challenges to globalization because democratically elected decision-makers end up with their hands tied, thanks to the intervention of an anonymous technocrat not obviously accountable to anyone. Dani Rodrik, for example, argues that whereas climate change requires a global response because there's a single climate system, the same does not – and should not – apply to the global economy. In Rodrik's words:

good economic policies – including openness – benefit the domestic economy first and foremost, and the price of bad economic policies is primarily paid domestically as well ... If economic openness is desirable, it is because such policies are in a country's own self-interest – not because it helps others.

He adds that 'the goal of global governance embodies a yearning for technocratic solutions that override and undercut public deliberation'.[5]

Rodrik is certainly right that resistance to international rules-based systems has inspired opposition to globalization. But the claim that good economic policies begin and end at home is not particularly robust. Partly, it is because many of our domestic economic decisions are also made by technocrats not held fully accountable for their actions: the tools of monetary policy, for example, are in the hands of unelected central bankers, who tinker with negative interest rates and quantitative easing with no direct regard for their distributional consequences. Mostly, however, it is because international economic agreements are not about economics alone: they are also about values, power and political influence.

To see why, imagine that the Trans-Pacific Partnership had been signed, sealed and delivered. The US would then have established itself as the dominant trading partner in the Asia-Pacific region, very much the 'first among equals'. Other TPP members would have been happy for the US to look after their collective security needs. China would have been left on the outside looking in, economically, politically and militarily diminished. Liberal democracy would have appeared, once again, to be on the move.

Instead, at the tail end of 2016, the US walked away from the Partnership, thanks in large part to growing domestic opposition to free trade revealed during the presidential election campaign. Washington's rejection of TPP creates an institutional vacuum in Asia, which China will doubtless be quick to fill. After all, Beijing already has the advantage, being the primary architect of the Regional Comprehensive Economic Partnership. At first, some would-be members of the TPP might have misgivings about joining RCEP, but, at the end of the day, China's magnetic economic attractions are likely to prove irresistible. What might have been a system sponsored by a Western liberal democracy will become, instead, a structure supported by the bureaucracy of the Chinese one-party state.

Whatever the relative merits of a China-led (rather than US-led) regional trading arrangement, it is difficult to see why anyone – those involved in the arrangement, those observing from the outside – can be indifferent to the outcome. And given the risk of Chinese dominance, it might seem odd to think that in 2016, neither Donald Trump nor Hillary Clinton was willing to endorse US participation in TPP with any degree of enthusiasm.

The underlying reasons, however, are not so difficult to fathom. National governments have been unable to marry global market outcomes with domestic social and political goals. Rich and poor nations alike have reasons to be suspicious of globalization. Being competitive globally threatens domestic labour standards, particularly in a world in which mobile capital hopes to seek out the cheapest pools of labour (ironically, TPP included an attempt to provide common labour standards). Bailing out banks for their far-flung misadventures leads only to austerity at home. Attempts to attract global capital can result in national tax authorities indulging in a corporation tax 'race to the bottom': indeed, corporate tax rates have plunged since the early 1980s.[6] Accepting the strictures of the World Trade Organization may only preserve a decidedly skewed playing field, preventing today's poor countries from using techniques employed by others in the past to foster economic progress. Without the use of protectionist measures to nurture infant industries, for example, it is unlikely that the nineteenth-century US economy or the East Asian economies of the late twentieth century would have made significant gains. Signing up to bilateral investment treaties might seem like a good way of attracting much-needed foreign investment into a country; but in the event that something goes wrong, whom does the treaty protect and who is left to pay the bill?

UNSTABLE BORDERS

All these are common criticisms of globalization in a world of nation states. Indeed, Dani Rodrik has suggested that they represent facets of what is ultimately a globalization 'trilemma'. Nations are faced with one of three awkward options: restrict democratic choice, in the hope that global economic and financial gains will be maximized; restrict globalization, in the hope that national democratic choice will be enhanced; or globalize democracy, creating institutions at the global or regional level to replace those that, until now, have been typically regarded as the sole preserve of nation states.[7] Of these options, the first no longer looks credible (particularly in the light of the global financial crisis); the second is uncomfortably redolent of the arguments used in the interwar period; and the third doesn't easily chime with an increasingly populist political environment.

One weakness of the 'trilemma' approach, however, is the assumption that the borders of nation states are effectively fixed. History suggests otherwise. British national pride (or, more accurately, English pride) may be bolstered by references to Crécy and Agincourt, but at the end of the Hundred Years' War the French won the Battle of Castillon and the English – who at one point considered large chunks of France to be their own – retreated back to Albion, where they briefly licked their wounds before going on to fight each other in the Wars of the Roses. In a twenty-first-century replay of medieval history, it is not difficult to imagine a further English retreat, this time away from Scotland and Northern Ireland. After all, their voters – unlike the majority of their English and Welsh counterparts – were heavily in favour of remaining in the European Union in the June 2016 referendum.

Meanwhile, in 1800, there were more than 300 separate German-speaking nations and principalities with little chance of a serious meeting of minds. Napoleon's escapades, however, helped instil a stronger sense of shared German identity against a common enemy. Following the 1815 Congress of Vienna, the case for a united Germany strengthened further, particularly given the growing economic linkages associated with the creation in 1818 of the Zollverein, a German customs union that was in effect a nineteenth-century Teutonic precursor of the European Union's single market. In the immediate aftermath of the 1870–71 Franco-Prussian War, Germany finally was unified, with King Wilhelm I of Prussia crowned German emperor in, of all places, the Hall of Mirrors in the Palace of Versailles. Yet Germany's borders remained unstable thanks to two world wars and the fall of the Berlin Wall. How those borders – and indeed the European Union's – will develop in the twenty-first century is an open question. At the time of writing, enthusiasm for further European federalism appears to be fading fast, but a newly assertive Russia, an increasingly isolationist US and the threat of a further influx of migrants from the east might change all that. There might even come a time when it could be useful to dust off maps of the Holy Roman Empire.

The truth is that any form of globalization will inevitably require some form of compromise between the advantages of openness and the benefits of sovereignty. That trade-off, in turn, will determine the relations that nation states have with each other and, *in extremis*, redraw the boundaries and institutions of nation states themselves. The international institutions that provide the framework within which countries can happily engage with each other, and thus avoid autarky, have to take this compromise into account. It is not clear that the institutions we have today satisfactorily deliver the best compromise. Nor is it obvious that agreement could be reached about the relevant institutions for tomorrow. After all, Rodrik's trilemma is expressed in democratic terms, yet, if anything, the evidence since the beginning of the twenty-first century is that democracy is in retreat. Is it really possible to create institutions to serve a world in which nation states continue to operate under entirely different political systems?

McCLOSKEY'S DOUBTS

To be fair, some argue that institutions themselves – domestic or international – are ultimately no more than a shoal of red herring when it comes to economic progress: we should instead focus on developing the ethical forces that underpin markets. In her monumental trilogy examining the economic and social success of the 'bourgeoisie', Deirdre McCloskey argues that the importance of institutions is hugely overrated. In her view, the key driver of economic advance is 'trade-tested betterment', an ethical approach to economic exchange first elucidated by – in their very different ways – Adam Smith, Jane Austen and Benjamin Franklin.[8] In McCloskey's world, the ethics of good business revolves around the idea that human beings are not merely profit-maximizing or utility-maximizing drones, but instead people capable of integrity, trust, respect, prudence, thrift, affection and the other 'bourgeois virtues'. Seen in this light, institutions may only serve to restrict the beneficial economic exchanges that ultimately have allowed so many billions of people to escape grinding poverty.

McCloskey makes a powerful point. After all, the existence of institutions says little about their effectiveness. A Londoner travelling to Mexico City, for example, will find traffic ostensibly governed in a similar way: there are traffic lights at road junctions and the police sit in their patrol cars apparently making sure that people obey the laws of the land. Yet Mexican drivers ignore red lights as a matter of course. And the police tend to intervene only when a car is sufficiently luxurious to suggest that the driver might be able to afford to pay an appropriate bribe.[9] In other words, while institutions may ostensibly be the same, their ethical foundations may differ enormously.

Yet there is no particular reason to assume that the bourgeoisie themselves are always on their best behaviour. For those tempted to stray, there are plenty of bourgeois vices: corruption, envy, jealousy, greed, adultery and the rest. Whatever their strengths – and, superficially, their God-fearing behaviour – the bourgeoisie are still human. Institutions don't necessarily make people behave better; but nor does being bourgeois.

Still, in McCloskey's world, even badly governed countries can still make progress, so long as there are opportunities for betterment. Only in modern-day North Korea, say, or the China of Mao's 1950s 'Great Leap Forward' is progress denied. Thankfully, the governments of most nations have no ambition to follow in the footsteps of the Great Leader. McCloskey reinforces her argument by pointing out that Italy and New Zealand have similar living standards, despite the fact that Italy is – at least according to McCloskey – known for its high levels of corruption, while New Zealand offers almost the perfect example of institutional probity.

Yet it is precisely this comparison that demonstrates that institutions do, in fact, matter. In 1990, the average Italian's standard of living was almost 20 per cent higher than the equivalent New Zealander's. Within a quarter-century, the gap had disappeared altogether. Should the same trends continue in decades to come, New Zealanders would be enjoying living standards almost double those of their Italian counterparts by 2100. Italians may be subject to 'trade-tested betterment', but *la dolce vita* seems to have turned into *la vita acida*.

What has gone wrong? Relative to its European peers, Italy's economic performance really began to deteriorate around the time that the euro was first created. Since then, the gap in living standards between Germany – seemingly the big 'winner' in the single currency system – and Italy has become what now appears to be an insurmountable gulf. Worse, Italian living standards in 2015 were no higher than they had been in 1999, marking a period of economic stagnation unprecedented in the developed world during the post-war era.

Before the single currency's creation, Italy had few problems keeping up with its European neighbours: when it had problems, it simply devalued its exchange rate. Since Italy first joined the euro, however, its economy has persistently lagged behind. Italy has become the equivalent of Wales in the UK or Saxony in Germany. The single currency is an institutional arrangement that appears – economically, at least – to be doing Italy more harm than good. Worse, Italy is increasingly under pressure from its northern neighbours to reform its domestic institutions, whether or not Italians themselves want the reforms. As a consequence, Italy's sovereignty is slowly being compromised and political populism is on the rise.

CROSS-BORDER CLAIMS IN A WORLD OF UNCERTAINTY

Italy's problems are symptomatic of a huge international challenge stemming from the globalization of capital markets. Recall from Chapter 4 that the ratio of foreign-held capital as a share of global income rose from little more than 5 per cent at the end of the Second World War to well over 200 per cent by the time of the global financial crisis, with much of the increase coming in the 1980s and beyond. In effect, there are now massive cross-border economic and financial claims made up of a vast number of pieces of paper and entries in electronic ledgers. Because these claims relate to capital markets, they essentially operate through time and space: when, for example, a German Landesbank buys a US collateralized debt obligation (CDO), it is essentially making a – legal – claim on future US economic output. The interest rate paid by the US issuer of the CDO to its proud owner will, in turn, reflect a combination of reward for consumption forgone, the perceived 'riskiness' of the underlying borrowers (to be precise, the danger that the borrowers will not be able to repay the principal in full), and the liquidity of the CDO (in other words, the ease with which it can be converted quickly into cash at little cost).

Risk, however, is not the same as uncertainty. One coin toss is risky, but the outcome of many repeated coin tosses should carry little in the way of uncertainty: the laws of probability suggest that the outcome following hundreds of such tosses should be 50 per cent heads, 50 per cent tails. Imagine a world, however, where coin tosses could not be repeated, and there was no way of knowing whether a particular coin toss involved either a scrupulously fair coin or one that was 'double-headed' or 'double-tailed'. This would represent a world that was more than just risky: it would be deeply uncertain. Imagine that all decisions in this world were governed by these fundamentally uncertain coin tosses: on an entirely random basis, some people may do very well, whereas others may fare very badly indeed. Both the winners and the losers might then be tempted to form their own narratives to explain their successes and failures – the winners extolling their (imaginary) skills, the losers blaming the winners for their (imaginary) exploitation.

When faith in financial markets peaked in the years before the financial crisis, both risk and uncertainty were – unhelpfully – assumed to be much the same thing. Financial markets would be able to do a decent job of resolving the 'riskiness' of a particular investment, so long as economies on the whole continued to make steady gains, consistent with the idea that the world would travel along the path determined by the 'Great Moderation'. In the event, however, Western economies in particular were not able to make steady gains. Even before the financial crisis, many of them were expanding at a much slower rate than had been witnessed in earlier decades. The post-crisis world simply made a bad situation even worse.

This, in turn, has revealed a fundamental problem regarding international capital markets in a world of uncertainty. So long as the world economy moves along a familiar path, there's every chance that the vast number of economic and financial claims that make up international capital markets will eventually be paid in full, with interest. If, however, the world moves along an unfamiliar path, there is only confusion and uncertainty. In the absence of a universally accepted process to divide up the losses between creditor and debtor nations, the natural tendency is for countries to withdraw into their shells. Those that are financially strong or reasonably liquid will have the advantage over those that, for reasons good or bad, have significant financial liabilities. The costs of global economic disappointment are then unfairly distributed, with little or no room to compensate those who, through no fault of their own, have lost out. Put another way, there are no international arrangements in place to allow nation states to resolve their contradictory financial claims in a world in which economic outcomes are persistently worse than expected.

THE DISUNITED STATES

To emphasize the importance that international institutions can potentially play in these circumstances, imagine that Washington, DC is abolished. Alongside its disappearance, all of the establishments associated with the US federal government vanish overnight. Suddenly it's each state for itself. And each state quickly wants to assess its financial relationship with all the other Disunited States. It soon becomes apparent that the educated (and wealthy) people of Massachusetts – who specialize in financial services, technology and life sciences – have been paying some of their tax dollars to support the disadvantaged (and poor) people of Mississippi – who are overly dependent on agriculture, low-cost manufacturing and gambling. In balance of payments terms, some of Massachusetts' hard-earned income has been transferred to the Deep South, allowing the good people of Mississippi to live better lives than their economic circumstances might otherwise suggest. On hearing this, the citizens of Massachusetts protest to the burghers of Boston, demanding that the effective subsidy to the South should stop. The burghers quickly agree. There are, after all, some important elections coming up and there is no reason to think that Massachusetts voters will be over the moon about on-going transfers to a newly independent state with a capital, Jackson, as distant from Boston as, say, Athens is from Berlin (to pick an example at random). Without the transfer, however, Mississippi's balance of payments lurches into huge deficit.

At first, the newly elected Jackson government is able to raise loans from nations with deep pockets elsewhere in the world – Germany, China, Japan – to maintain its previous standard of living. Even better, after a while Mississippi begins to attract some modest investment inflows from foreign companies keen to take advantage of relatively low labour costs. However, following a deep and prolonged global economic crisis, creditor nations soon become frustrated with Mississippi's lack of immediate economic progress. They turn their backs on the Magnolia State. No one, it seems, sees a long-term future in agriculture or low-productivity manufacturing, and only a handful really think gambling will offer a major contribution to Mississippi's economic progress. With a heavy heart, the new Mississippi president declares a state of emergency and imposes draconian austerity measures: all the magnolias can do is wilt.

WHERE OUR OBLIGATIONS BEGIN AND END

This 'Disunited States' parable reveals many of the fundamental weaknesses associated with blind faith in globalization. Too much economic analysis habitually assumes that whilst human beings may have differing tastes, they are nevertheless all 'super-rational' and at all times are trying to 'maximize their utility'. Any basic microeconomics textbook will argue that utility maximization is most likely to be achieved in a world of perfect competition where there are no 'barriers to entry', including, most obviously, the borders that surround sovereign nation states. This is, of course, mostly nonsense. Human beings tend instead to use simple rules of thumb – or, to use the jargon, heuristics – to make decisions. Often, those rules of thumb are so deeply embedded in the subconscious that we are blissfully unaware of what is going on. Our brains may be the biological equivalent of supercomputers, but for much of the time we rely on what might best be described as 'gut instinct' or even 'tribal loyalty'. Moreover, even when we try to act in a certain way, based on some kind of clever calculus, we may well discover that the actions of others – or indeed random events – prevent us from achieving our goals. And we are unsure of how far our obligations stretch. Charity may begin at home, but how should 'home' be defined: is it our abode, our local village, the town we live in, the big city down the road, the country, the region, the empire or the world?

Institutional arrangements are important because they help determine the obligations we have to each other both locally and internationally. In the parable, as the United States fragments into its 50 component parts, the citizens of Massachusetts begin to limit the radius of their obligations: with their new-found independence, life becomes more difficult for poorer states. If the people of Massachusetts are no longer under an obligation to support the incomes of the citizens of Mississippi, the Magnolia State crumbles.

In the real world, there is no shortage of examples that demonstrate the importance of obligation – and indeed its limits.

Germany is undoubtedly the equivalent of Massachusetts within the Eurozone: a rich nation, it is also financially very stable and blessed with a series of industries that have thrived over the last 25 years – thanks in part to strong demand from China and other emerging nations for Germany's capital goods. Greece, arguably, is the equivalent of Mississippi: a poorer country that for many years relied on capital inflows from abroad, notably from Germany. Had Germany and Greece both been part of a federal fiscal system, the global financial crisis might have led to an automatic transfer of German tax revenues in order to support the poorer people of Greece in the light of a – hopefully temporary – collapse in those inflows. Instead, the crisis only served to highlight the competitive gulf between the two nations, leading in turn to a crunching adjustment in Greece, even as Germany appeared to emerge from the financial crisis relatively unscathed. Where did Germany's obligations end? And where did Greece's obligations begin? How does Italy – which, as already noted, has had a terrible economic experience within the single currency – fit in?

Then consider the claims made back in 2008 by Alex Salmond, at the time leader of the Scottish National Party and the cheerleader for Scottish independence. In a speech given at Harvard University, Salmond claimed that:

> the winds of globalisation are blowing strongly in [Scotland's] favour . . . among the big winners of globalisation are the small, dynamic trading nations of Europe . . . among the top five nations in the world [as measured by the United Nations Human Development Index] we see three of our European cousins – Ireland, Iceland and Norway. These countries are of course being affected by global forces just like their larger neighbours but all recent evidence suggests they will rebound quickest and strongest from current difficulties.[10]

They didn't. The Icelandic and Irish economies both collapsed (even if Ireland subsequently rebounded), while Norway only did well initially because of its enormous exposure to oil at a time of China-led oil price increases.

Buried within Salmond's impressive rhetorical flourishes – the most striking of which was surely the claimed 'Arc of Prosperity' supposedly linking the small, Celtic, nations of Northern Europe – were assertions which in hindsight only served to emphasize the importance of obligation and, in Scotland's case, economic dependency. Specifically, 'With RBS and HBOS – two of the world's biggest banks – Scotland has global leaders today, tomorrow and for the long-term.' Seven months later, both banks were nationalized – at a cost to the British (not Scottish) taxpayer by 2016 of around £30 billion, roughly 5 per cent of annual UK tax revenue.

What if Scotland had been an independent state? It would presumably have found itself on the hook for a taxpayer bailout amounting to around 70 per cent of annual Scottish tax revenue. Scotland would then have had to declare itself bankrupt, defaulting to its foreign creditors, and the two banks in question would have collapsed, sending a particularly chilly wind through the global economy and its network of financial capillaries. Scotland was lucky: the taxpayers of the UK as a whole were obliged to help it out in its time of need. Had borders existed between England and Scotland, the results might have been very different.

It's not impossible to think of ways of solving the obligation issue across borders. When the global economy is expanding rapidly and debtors can easily service their debts, both creditors and debtors are happy. When the global economy nosedives or stagnates, the likelihood that debtors will be either willing or able to repay their creditors diminishes significantly. At that point, creditors panic, withdraw their funds and leave the debtors facing an even bigger problem. To regain access to global capital markets, they now have to tighten their belts with sufficient vigour to show that creditors' future investments will be safe: in the attempt to demonstrate that they are creditworthy, however, they may have to deliver painful – and self-defeating – austerity.

BACK TO FLOATING CURRENCIES?

In a persistently low-growth world, this process is dangerous. If the costs of demonstrating creditworthiness are simply too great, countries will increasingly be incentivized not to borrow at all. At that point, the world may end up in a deflationary funk, with too many countries hoping to save and too few planning to borrow – precisely the situation in the years following the 1997/98 Asian crisis, and again in the aftermath of the Eurozone crisis. To avoid this, there needs to be a better burden-sharing arrangement between creditors and debtors, such that creditors have less incentive to export their savings in ways that are only likely to cause trouble for debtors following an unexpected future economic setback.

One option is simply to move back to a world in which exchange rates are completely flexible. That would mean, most obviously, allowing the euro to break up. Currency flexibility would, by definition, introduce currency risk. German savers – to take an obvious example – would then have to think twice about investing their money in Southern Europe because, even in the absence of a formal default, countries like Italy and Greece would then have the option of devaluation to bail themselves out if faced with difficult circumstances. The prospect of currency losses would presumably persuade German savers to find better uses for their money at home.

RESOLVING FINANCIAL DISPUTES: THE GLOBAL ORGANIZATION FOR FINANCIAL FLOWS

Another option is to create a formal reconciliation procedure – a dispute mechanism with financial pockets – for capital markets. It would operate along similar lines to the World Trade Organization and be funded in a similar way to the IMF. It might be called, say, the Global Organization for Financial Flows (GOFF). In the event of a cross-border financial crisis in which savers walked away from a particular country, that country would have the right to appeal to GOFF. GOFF, in turn, would provide the troubled country with temporary funding – for a year or so – on better terms than those now prevailing in the capital markets (although, to limit moral hazard risks, on worse terms than had been on offer pre-crisis).

Having provided the loan, GOFF would then attempt to assess precisely who was responsible for the underlying imbalance. If it turned out that the borrowing country was basically corrupt and had raised loans fraudulently, GOFF would end the funding and also deliver a downgraded credit rating. Admittedly, GOFF would then have made losses on its 'investment', but having been found guilty, the country would also be in considerable trouble. If instead the country had been a victim of 'hot money' inflows from avaricious investors elsewhere in the world, GOFF would have the power either to impose an orderly default – deliberately designed to damage the creditors – or instead impose a fine on those countries that were 'harbouring' most of the creditors. That, in turn, would act as a powerful incentive for those countries to improve their financial regulation, to invest more at home (in infrastructure, for example) and to encourage more in the way of domestic consumption (raising the minimum wage, offering reductions in sales taxes). In other words, it would no longer be acceptable to regard a large current account surplus as a 'good thing' at all times.

In that sense, GOFF would be an overdue addition to the existing Bretton Woods institutions. It would underscore the principle that creditors and debtors have obligations to each other, thereby removing the inherent bias that for centuries has favoured the former over the latter. By encouraging creditors to invest more of their savings at home, it would reduce the risk of excessive savings globally, limiting any demand shortfall and reducing the risk of a descent into a world of deflation.

Most importantly, GOFF would be a decisive response to the massive increase in cross-border capital flows witnessed in the decades before the 2008 global financial crisis. It would be a direct attempt to recognize both the advantages of such flows (most obviously, their ability to spread economic wealth far and wide) and their obvious disadvantages (including both the burden placed on recipient countries during periods of economic disappointment and the contribution of capital flows to systemic instability). Unlike the suggestions from Varoufakis and Stiglitz, however, GOFF would not pre-judge or limit the size of capital flows; it would instead offer the equivalent of 'conflict resolution' after the event. And crucially, its existence would provide a powerful incentive for both creditor and debtor nations to consider very carefully their contributions to global financial imbalances.

GOFF, however, has one very obvious drawback in a world in which globalization appears to be in retreat. It would be yet another international institution that, for many voters, would appear to be both technocratic and unaccountable. Would political leaders be prepared to support it? Would they dare? Can globalization only be saved by creating institutions that voters are already opposing?

A BORDERLESS WORLD

A third option would be to dispense with borders altogether. The nearest we have got to this is perhaps the European Union – or, more specifically, the 19 members that make up the Eurozone. Yet the single currency project is only half-finished – and arguably only half-baked. The Eurozone has some aspects of nationhood: a single currency, a single monetary policy, a single (although incomplete) market and, for those who also happen to be members of Schengen, a common external border. Yet it lacks other aspects: there is no common fiscal policy and no common border force; the European Parliament is a weak and distant institution; and a common European defence policy has so far proved be more a matter of words than deeds. Moreover, the strategic direction of the EU is determined by a European Council that is not much more than a talking shop for the various European heads of state or government – in other words, it is a bit like a White House occupied not only by a president, but also by assorted state governors, each of whom is entitled to promote his or her legitimate point of view.

On paper, it is not hard to imagine what needs to be done to resolve the single currency's contradictions. The president of the Council would be given full executive powers. He or she would serve a maximum of two full four-year terms in office and would be elected directly by the people of Europe. The various heads of state would have their own powers severely curtailed: they would become the equivalent of US state governors, and their national parliaments would have powers more commonly associated with principalities. The members of the European Commission would become the heads of new EU ministries, which in turn would recruit the brightest and the best from existing national ministries. There would be common European fiscal, foreign and defence policies. The Eurozone would, in effect, become a single nation state, just as Italy and Germany did in the nineteenth century.

There are those skulking around on the various floors of the Berlaymont building, the Brussels headquarters of the European Commission, who might hope that one day these arrangements will eventually come about. Indeed, Jean-Claude Juncker, president of the European Commission, announced in August 2016 that 'borders are the worst invention ever made by politicians' – an odd remark coming from someone who, in a previous life, had diligently turned Luxembourg into a tax haven.

FROM GRAVE NEW WORLD TO *NINETEEN EIGHTY-FOUR*

In the real world, however, the political 'mood music' is rather different. The key drivers of globalization in the modern era – flows of capital, people and technology – have left many people feeling distinctly uncomfortable. They have no time for further integration, and they no longer trust those who argue that globalization is in everyone's best interests. And if European countries – with a common (if bloody) history, shared democratic values, similar laws and broadly comparable welfare arrangements – are unable to present a united front, it's difficult to see how the world as a whole could make much in the way of further progress. Even if separate regions could get their acts together, differences in both politics and history suggest that the world as a whole might end up in a state of permanent rivalry, a real-life version of George Orwell's Oceania, Eurasia and Eastasia.

Indeed, it may well be that Orwell's *Nineteen Eighty-Four* proves to be prescient not just in terms of 'Big Brother' and 'doublethink', both of which neatly anticipated the impact of technology on our lives and, in particular, the role of social media in promoting a 'post-truth' society. Orwell may also have offered an accurate vision of geopolitical arrangements in the twenty-first century. The three empires in Orwell's world constantly change allegiances, so that at any point in time two are at war against the third. As the US loses its appetite for supporting the global institutions that have established the 'rules of the game', it is not impossible to imagine that the twenty-first century will increasingly be characterized by *Nineteen Eighty-Four*-style superpower rivalry, with Oceania dominated by the US, Eurasia by Russia and Eastasia by China. In this world, Europe's old fault lines could easily re-emerge, with Western European nations keen to align with Oceania and Eastern European nations attracted to opportunities (or sucked in by threats) dangled by Eurasia and Eastasia. One day, perhaps Brexit will have to be seen in this context.

FROM OBLIGATION TO BLAME

Obligations matter. Yet when the global economy appeared to be flourishing in the years before the global financial crisis, no one really had to think about them: the institutions that might eventually have helped simply had not been created – or if they had, they were only half-finished. Globalization appeared to be lifting all boats, even if the distribution of income and wealth within some hulls was increasingly unequal. The aftermath of the financial crisis, however, revealed that more and more voters had serious qualms about globalization. Whilst in theory its weaknesses could be fixed, the political narrative was rapidly changing. It was time to look for scapegoats.

International institutions matter, because they provide frameworks through which countries interact in what might informally be described as a 'grown-up' way. With increasing frequency, however, both the institutions themselves and some of the countries they represent are treated as convenient scapegoats. While Hillary Clinton ultimately proved successful in winning the Democratic nomination for the 2016 presidential election, her main rival, Bernie Sanders, spent a lot of time blaming globalization for ordinary people's woes. In his words: 'Let's be clear. The global economy is not working for the majority of people in our country and in the world. This is an economic model developed by the economic elite to benefit the economic elite. We need real change.' Sanders appeared to prefer sound bites to facts.

Whilst there may be serious differences of opinion about the distribution of the spoils of globalization within the US, it is much more difficult to support the claim that 'the global economy is not working for the majority of people . . . in the world'. According to the World Bank:

The world attained the first Millennium Development Goal target – to cut the 1990 poverty rate in half by 2015 – five years ahead of schedule, in 2010. In October 2015, the World Bank projected for the first time that the number of people living in extreme poverty was expected to have fallen below 10 per cent.[11]

Over much of this period, the biggest reductions in poverty took place in East Asia, with China accounting for a big chunk of the story. This leaves populists in the US in an awkward position. Either they deny the facts and pretend the entire model is at fault (the Sanders approach) or they use the facts to suggest that the future of Americans is imperilled by the success of others (the Donald Trump approach). This latter version is inevitably tinged with nationalism: according to one narrative, Americans have suffered thanks to the Chinese, the Mexicans or others, some of whom have, apparently, conspired to damage American interests.

Given the views of Republican grandees – and, for that matter, the mainstream media – Donald Trump was an unlikely candidate to win the Republican nomination, let alone the 2016 presidential election. As was argued in Chapter 6, his success was a function of his ability to subvert Republican party elites and to reach out to voters directly. And he was prepared to recognize their concerns rather than dismiss them. He proved adept at tapping into American angst. That angst, in turn, had less to do with inequality or poverty than is often perceived. There is, according to Gallup's senior economist, Jonathan Rothwell,

> mixed evidence that economic distress has motivated Trump support. His supporters are less educated and more likely to work in blue collar occupations, but they earn relatively high household incomes, and living in areas more exposed to trade or immigration does not increase Trump support. There is stronger evidence that racial isolation and less strictly economic measures of social status, namely health and intergenerational mobility, are robustly predictive of more favorable views towards Trump, and these factors predict support for him but not other Republican presidential candidates.[12]

If economics mattered in the 2016 US presidential election, it did so through people's perceptions of their well-being. According to a Pew Research Center poll, 81 per cent of Trump supporters thought life for people like them had got worse over the previous 50 years, while only 11 per cent thought life had got better; for Clinton supporters, the equivalent figures were 19 per cent and 59 per cent respectively. Many Trump supporters were deeply pessimistic about the future: 68 per cent thought the next generation's lives would be worse than the current generation's, compared with 30 per cent (still a depressingly high number) for Clinton supporters.

On the problems facing American society, Trump supporters were particularly worried about immigration and terrorism, whereas Clinton supporters were much more concerned about the gap between rich and poor. As for free trade deals, Trump supporters were very much opposed, while Clinton supporters were, on balance, more enthusiastic. Still, their enthusiasm did not stop Clinton pouring cold water on the Trans-Pacific

Partnership in a bid to win the support of those in swing states who might otherwise have been tempted to vote for Trump. Within the poll, the only area in which many voters appeared to be in agreement – whatever their political view – was that there was a relatively high probability that neither a Clinton nor a Trump presidency would be a good experience. We're back to the idea of political decay and a breakdown of trust between voters and their representatives in Washington.

Admittedly, there is nothing particularly new about any of this. There has always been a strand in American politics of what Richard Hofstadter described in 1964 as the 'Paranoid Style'.[13] Hofstadter highlighted Senator Joe McCarthy's claim that Secretary of State George Marshall – he of the Marshall Plan – had been busily betraying American interests from before the onset of the Second World War. In the senator's words, America's supposed post-war decline did not 'just happen'. It was the consequence of a treasonous 'conspiracy on a scale so immense as to dwarf any previous such venture in the history of man'. Modern-day rhetoric – from Trump and his fellow travellers – is not so different.

Nor is Paranoid Style confined to the US. In the UK, some in the EU 'Leave' campaign argued passionately that somehow the nations of the EU had been persistently blocking British interests, suggesting that it was time for the UK to 'take back control'. And, as noted in Chapter 5, the evidence from 150 years of European political and economic history strongly suggests that, after extended financial crises – as opposed to recessions – mainstream political movements are too often shunned in favour of what might usefully be described as paranoid movements on both left and right, often linked to racism, anti-Semitism, nationalism and the rejection of the international institutions that, in better times, are able to provide the ground rules for economic and political engagement across borders. Under these circumstances, globalization can only retreat, leaving dangerous political and economic rivalry in its wake.

BELIEF, TRUTH AND CONSISTENCY

Persistent economic disappointments demand a new political narrative. Those in favour of greater integration have, to date, mostly failed to supply one. British politicians who campaigned in support of the UK staying in Europe in effect argued that 'If you think it's bad now, it'll be a lot worse if we leave.' It was hardly an inspiring message. Those in favour of globalization tend either to make the – false – claim that it will make everyone better off or, instead, offer technocratic solutions that do not have the support of the people. And they have struggled to promote what arguably has been globalization's greatest success. To paraphrase Winston Churchill, globalization is the worst form of economic arrangement, except for all the others. Whatever its weaknesses and frustrations, globalization has been associated with sustained and enduring increases in living standards for an ever-larger share of the world's ever-expanding population.

Still, Churchill also knew the limitations of his line of thinking. On another occasion (allegedly), he noted that 'The best argument against democracy is a five-minute conversation with the average voter.' Amusing, unfair, probably apocryphal, but nevertheless a potential weakness of democratic politics, particularly during periods of extended economic and financial disappointment. Although living standards in the West continue to rise on average, the pace of increase is much slower than expected, and for some there has been no progress whatsoever. Debts are too high and, in time, some of the promises societies have made to themselves – on pensions, healthcare and education, for example – will have to be abandoned. Finding a narrative to explain this looming disappointment is hardly easy – economists themselves struggle to agree on precisely why productivity and investment growth have been so disappointing at the beginning of the twenty-first century – but the path of least resistance is, all too often, to blame the 'other': the foreigner, the immigrant, the elites and the alleged conspirators. Building barriers – physical or metaphorical – allows us to return to our 'tribe'. Our nation states suddenly feel cosily safe. They become sanctuaries away from the uncertainties of globalization.

All the evidence, however, suggests that this is a very dangerous game. As soon as the world descends into an argument between 'them and us', it is only a few steps from initial mistrust to outright conflict – economically, financially and even militarily. And in the years ahead, the challenges to the process of globalization are only going to get worse. Rising incomes in Africa will encourage a much larger number of migrants to make the journey across the Mediterranean Sea, an especially porous border. Social media will encourage greater 'herding' of ideas, with debate shut down via cyber intimidation. To gain power, politicians may have to pursue increasingly polarized positions, further undermining the public's trust in its elected representatives. Regulatory frameworks that will inevitably reflect the interests of nation states over and above the interests of nations collectively will increasingly stymie global market forces. The current temples of globalization may need to be demolished. The euro may not be able to survive if some countries (Italy, for example) are condemned to permanent stagnation, even as others (most obviously Germany) continue to flourish, while international trade may collapse if the World Trade Organization is undermined by increasingly nationalist attitudes from the world's most powerful nations. Capital markets may no longer be able to perform their function if, increasingly, prices are distorted by the activities of central banks. If so, capital will be allocated inefficiently, with a permanent cost in the form of diminished productivity and lower incomes. And as Western democracies focus increasingly on their own sovereign interests at the expense of the world's collective interests, the resulting vacuum will be quickly filled by countries – neither liberal nor democratic – keen to establish their own power and influence on the grandest of stages.

Successful globalization cannot be just a market-driven process. It must also involve cross-border sponsorship of both ideas and institutions that help underwrite our obligations and responsibilities to each other. In its twentieth-century heyday – from the 1950s through to the end of the 1990s – the chief sponsor of this process was the US, an admittedly reluctant imperium. Unlike previous superpowers, the US was not so interested in controlling the rest of the world. Instead it played its role as the first among equals, supporting international institutions in its own image, acting from time to time as a global policeman and offering a beacon of hope to countries that might otherwise have remained under the yoke of Soviet communism. Yet, after a prolonged period of economic underperformance which, in turn, has exposed huge inequality problems at home, the US no longer appears willing or able to offer continued sponsorship. For many Americans, the job is done. The collapse of the Soviet Empire and the failure to deliver peace in the Middle East have encouraged the US to become inward-looking again, focusing on its own narrow self-interest in the hope that it can insulate itself from an increasingly chaotic world. Yet the US retreat is only adding to that chaos. Who could sponsor a twenty-first-century Marshall Plan? Who could support the creation of a twenty-first-century version of the IMF for a global economy with a multitude of competing political systems?

In the absence of firm US leadership – and persistently weak economic activity in the developed world – is there any future for Western-style globalization? It is tempting to suggest not, particularly given both the rise of competing superpowers in pursuit of their own self-interests and the growing opposition to an increasingly integrated world from within the West's own borders. Yet, in a bid to save globalization, governments, policymakers and commentators could at least attempt to challenge the inconsistencies of those who seek to pursue policies of disintegration.

Those, for example, who seek to limit immigration tend also to be in favour of cutting foreign aid budgets. Admittedly, there are plenty of reasons for questioning the efficacy of aid, but unless economic opportunities in, say, Africa grow rapidly, its demographics suggest that many

African people will eventually go in search of opportunities elsewhere. Borders are there to be breached. If we are nervous about accelerated immigration, we need to think more about supporting development in poorer parts of the world.

Those who are opposed to the European Union need to explain how a divided Europe would more easily cope with a nervous Russian bear next door, particularly if Washington becomes increasingly isolationist. Given that Moscow appears quite comfortable with the idea of a de-stabilized and, hence, weakened Europe, why would a European Union break-up be in any sense a good idea?

Those who are against the WTO and its various regional offspring should be asked why the old world, in which there was no process by which Ecuador could triumph in its trade dispute with the US over shrimps (of all things),[14] was somehow fairer than the world we live in today. The US has been subject to 126 complaints under the WTO, more than any other country or region. In the absence of a dispute resolution mechanism, would it really be so easy to ensure that trade disputes between David and Goliath would ever be resolved fairly?

Those who threaten to disband NATO may see it only as a relic of the Cold War but, in the absence of a credible alternative, it has been the best way of ensuring that like-minded liberal democracies can protect their collective interests. It is certainly more costly for the US than for NATO's other member states, but the US benefits hugely from a more stable world than might otherwise be the case – in the same way that the British Empire benefited following the end of the Napoleonic Wars. Peace comes at a – worthwhile – price.

And, lastly, those who favour insularity and protectionism should be challenged to explain how they could possibly think that history is on their side.

Should their views prevail, it really will be a Grave New World.

EPILOGUE
A 2044 Republican Fundraiser

'Trump, Trump, Trump', they exclaimed. She was approaching the climax of a campaign that had left the gifted orator's would-be competitors floundering in her wake. Onto the stage she came, all smiles as she soaked up the adulation. Approaching the podium, she signalled to the huge crowds for hush.

Unlike one of her stepmothers all those years ago, she wasn't going to be accused of plagiarism. Her foreign policy speech had been checked and rechecked – not just for its content but, importantly, for its originality. Looking to her audience, she took a deep breath.

Ladies and gentlemen, I'm truly honoured to be the Republican party's first female presidential candidate. It's been too long. Look at our friends across the Atlantic. They're now on to their fifth woman prime minister!

The world is a dangerous place. If I win the race to the White House, I will absolutely make sure that America can protect itself. I will invest in the most advanced weapons technology. I will make sure our military boffins more than match the Chinese and the

Russians in the cybersphere. I will demand that America's borders are impenetrable.

You and I know there are many threats.

Ever since the collapse of the European Union five years ago, Europe has been dangerously unstable.

Following the 47th president's decision to leave NATO – totally justified given how much we Americans had been paying to fund a relic of the Cold War – the Europeans proved wholly incapable of creating their own Defence Force. Given their welfare commitments, they simply couldn't afford it. And, between them, they couldn't decide how big a threat Russia would be. Foolishly, they decided to go their separate ways.

Of course, the European Union was already on its last legs economically following the break-up of the single currency. The row over defence was simply the final straw. But, let's be honest. We all knew the Union was going to implode eventually.

True, Russia probably shouldn't have taken advantage. But the 47th president made it clear to the Europeans that they could not rely on American military support indefinitely. We had been contributing too much for too long. Things had to change.

Still, at least we are now using our expertise in building walls to help secure Europe's eastern border. And it's great news for American engineering jobs!

The Pacific is a dangerous place, too. You may remember a crazy debate in my father's day about something called the Trans-Pacific Partnership. Well, let me tell you something. We were right to have ignored the free-traders. We'd have lost even more jobs had the Partnership gone ahead. I'm glad it didn't.

Yes, there were the usual naysayers criticizing my father's America-first policy. But facts are facts. Our former allies in the Pacific were hopelessly untrustworthy. Who would have thought they'd all jump into bed with the Chinese?

So we have to face some home truths. East Asia and the Pacific are now in China's sphere of influence, particularly after those island disputes were resolved to Beijing's advantage. As for the rest of Asia – and, for that matter, Europe and the Middle East – well, it's best that China, India and Russia sort those problems out between themselves.

And despite our occasional disagreements, Moscow has at least achieved many things that Washington simply couldn't pull off. The peace deal between Israel and Palestine was impressive. The New Ottoman Territories were a stroke of genius, even if a lot of blood was spilled along the way. One day, perhaps we'll even be able to trade on better terms with the Eurasian Comprehensive Economic Partnership (ECEP).

They used to think that 'splendid isolation' was an insult. Let me tell you the truth. I'm proud that we're 'splendidly isolated'. Even if, following the default, the world no longer trusts us financially, we are very much masters of our own destiny.

And, yes, we still have friends.

Every day, I look at NAFTA 2.0. I feel proud. Far better to have a North Atlantic trade deal than the old North American version. At least we're competing on a level playing field with the Brits. Oops . . . I mean the English!

They, after all, showed us the way all those years ago. They took back control. We've done the same. And in a world that's becoming ever more dangerous, I'm delighted that, as secretary of state, I followed the late Lord Farage's example – a true English great, up there with Winston Churchill and Margaret Thatcher. Should I win, Farage's bust will definitely be on display in the Oval Office. He's their Thomas Jefferson and George Washington rolled into one.

Ladies and gentlemen. As your president, I will always make sure that the United States of America is in control. I will engage only with those countries that believe 100 per cent in the American way.

And those who don't can expect to be faced with the full force of my proposed Pacifying Protectionist Regime (PPR). I'm fed up with countries using their cheap labour to steal from good, honest, American workers. So, tonight, I pledge to protect remaining American jobs come what may!

Ladies and gentlemen. I have only one more thing to say. God bless America!

* * *

Ms Trump's speech was followed by a standing ovation, which a number of foreign observers reckoned lasted around 4 minutes and 33 seconds.

NOTES

INTRODUCTION: THE ANDALUCÍAN SHOCK

1. The Americans themselves were no strangers to imperial activities in the nineteenth century: in 1812, Washington declared war on Great Britain with the aim of taking control of Canada (in return, the British burnt down the White House) while the 1898 Spanish–American War concluded with the Treaty of Paris, which handed the Philippines over from Spanish to American control. Meanwhile, the Mexican–American War beginning in 1846 led to the American annexation of California.
2. See, most obviously, T. Friedman, *The World is Flat: The globalized world in the twenty-first century*, Allen Lane, New York, 2005.

CHAPTER 1: FALSE PROPHETS, HARSH TRUTHS

1. P. Hartshorn, *I Have Seen the Future: A life of Lincoln Steffens*, Counterpoint Press, Berkeley, 2011.
2. The Maddison Project, http://www.ggdc.net/maddison/maddison-project/home.htm, 2013 version.
3. G.B. Shaw et al., 'Social conditions in Russia: Recent visitors' tribute', Letters to the Editor, *Manchester Guardian*, 2 March 1933.
4. For a detailed discussion of the Soviet Union's warped morality, see J. Glover, *Humanity: A moral history of the twentieth century*, Vintage, London, 2001, particularly Part Five: 'Belief and Terror: Stalin and his heirs'.
5. F. Fukuyama, *The End of History and the Last Man*, Free Press, New York, 1992.
6. F. Fukuyama, 'The end of history', *National Interest*, 16 (1989).
7. F. Fukuyama, *Political Order and Political Decay: From the Industrial Revolution to the globalization of democracy*, Farrar, Straus and Giroux, New York, 2014.
8. See, for example, http://www.theguardian.com/world/datablog/2015/jul/23/vladimir-putins-approval-rating-at-record-levels

9. http://www.ned.org/remarks-by-president-george-w-bush-at-the-20th-anniversary/

10. https://www.theguardian.com/world/2016/nov/15/mohamed-morsi-death-sentence-overturned

11. Escaping the so-called middle-income trap has not been easy. See, for example, R. Cherif and F. Hasanov, *The Leap of the Tiger: How Malaysia can escape from the middle income trap*, IMF Working Paper WP/15/131, Washington, DC, June 2015, available at https://www.imf.org/external/pubs/ft/wp/2015/wp15131.pdf

12. Hillary Clinton would have killed it off, too.

13. J. Darwin, *After Tamerlane: The rise and fall of global empires, 1400–2000*, Allen Lane, London, 2007.

14. IMF World Economic Outlook database.

15. R. Lyman and J. Berendt, 'As Poland lurches to the right, many in Europe look on in alarm', *New York Times*, 14 December 2015, available at: http://www.nytimes.com/2015/12/15/world/europe/poland-law-and-justice-party-jaroslaw-kaczynski.html

16. There are other reasons for optimism, as Stephen Pinker and Andrew Mack note in 'The world is not falling apart', *Slate*, 2014, available at: http://www.slate.com/articles/news_and_politics/foreigners/2014/12/the_world_is_not_falling_apart_the_trend_lines_reveal_an_increasingly_peaceful.html They point to data showing significant declines in homicide rates, rape and other forms of sexual assault, mass killings, genocides and wars. All of this is very good news. Their data, however, only tell us what has happened, not what may happen in a future in which globalization goes into reverse.

17. Freedom House, 'Discarding democracy: Return to the iron fist', available at: https://freedomhouse.org/report/freedom-world-2015/discarding-democracy-return-iron-fist

18. M. MacMillan, *The War that Ended Peace: How Europe abandoned peace for the First World War*, Profile Books, London, 2014.

19. Fukuyama, *The End of History and the Last Man*.

CHAPTER 2: THE NEW IMPERIUM

1. The word 'ultimately' is there for a reason. Officially called the 'Program to Prevent Germany from Starting a World War III' – or more informally the Morgenthau Plan – the plan put together in September 1944 by the US Treasury Department, led by Henry Morgenthau, aimed to de-industrialize the German economy, in effect turning Germany into an eighteenth-century pastoral wasteland. Roosevelt appeared supportive. So, too, did Winston Churchill, although that was largely because the UK was desperate for US financial help and, to get it, Churchill felt he had no choice but to sign up to the plan. As Churchill said to his foreign secretary, Anthony Eden, 'The future of my people is at stake and when I have to choose between my people and the German people, I am going to choose my people.' See B. Steil, *The Battle of Bretton Woods: John Maynard Keynes, Harry Dexter White and the making of a new world order*, Princeton University Press, Princeton, 2013.

2. J.M. Keynes, *A Treatise on Monetary Reform*, Macmillan, London, 1924.

3. The arrangement was agreed at the 1932 Imperial Economic Conference in Ottawa, Canada.

4. Ben Steil's *The Battle of Bretton Woods* repeats an oft-made claim that White was a Soviet spy. Others, however, have serious doubts. In a 2013 review of Steil's book for *The Nation*, James M. Boughton, at the time the IMF's official historian, suggested that there was no evidence whatsoever to support the claim, and the supposed 'smoking gun' document uncovered by Steil had been given meaning only by being taken out of context. The review is available at http://www.thenation.com/article/dirtying-white/

5. D. Leech, 'Voting power in the governance of the International Monetary Fund', London School of Economics, 2002, available at: http://eprints.lse.ac.uk/648/1/ANOR109Leech. pdf

6. G. Kennan, 'The charge in the Soviet Union (Kennan) to the Secretary of State', 22 February 1946, available at: http://nsarchive.gwu.edu/coldwar/documents/episode-1/ kennan.htm

7. G. Marshall, 'Speech at Harvard University', 5 June 1947, available at: http://www.oecd. org/general/themarshallplanspeechatharvarduniversity5june1947.htm

8. R. Schuman, 'The Schuman Declaration', 9 May 1950, available at: http://europa.eu/ european-union/about-eu/symbols/europe-day/schuman-declaration_en

9. European Union, Treaty on European Union (Maastricht Treaty), 1992, available at: https://europa.eu/european-union/sites/europaeu/files/docs/body/treaty_on_ european_union_en.pdf

10. The founding nations were Belgium, Canada, Denmark, France, Iceland, Italy, Luxembourg, the Netherlands, Norway, Portugal, the UK and the US. Greece and Turkey joined in 1952, West Germany in 1955, Spain in 1982, the Czech Republic, Hungary and Poland in 1999, Bulgaria, Estonia, Latvia, Lithuania, Romania, Slovakia and Slovenia in 2004, and Albania and Croatia in 2009.

11. T. Kane, *Global US Troop Deployment, 1950–2003*, Center for Data Analysis Report No. 04/11, Heritage Foundation, Washington, DC, 27 October 2004.

12. H. Kissinger, *World Order: Reflections on the character of nations and the course of history*, Allen Lane, London, 2014.

13. G. Cleveland, 'First Inaugural Address', 4 March 1885, available at: http://avalon.law. yale.edu/19th_century/cleve1.asp

14. W. Wilson, 'Address to a joint session of Congress requesting a declaration of war against Germany', 2 April 1917, available at: http://www.presidency.ucsb.edu/ws/?pid=65366

15. N. Rose, *Churchill: An unruly life*, Tauris, London, 2009 (first published by Simon & Schuster, New York, 1994), p. 290.

16. T. Jefferson, 'Letter to Joseph Priestley', 19 June 1802, available at: http://founders. archives.gov/documents/Jefferson/01-37-02-0515

CHAPTER 3: RELATIVE SUCCESS

1. The definition of Northern European used here includes Austrians, Belgians, Danes, French, Finns, Germans, northern Italians, Dutch, Norwegians, Swedes, Swiss and British.

2. http://www.imf.org/external/np/exr/center/mm/eng/sc_sub_3.htm

3. The American Presidency Project, available at: http://www.presidency.ucsb.edu/ws/? pid=3115

4. W. Silber, *Volcker: The triumph of persistence*, Bloomsbury, New York, 2012.

5. National Archives, 'Conclusions of a meeting of the Cabinet held at 10 Downing Street on Tuesday 23 November 1976 at 10.00am', available at: http://filestore.nationalarchives. gov.uk/pdfs/small/cab-128-60-cm-76-33.pdf

6. Ibid.

7. National Archives, 'The real choices facing the Cabinet, memorandum by the secretary of state for energy, 29 November 1976', available at: http://filestore.nationalarchives.gov. uk/pdfs/small/cab-129-193-cp-76-117-7.pdf

8. See, for example, J. Moran, 'Defining moment: Denis Healey agrees to the demands of the IMF', *Financial Times*, 4 September 2010, available at: https://www.ft.com/content/ 11484844-b565-11df-9af8-00144feabdc0

9. Remarkable not only because so many countries sat round a table together, but also because, when the United Nations was founded in 1945, there were only 51 members.
10. J.S. Nye, *Soft Power: The means to success in world politics*, PublicAffairs, New York, 2004.
11. http://www.forbes.com/powerful-brands/list/#tab:rank
12. Coca-Cola Company, '125 years of sharing happiness: A short history of the Coca-Cola Company', available at: https://www.coca-colacompany.com/content/dam/journey/us/en/private/fileassets/pdf/2011/05/Coca-Cola_125_years_booklet.pdf
13. Reputation Institute, '2015 Country RepTrak®: The world's most reputable countries', available at: https://www.reputationinstitute.com/CMSPages/GetAzureFile.aspx?path=~\media\media\documents\country-reptrak-webinar-2015-forweb.pdf&hash=3e386f19a737277500c8c2c5f651f5810028665ad3c2af218dccc1e5856eacfd&ext=.pdf
14. Stockholm International Peace Research Institute, 'Military Expenditure Database', available at: http://www.sipri.org/research/armaments/milex/milex_database
15. P. Kennedy, *The Rise and Fall of the Great Powers: Economic change and military conflict from 1500 to 2000*, Random House, New York, 1988.

CHAPTER 4: PRIDE AND THE FALL

1. G.W. Bush, 'Address to Joint Session of Congress', 20 September 2001, available at: http://edition.cnn.com/2001/US/09/20/gen.bush.transcript
2. Al Qaeda's attacks began with the bombing of hotels in Yemen in 1992, followed by a truck bomb detonated in a car park below the World Trade Center in 1993, the bombing of the US embassies in Kenya and Tanzania in 1998, and an attack on the USS *Cole* in 2000.
3. The original list of ten came from John Williamson while he was at the Institute of International Economics in 1989. The others were: the ending of indiscriminate subsidies; market-determined interest rates; a competitive exchange rate; and deregulation.
4. Source: *Guinness Book of Records*.
5. https://www.youtube.com/watch?v=xhYJS80MgYA
6. In 1981, 364 economists wrote to *The Times* objecting to the degree of deflation imposed on the UK economy by Margaret Thatcher's government. In their statement, they noted: 'We, who are all present or retired members of the economics staffs of British universities, are convinced that: a) there is no basis in economic theory or supporting evidence for the government's belief that by deflating demand they will bring inflation permanently under control and thereby induce an automatic recovery in output and employment; b) present policies will deepen the depression, erode the industrial base of our economy and threaten its social and political stability; c) there are alternative policies; and d) the time has come to reject monetarist policies and consider urgently which alternative offers the best hope of sustained economic recovery.' The signatories included Mervyn King, Willem Buiter, Stephen Nickell and Martin Weale, all of whom ended up at the Bank of England with responsibility for the implementation of an inflation-targeting framework through what might be reasonably described as 'monetarism mark II', and Nicholas Stern, later to become HM Treasury's chief economic adviser.
7. O. Blanchard and J. Simon, 'The long and large decline in US output volatility', *Brookings Papers on Economic Activity*, 1 (2001), pp. 135–64.
8. B. Bernanke, 'The Great Moderation', remarks at the meeting of the Eastern Economic Association, Washington, DC, 20 February 2004, available at: http://www.federalreserve.gov/Boarddocs/Speeches/2004/20040220/

9. R.E. Lucas, 'Macroeconomic priorities', *American Economic Review*, 93:1 (2003), pp. 1–14.

10. J.M. Keynes, *The General Theory of Employment, Interest and Money*, Macmillan, London, 1936.

11. Ibid., specifically Chapter 12: 'The State of Long Term Expectation'.

12. Some have suggested that Minsky's explanation is lacking. In *The End of Alchemy*, Mervyn King notes that Minsky's periods of excess are not just in financial markets, but also in economic activity; yet, prior to the financial crisis, there was no evidence that economic growth was unusually rapid. King also notes that Minsky's view is not helpfully predictive, relying too much on the idea that people can sometimes be irrational. Yet these arguments are not fatal to Minsky's view: in the aftermath of the technology bubble, growth in the US only accelerated thanks to remarkably supportive monetary and fiscal policies. We now know that underlying economic performance – as measured by productivity growth – was already slowing rapidly. And an important part of Minsky's argument is that behaviour by central bankers can encourage irrational behaviour by others. See M. King, *The End of Alchemy: Money, banking and the future of the global economy*, Little, Brown, London, 2016.

13. Sherman McCoy, the protagonist in Wolfe's *Bonfire of the Vanities*, is a Wall Street trader whose life goes horribly wrong just when it seemed to be going so well: he was a self-styled Master of the Universe.

14. For a discussion of the effects of dysfunctional belief systems, see R. Hausmann, 'Through the Venezuelan looking glass', Project Syndicate, August 2016, available at: https://www.project-syndicate.org/commentary/venezuela-destructive-belief-systems-by-ricardo-hausmann-2016-08

15. The classic article on asymmetric information is George Akerlof, 'The market for lemons: Quality, uncertainty and the market mechanism', *Quarterly Journal of Economics*, 84:3 (1970), pp. 488–500.

16. See, for example, E. Passari and H. Rey, *Financial Flows and the International Monetary System*, National Bureau of Economic Research Working Paper No. 21172, Cambridge, MA, May 2015.

17. The pre-2000 figures come from M. Obstfeld and A.M. Taylor, *Global Capital Markets: Integration, crisis, and growth*, Cambridge University Press, New York, 2004. The later figures come from an updated and extended version of the dataset constructed in P.R. Lane and G.M. Milesi-Ferretti, 'The external wealth of nations mark II: Revised and extended estimates of foreign assets and liabilities, 1970–2004', *Journal of International Economics*, 73:2 (2007), pp. 223–50.

18. The OECD attempted to provide such governance in a series of negotiations carried out at ministerial level beginning in May 1995, as part of the proposed Multilateral Agreement on Investment. In the OECD's own words, 'after intense negotiations during a three-year period until May 1998, and a six-month pause during which no official meetings of the negotiators took place, negotiations ceased in December 1998'. Interestingly, China was present at the negotiations, but was only granted 'observer status'.

CHAPTER 5: GLOBALIZATION AND NATION STATES

1. It didn't always work out. In 1890, Barings Bank faced insolvency following excessive risk-taking in Argentina. Still, its debts were guaranteed by a consortium led by the Bank of England, thus avoiding a wider crisis.

2. His views, in turn, built on the thoughts of Enlightenment philosophers, who thought that Europe's multiple-state model was superior to that of Asian autocracies thanks to the benefits of trade and the exchange of ideas. There is probably some truth to this: China's rapid economic development since the 1980s owes a lot to its new-found willingness to engage with the rest of the world after centuries of – mostly self-imposed – isolationism.

3. For a detailed discussion of nineteenth-century attempts at 'internationalization', see M. Mazower, *Governing the World: The history of an idea, 1815 to the present*, Penguin, New York, 2012.

4. To this day, socialists have struggled to cope with the 'patriotism' of the working class. Emily Thornberry was sacked from the Labour frontbench ahead of the 2015 UK general election for tweeting a photograph – with a derogatory implication – of a house in Rochester resplendent in the flag of St George with a white van parked in the driveway.

5. Japan was admitted to the club in 1905, following its remarkable and unexpected defeat of Russia in the Russo-Japanese War. As a Japanese diplomat put it at the time, 'We show ourselves at least your equals in scientific butchery and at once are admitted to your council tables as civilised men.' See G. Best, *Humanity in Warfare: The modern history of the international law of armed conflicts*, Weidenfeld and Nicolson, London, 1980.

6. Estimates vary, but it is thought that roughly 10 million died in Congo Free State, at the time privately controlled by Belgium's King Leopold II. Mutilation – most frequently in the form of severed hands – was common practice. The horror was captured in Joseph Conrad's *Heart of Darkness*, which, in turn, underpinned Francis Ford Coppola's *Apocalypse Now*.

7. It is worth noting, however, that it has never been easy to spot the difference between insolvency and illiquidity – as many financial institutions and policymakers discovered during the 2007–08 global financial crisis.

8. Federal Deposit Insurance Corporation, 'A brief history of deposit insurance in the United States', presentation prepared for the International Conference on Deposit Insurance, Washington, DC, September 1998.

9. For a useful discussion of the history of the lender of last resort, see T.M. Humphrey, 'Lender of last resort: The concept in history', *Federal Reserve Bank of Richmond Economic Review*, March/April (1989), pp. 8–16.

10. T. Clark and A. Dilnot, *Long-Term Trends in British Taxation and Spending*, Institute for Fiscal Studies Briefing Note No. 25, London, 2002.

11. Even this claim is false: in 1789, only half of the population of France spoke French. By 1871, it was down to a quarter. See J. Merriman, 'France since 1871: The birth of national identity and agents of modernization', Yale Open Courses Lecture, 17 September 2007, available at: http://oyc.yale.edu/transcript/357/hist-276

12. All data in this paragraph are sourced from A. Alesina, A. Devleeschauwer, W. Easterly, S. Kurlat and R. Wacziarg, *Fractionalization*, Harvard Institute of Economic Research Discussion Paper No. 1959, Cambridge, MA, June 2002, available at: https://dash.harvard.edu/handle/1/4553003

13. He would have been a staunch opponent of utilitarianism: he did not think society as a whole would be able to agree on what would make people happy.

14. Suicide bombers suggest that Hobbes may have been wrong.

15. In Latin, the phrase is – famously – expressed as *bellum omnium contra omnes*.

16. As John Locke (1632–1704) argued, citizens must delegate to government the right of self-defence, because no one, on his own, should be able to be judge, jury and executioner.

17. C. Montesquieu, *The Spirit of the Laws*, ed. A. Cohler, B. Miller and H. Stone, Cambridge University Press, Cambridge, 1989, specifically Book 5.
18. J.M. Buchanan, 'An economic theory of clubs', *Economica*, 32:125 (1965), pp. 1–14.
19. H. Morgenthau, *Politics among Nations: The struggle for power and peace*, rev. K. Thompson, McGraw-Hill, New York, 1993. The first edition of Morgenthau's book was published in 1948.
20. I once heard a former European Commissioner complain that national politicians spent too much time 'pandering to the interests of their voters'.
21. One obvious example is the discrepancy in pay between the chair of the Federal Reserve and the managing director of the IMF. The former is paid an annual salary of $199,700, on which tax is paid; while the latter receives a tax-free income of approaching $500,000, with a whole range of perks on top. The former is directly accountable to US Congress, the latter is not.
22. Bureau of Labor Statistics, Washington, DC.
23. A.B. Atkinson and S. Morelli, *Chartbook of Economic Inequality*, 2014, available at: http://www.chartbookofeconomicinequality.com/
24. A. Mian and A. Sufi, *House of Debt: How they (and you) caused the Great Recession and how we can prevent it from happening again*, University of Chicago Press, Chicago, 2014
25. Source for the data in this paragraph is E.N. Wolff, *Household Wealth Trends in the United States, 1961–2013: What happened over the Great Recession?*, National Bureau of Economic Research Working Paper No. 20733, Cambridge, MA, December 2014.
26. C. Góes, *Testing Piketty's Hypothesis on the Drivers of Income Inequality: Evidence from panel VARs with heterogeneous dynamics*, IMF Working Paper WP/16/160, Washington, DC, August 2016.
27. D. Acemoglu and J. Robinson, 'The rise and decline of general laws of capitalism', *Journal of Economic Perspectives*, 29:1 (2015), pp. 3–28.
28. C. Rhodes, 'Public sector employment and expenditure by region', House of Commons Library, London, July 2014, available at: http://researchbriefings.parliament.uk/ResearchBriefing/Summary/SN05625
29. J.M. Keynes, 'The economic consequences of Mr Churchill', in *Essays in Persuasion*, Norton, New York, 1963; '2s' refers to the old shilling, which was worth 12 old pennies or, in decimal money, 5 pence. In the old system – thankfully phased out in the early 1970s – the pound was made up of 20 shillings or 240 pennies. Madness.
30. True, interest rates on bank deposits and government debt can fall below zero – and indeed did so in parts of the Eurozone in 2014 and 2015 – but as cash by definition offers a zero interest rate, it is unlikely that borrowing costs overall could stray too far below the so-called 'zero bound': savers would ultimately prefer to keep their money in cash and stuff it under the mattress, leading to the potential collapse of the credit system.
31. For a detailed analysis of these historical patterns, see M. Funke, M. Schularick and C. Trebesch, 'Politics in the slump: Polarization and extremism after financial crises, 1870–2014', Berlin, September 2015, available at: http://ec.europa.eu/economy_finance/events/2015/20151001_post_crisis_slump/documents/c._trebesch.pdf
32. The survey by GlobeScan and commissioned by the BBC can be found at: http://www.globescan.com/images/images/pressreleases/BBC2016-Identity/BBC_GlobeScan_Identity_Season_Press_Release_April%2026.pdf

CHAPTER 6: THE SPIRIT OF ELITISM

1. http://www.ambrosetti.eu/en/summits-workshops-forums/forum-villa-deste/
2. All quotes in this paragraph come from T. Mann, *The Magic Mountain*, trans. J.E. Woods, Vintage Everyman's Library Edition, New York, 2005. The book was first published in German as *Der Zauberberg* in 1924.
3. See, for example, B. Milanović, *Global Inequality: A new approach for the age of globalization*, Belknap Press, Cambridge, MA, 2016. Milanović made considerable use of the so-called 'elephant chart'. Others have subsequently criticized his findings, largely because of changes in the composition of income deciles over time, the dominance of China and some serious doubts about the reliability of Japanese data. See, for example, A. Corlett, 'Examining an elephant: Globalisation and the lower middle class of the rich world', Resolution Foundation, London, September 2016, available at: http://www.resolutionfoundation.org/wp-content/uploads/2016/09/Examining-an-elephant.pdf. Still, this wasn't the end of the matter: Milanović offered a response in C. Lakner and B. Milanović, 'Response to Adam Corlett's "Examining an elephant: Globalisation and the lower middle class of the rich world" ', September 2016, available at http://www.gc.cuny.edu/CUNY_GC/media/CUNY-Graduate-Center/LIS%20Center/elephant_debate-4,-reformatted.pdf
4. YouGov Survey, fieldwork conducted on 13–14 June 2016; sample size – 1,656 British adults.
5. C. Murray, *Coming Apart: The state of white America 1960–2010*, Crown Forum, New York, 2012.
6. R. Chetty, N. Hendren, P. Kline, E. Saez and N. Turner, *Is the United States Still a Land of Opportunity? Recent trends in intergenerational mobility*, National Bureau of Economic Research Working Paper No. 19844, Cambridge, MA, January 2014.
7. G. Clark, *The Son Also Rises: Surnames and the history of social mobility*, Princeton University Press, Princeton, NJ, 2014.
8. R. Chetty, N. Hendren and L. Katz, 'The effects of exposure to better neighborhoods on children: New evidence from the moving to opportunity experiment', *American Economic Review*, forthcoming.
9. http://www.thetimes.co.uk/article/ending-poverty-need-not-be-a-utopian-dream-qjfrrjrcr
10. W.A. Lewis, 'Economic development with unlimited supplies of labour', *The Manchester School*, 22:2 (1954), pp. 139–91.
11. See, for example, L.M. Bartels, *Unequal Democracy: The political economy of the new gilded age*, Princeton University Press, Princeton, NJ, 2010 or M. Gilens, *Affluence and Influence*, Princeton University Press, Princeton, NJ, 2012.

CHAPTER 7: COMPETING COMMUNITIES, COMPETING HISTORIES

1. 'Talking points for Ambassador Rumsfeld's meeting with Tariq Aziz and Saddam Hussein', cited in P. Frankopan, *The New Silk Roads*, Bloomsbury, London, 2015.
2. Reinterpretation of history is particularly prevalent among university students: witness the campaign to have a statue of Cecil Rhodes removed from University College, Oxford and the decision by Harvard Law School to abandon its crest, which had been inspired by an eighteenth-century slaveholder, Isaac Royall: his son had endowed Harvard with its first law professorship.
3. To be fair, most of the vetoes relate to a single issue – Israel and Palestine – where the number of resolutions sponsored by Arab countries with vested interests has been

remarkably large. The outcome in each case – a US veto – would have been a foregone conclusion.

4. It is worth noting that in Grenada the date of the invasion is now known as Thanksgiving Day: most Grenadians have nothing but thanks to offer for the widely condemned US-led invasion.

5. For a detailed discussion of this, see G. Clark, *A Farewell to Alms: A brief history of the world*, Princeton University Press, Princeton, NJ, 2007.

6. The divisions were mostly made by the French and British – with Russian assent – in the secret Sykes–Picot Agreement of 1916.

7. Alaska was sold to the US in 1867.

8. Iran's leadership ambitions suffer from two problems: first, Iranians are part of a Shi'a minority and, second, they are Persian, not Arab.

9. All of this is, at the time of writing, available at: https://ustr.gov/tpp/

10. Ricardo's comparative advantage was a ground-breaking contribution to economics. He simply pointed out that if country A was absolutely better at producing goods X and Y than country B, but was relatively better than B at producing X than Y, it would make sense for country A to specialize in X, country B to specialize in Y and for the two countries to trade with each other: they would both be better off than before.

11. For a useful discussion of the economic effects of TPP, see P. Petri and M. Plummer, *The Economic Effects of the Trans-Pacific Partnership: New estimates*, Peterson Institute for International Economics Working Paper 16-2, Washington, DC, January 2016.

12. The US offers Trade Adjustment Assistance, but the jury is out regarding its effectiveness.

13. The nine-dash line was originally an eleven-dash line that first appeared on Taiwanese maps in 1947. The People's Republic of China thereafter adopted a similar approach: both cases in effect make territorial claims on disputed parts of the South China Sea.

14. The press release accompanying the ruling can be found at https://pca-cpa.org/wp-content/uploads/sites/175/2016/07/PH-CN-20160712-Press-Release-No-11-English.pdf

15. Tibetans might well disagree, but while the Tibetan landmass is huge, it is sparsely populated: at the last count, there were around 3.2 million inhabitants, of whom 90 per cent were ethnically Tibetan. That compares with a Chinese population well in excess of a billion.

16. At the end of 2014, Japan was the Asian Development Bank's largest shareholder. Haruhiko Kuroda, who led the Asian Development Bank between 2005 and 2013, went on to become governor of the Bank of Japan.

17. China has attempted to allay such fears by working initially with the World Bank on joint-finance projects.

18. Uzbekistan was the sixth member to join.

19. Brunei, Myanmar, Cambodia, Indonesia, Laos, Malaysia, the Philippines, Singapore, Thailand and Vietnam.

20. Programme for International Student Assessment, published by the OECD. The latest results – for 2015 – can be found at: http://www.oecd.org/publications/pisa-2015-results-volume-i-9789264266490-en.htm

21. In science, the US ranks 25th while the UK ranks 15th. In literacy, the US ranks 24th while the UK ranks 22nd.

CHAPTER 8: PEOPLE AND PLACES

1. The three dominant nations supplying emigrants in the mid-nineteenth century were Great Britain, Germany and Ireland. Irish emigrants were mostly poor; the others less so.
2. See, for example, T. Bartlett, *Ireland: A history*, Cambridge University Press, Cambridge, 2010.
3. Many of these immigrants came from just three countries/empires: Italy, the Austro-Hungarian Empire and Russia.
4. Office of Immigration Statistics, *2013 Yearbook of Immigration Statistics*, Department of Homeland Security, Washington, DC, available at: http://www.dhs.gov/sites/default/files/publications/ois_yb_2013_0.pdf
5. Instituto Cervantes, 'El español, una lengua viva', available at: http://eldiae.es/wp-content/uploads/2015/06/espanol_lengua-viva_20151.pdf
6. See, for example, G.J. Borjas, *Making It in America: Social mobility in the immigrant population*, National Bureau of Economic Research Working Paper No. 12088, Cambridge, MA, March 2006.
7. Powell's full speech can be read here: http://www.telegraph.co.uk/comment/3643823/Enoch-Powells-Rivers-of-Blood-speech.html
8. At the time, Powell, was shadow secretary of state for defence.
9. Article in a 1960 edition of the *Daily Herald*, available at the National Archives website: http://www.nationalarchives.gov.uk/pathways/citizenship/brave_new_world/docs/strange_voices.htm
10. https://www.indy100.com/article/these-are-the-10-most-popular-foreign-dishes-in-britain—WJqyFdk5mx
11. Economic miracle.
12. Most are fully signed-up members, others – Bulgaria, Croatia, Cyprus and Romania – have a commitment to join at an unspecified future date.
13. See, for example, D. Davis and T. Gift, 'The positive effects of the Schengen Agreement on European trade', *World Economy*, 37:11 (2014), pp. 1541–57.
14. The majority of academic studies suggest that its impact over the medium term is relatively small and ultimately outweighed by the impact on all incomes of efficiency gains.
15. See, most obviously, W. Easterly and R. Levine, 'Africa's growth tragedy: Policies and ethnic divisions', *Quarterly Journal of Economics*, 112:4 (1997), pp. 1203–50.
16. While country corruption indices in themselves say little about the behaviour of migrants who hail from those countries, it is worth noting that Syria ranks 154th out of 167 countries in Transparency International's list of countries from the least to the most corrupt. See http://www.transparency.org/cpi2015#results-table
17. One reason for this was the requirement for asylum seekers to be processed in the first EU country in which they arrived after crossing the Schengen border. This placed an unusually large strain on the immigration authorities in Greece and Italy, the first ports of call for asylum seekers entering the EU.
18. Sources for all projections in this section are: http://esa.un.org/unpd/wpp/Publications/Files/WPP2015_Volume-I_Comprehensive-Tables.pdf and http://esa.un.org/unpd/wpp/Publications/Files/WPP2015_Volume-II-Demographic-Profiles.pdf. I have used the UN's 'medium variant' numbers: the UN also provides 'high' and 'low' variant numbers, at the very least to illustrate the inherent uncertainties associated with long-term demographic projections.
19. Nigeria, in contrast, had only five equivalent 'oldies' for every 100 of working age.

20. United Nations, *World Population Prospects: The 2015 revision*, Volume II: *Demographic Profiles*, United Nations Department of Economic and Social Affairs/Population Division, New York, 2015.
21. Available at: http://economicsandpeace.org/wp-content/uploads/2015/06/Global-Peace-Index-Report-2015_0.pdf
22. http://www.bbc.co.uk/news/world-africa-13951696
23. N. Myers and J. Kent, *Environmental Exodus: An emergent crisis in the global arena*, Climate Institute, Washington, DC, 1995.
24. It is important to stress that these worries are not necessarily supported by hard evidence. See, for example, C. Dustmann and T. Frattini, 'The fiscal effects of immigration to the UK', *Economic Journal*, 124:580 (2014), pp. 593–643.

CHAPTER 9: THE DARK SIDE OF TECHNOLOGY

1. Although it is worth noting that we may be close to reaching the physical limits of miniaturization: quantum mechanics suggests life could become a lot less certain.
2. The phrase 'mass production' wasn't coined until the 1920s. It originally referred to the Ford Motor Company.
3. For a useful summary of the evolution of global supply chains, see R. Baldwin, *Global Supply Chains: Why they emerged, why they matter, and where they are going*, Centre for Trade and Economic Integration Working Paper CTEI-2012-13, Graduate Institute, Geneva, 2012.
4. Lord Reith, director general of the BBC between 1927 and 1938, was keen to deliver to his audience 'All that is best in every department of human knowledge, endeavour and achievement ... The preservation of a high moral tone is obviously of paramount importance.'
5. Winston Churchill appeared to thrive on alcohol in ways that would likely be unacceptable today, yet he was rarely criticized. John Profumo, the British secretary of state for war in the 1960s, eventually admitted having slept with a woman – Christine Keeler – who also happened to have been sleeping with Yevgeni Ivanov, the senior naval attaché at the Soviet embassy. As this was at the height of the Cold War, Profumo had to fall on his sword.
6. Peter Oborne, a journalist at the *Daily Telegraph*, resigned in protest because he believed that the *Telegraph*'s independence had been compromised by its advertising relationship with HSBC. His views can be read at: https://www.opendemocracy.net/ourkingdom/peter-oborne-why-i-have-resigned-from-telegraph
7. http://graphics.wsj.com/blue-feed-red-feed/#/pres-debate
8. S. Bond, 'Digital is reshaping the world of advertising', *Financial Times*, 28 April 2015, available at: http://www.ft.com/cms/s/2/60b8747e-bc1f-11e4-a6d7-00144feab7de.html #axzz43CXb1TWE
9. See, for example, L. Barnard, 'The cost of creepiness: How online behavioral advertising affects consumer purchase intention', dissertation, University of North Carolina at Chapel Hill, 2014.
10. See, for example, W. Nordhaus, 'Two centuries of productivity growth in computing', *Journal of Economic History*, 67:1 (2007), pp. 128–59.
11. Two of the best papers on this issue are M. Goos and A. Manning, 'Lousy and lovely jobs: The rising polarization of work in Britain', *Review of Economics and Statistics*, 89:1 (2007), pp. 118–33, and D. Autor, 'Polanyi's paradox and the shape of employment growth', presentation to the Federal Reserve Bank of Kansas City's Jackson Hole central banking conference, September 2014.

12. M. Ford, *The Rise of the Robots: Technology and the threat of mass unemployment*, Oneworld, London, 2015.

CHAPTER 10: DEBASING THE COINAGE

1. The then Brazilian finance minister, Guido Mantega, first referred to currency wars in September 2010.
2. Although, given that China's growth rate was well above the global average, China's surplus rose more quickly as a share of non-Chinese global national income.
3. The Juncker plan – a €315 billion infrastructure plan for the European Union – was supposed to deliver the spending over a three-year period beginning on 1 January 2015. How much of this was net new money was unclear. However, at an average annual rate of 0.7 per cent of EU national income, the plan was never likely to transform EU growth prospects, even if some of the investments contained within the plan were, in themselves, worthwhile.
4. For a useful discussion of pre-crisis thinking on the subject, try J. Bullard, 'Testing long-run monetary neutrality propositions: Lessons from the recent research', *Federal Reserve Bank of St Louis Review*, November/December 1999, available at: https://research.stlouisfed.org/publications/review/99/11/9911jb.pdf
5. The Marshall–Lerner condition states that there will be an improvement in the balance of trade following a devaluation so long as the absolute sum of the export and import elasticities is greater than one.
6. For a discussion of the impact of global value chains on the effects of exchange rate declines, see S. Ahmed, M. Appendino and M. Ruta, *Depreciations without Exports? Global value chains and the exchange rate elasticity of exports*, Policy Research Working Paper No. 7390, World Bank, Washington, DC, August 2015.
7. Robert Triffin described the dilemma in testimony to US Congress in 1960. For a good description of his view, see: https://www.imf.org/external/np/exr/center/mm/eng/mm_sc_03.htm
8. I am indebted to Gideon Bloom for this hybrid term.
9. See, for example, K.S. Rogoff, *The Curse of Cash*, Princeton University Press, Princeton, NJ, 2016. To be fair, Rogoff is more interested in abolishing high-denomination notes to reduce the practicality of holding cash for nefarious purposes. When India introduced precisely this reform, sales of Rolex watches went through the roof: there's more than one way of keeping 'cash' hidden from the taxman.
10. S. King, 'The alchemist's puzzle: The monetary threat to productivity growth', HSBC, London, November 2016 and D. Andrews, C. Criscuolo and P. Gal, *The Global Productivity Slowdown, Technology Divergence and Public Policy: A firm level perspective*, Economics Department, OECD, Paris, 2016.
11. See, for example, Bank for International Settlements, *Quarterly Review*, 6 March 2016, available at: http://www.bis.org/publ/qtrpdf/r_qt1603b.htm

CHAPTER 11: OBLIGATIONS AND IMPOSSIBLE SOLUTIONS

1. I argued this point forcefully in *Losing Control: The emerging threats to Western prosperity*, Yale University Press, London, 2010.
2. See, for example, D. Rodrik, 'The abdication of the left', Project Syndicate, July 2016, available at: https://www.project-syndicate.org/commentary/anti-globalization-backlash-from-right-by-dani-rodrik-2016-07

3. Y. Varoufakis, 'Imagining a new Bretton Woods', Project Syndicate, May 2016, available at: https://www.project-syndicate.org/commentary/imagining-new-bretton-woods-by-yanis-varoufakis-2016-05

4. J. Stiglitz, 'A split euro is the solution for Europe's single currency', Financial Times, 17 August 2016, available at: http://www.ft.com/cms/s/0/dbbd151c-62f4-11e6-8310-ecf0bddad227.html#axzz4HY4gzCzn

5. D. Rodrik, 'The false economic promise of global governance', Project Syndicate, August 2016, available at: https://www.project-syndicate.org/commentary/global-governance-false-economic-promise-by-dani-rodrik-2016-08

6. In 1981, the average OECD corporation tax rate was 47.5 per cent. By 2013, it had dropped to 25.5 per cent. Weighted by size of GDP, the average rate dropped from 49.1 per cent to 32.5 per cent over the same period. At 49.7 per cent, the US had a typical OECD corporation tax rate in 1981 but, by 2013, it had the highest, at 39.1 per cent. Interestingly, one of the US economy's main failings over that period was a sustained reduction in the number of thriving businesses.

7. See, most obviously, D. Rodrik, The Globalization Paradox: Why global markets, states and democracy can't coexist, Oxford University Press, Oxford, 2011.

8. McCloskey's three volumes are a remarkable journey through the ideas of free markets, capitalism, English literature and bourgeois behaviour. See D. McCloskey, The Bourgeois Virtues (2006), Bourgeois Dignity (2010) and Bourgeois Equality (2016), all published by University of Chicago Press.

9. A suspicious reader might think the author had been involved in an experience of this kind. The author couldn't possibly comment.

10. A. Salmond, 'Free to prosper: Creating the Celtic Lion economy', speech to Harvard University, 31 March 2008, available at: http://www.gov.scot/News/Speeches/Speeches/First-Minister/harvard-university

11. http://www.worldbank.org/en/topic/poverty/overview

12. J. Rothwell, 'Explaining nationalist political views: The case of Donald Trump', Gallup, August 2016, available at: http://www.umass.edu/preferen/You%20Must%20Read%20This/Rothwell-Gallup.pdf

13. R. Hofstadter, 'The paranoid style in American politics', Harper's Magazine, November 1964, available at: http://harpers.org/archive/1964/11/the-paranoid-style-in-american-politics/?single=1

14. Ecuador won its case against the US in 2007. The full list of disputes can be found at: https://www.wto.org/english/tratop_e/dispu_e/dispu_by_country_e.htm

BIBLIOGRAPHY

Acemoglu, D. and J. Robinson. *Why Nations Fail: The origins of power, prosperity and poverty*, Profile Books, New York, 2013

Acemoglu, D. and J. Robinson. 'The rise and decline of general laws of capitalism', *Journal of Economic Perspectives*, 29:1 (2015), pp. 3–28

Admati, A. and M. Hellwig. *The Bankers' New Clothes: What's wrong with banking and what to do about it*, Princeton University Press, Princeton, NJ, 2013

Ahmed, S., M. Appendino and M. Ruta. *Depreciations without Exports? Global value chains and the exchange rate elasticity of exports*, Policy Research Working Paper No. 7390, World Bank, Washington, DC, August 2015

Akerlof, G. 'The market for lemons: Quality, uncertainty and the market mechanism', *Quarterly Journal of Economics*, 84:3 (1970), pp. 488–500

Alesina, A., A. Devleeschauwer, W. Easterly, S. Kurlat and R. Wacziarg. *Fractionalization*, Harvard Institute of Economic Research Discussion Paper No. 1959, Cambridge, MA, June 2002, available at: https://dash.harvard.edu/handle/1/4553003

Andrews, D., C. Criscuolo and P. Gal. *The Global Productivity Slowdown, Technology Divergence and Public Policy: A firm level perspective*, Economics Department, OECD, Paris, 2016

Atkinson, A.B. *Inequality: What can be done?*, Harvard University Press, Cambridge, MA, 2015

Atkinson, A.B. and S. Morelli. *Chartbook of Economic Inequality*, 2014, available at: http://www.chartbookofeconomicinequality.com/

Autor, D. 'Polanyi's paradox and the shape of employment growth', presentation to the Federal Reserve Bank of Kansas City's Jackson Hole central banking conference, September 2014

Baldwin, R. *Global Supply Chains: Why they emerged, why they matter, and where they are going*, Centre for Trade and Economic Integration Working Paper CTEI-2012-13, Graduate Institute, Geneva, 2012

Baldwin, R. *The Great Convergence: Information technology and the new globalization*, Harvard University Press, Cambridge, MA, 2016

Bank for International Settlements. *Quarterly Review*, 6 March 2016, available at: http://www.bis.org/publ/qtrpdf/r_qt1603b.htm

Barnard, L. 'The cost of creepiness: How online behavioral advertising affects consumer purchase intention', dissertation, University of North Carolina at Chapel Hill, 2014

Bartels, L.M. *Unequal Democracy: The political economy of the new gilded age*, Princeton University Press, Princeton, NJ, 2010

Bartlett, T. *Ireland: A history*, Cambridge University Press, Cambridge, 2010

Beckwith, C. *Empires of the Silk Road: A history of Central Eurasia from the Bronze Age to the present*, Princeton University Press, Princeton, NJ, 2009

Bernanke, B. 'The Great Moderation', remarks at the meeting of the Eastern Economic Association, Washington, DC, 20 February 2004, available at: http://www.federalreserve.gov/Boarddocs/Speeches/2004/20040220/

Bernanke, B. *The Federal Reserve and the Financial Crisis*, Princeton University Press, Princeton, NJ, 2013

Best, G. *Humanity in Warfare: The modern history of the international law of armed conflicts*, Weidenfeld and Nicolson, London, 1980

Blanchard, O. and J. Simon. 'The long and large decline in US output volatility', *Brookings Papers on Economic Activity*, 1 (2001), pp. 135–64

Bond, S. 'Digital is reshaping the world of advertising', *Financial Times*, 28 April 2015, available at: http://www.ft.com/cms/s/2/60b8747e-bc1f-11e4-a6d7-00144feab7de.html#axzz43CXb1TWE

Borjas, G.J. *Making It in America: Social mobility in the immigrant population*, National Bureau of Economic Research Working Paper No. 12088, Cambridge, MA, March 2006

Boughton, J. 'Dirtying White: Why does Benn Stell's history of Bretton Woods distort the ideas of Harry Dexter White?', *The Nation*, 5 June 2013, available at https://www.thenation.com/article/dirtying-white/

Brynjolfsson, E. and A. McAfee. *The Second Machine Age: Work, progress, and prosperity in a time of brilliant technologies*, Norton, New York, 2014

Buchanan, J.M. 'An economic theory of clubs', *Economica*, 32:125 (1965), pp. 1–14

Bullard, J. 'Testing long-run monetary neutrality propositions: Lessons from the recent research', *Federal Reserve Bank of St Louis Review*, November/December 1999, available at: https://research.stlouisfed.org/publications/review/99/11/9911jb.pdf

Bush, G.W. 'Address to Joint Session of Congress', 20 September 2001, available at: http://edition.cnn.com/2001/US/09/20/gen.bush.transcript

Chang, Ha-Joon. *Kicking Away the Ladder: Development strategy in historical perspective*, Anthem Press, London, 2002

Chang, Ha-Joon. *Bad Samaritans: The myth of free trade and the secret history of capitalism*, Bloomsbury, New York, 2008

Cherif, R. and F. Hasanov. *The Leap of the Tiger: How Malaysia can escape from the middle income trap*, IMF Working Paper WP/15/131, Washington, DC, June 2015, available at https://www.imf.org/external/pubs/ft/wp/2015/wp15131.pdf

Chetty, R., N. Hendren and L. Katz. 'The effects of exposure to better neighborhoods on children: New evidence from the moving to opportunity experiment', *American Economic Review*, forthcoming

Chetty, R., N. Hendren, P. Kline, E. Saez and N. Turner. *Is the United States Still a Land of Opportunity? Recent trends in intergenerational mobility*, National Bureau of Economic Research Working Paper No. 19844, Cambridge, MA, January 2014

Clark, G. *A Farewell to Alms: A brief history of the world*, Princeton University Press, Princeton, NJ, 2007

Clark, G. *The Son Also Rises: Surnames and the history of social mobility*, Princeton University Press, Princeton, NJ, 2014

Clark, T. and A. Dilnot. *Long-Term Trends in British Taxation and Spending*, Institute for Fiscal Studies Briefing Note No. 25, London, 2002

Cleveland, G. 'First Inaugural Address', 4 March 1885, available at: http://avalon.law.yale. edu/19th_century/cleve1.asp

Coca-Cola Company. '125 years of sharing happiness: A short history of the Coca-Cola Company', available at: https://www.coca-colacompany.com/content/dam/journey/us/en/private/fileassets/pdf/2011/05/Coca-Cola_125_years_booklet.pdf

Conrad, J. *Heart of Darkness*, Penguin, London, 2007

Conway, E. *The Summit: The biggest battle of the Second World War – fought behind closed doors*, Little, Brown, London, 2014

Corlett, A. 'Examining an elephant: Globalisation and the lower middle class of the rich world', Resolution Foundation, London, September 2016, available at: http://www.resolutionfoundation.org/wp-content/uploads/2016/09/Examining-an-elephant.pdf

Darwin, J. *After Tamerlane: The rise and fall of global empires, 1400–2000*, Allen Lane, London, 2007

Davis, D. and T. Gift. 'The positive effects of the Schengen Agreement on European trade', *World Economy*, 37:11 (2014), pp. 1541–57

Dustmann, C. and T. Frattini. 'The fiscal effects of immigration to the UK', *Economic Journal*, 124:580 (2014), pp. 593–643

Easterly, W. *The Tyranny of Experts: Economists, dictators and the forgotten rights of the poor*, Basic Books, Philadelphia, 2013

Easterly, W. and R. Levine. 'Africa's growth tragedy: Policies and ethnic divisions', *Quarterly Journal of Economics*, 112:4 (1997), pp. 1203–50

Eichengreen, B. *Hall of Mirrors: The Great Depression, the Great Recession and the uses – and misuses – of history*, Oxford University Press, Oxford, 2015

European Union. Treaty on European Union (Maastricht Treaty), 1992, available at: https://europa.eu/european-union/sites/europaeu/files/docs/body/treaty_on_european_union_en.pdf

Federal Deposit Insurance Corporation. 'A brief history of deposit insurance in the United States', presentation prepared for the International Conference on Deposit Insurance, Washington, DC, September 1998

Ferguson, N. *The Great Degeneration: How institutions decay and economies die*, Allen Lane, London, 2013

Findlay, R. and K. O'Rourke. *Power and Plenty: Trade, war and the world economy in the second millennium*, Princeton University Press, Princeton, NJ, 2007

Ford, M. *The Rise of the Robots: Technology and the threat of mass unemployment*, Oneworld, London, 2015

Frankopan, P. *The New Silk Roads*, Bloomsbury, London, 2015

Freedom House. 'Discarding democracy: Return to the iron fist', available at: https://freedomhouse.org/report/freedom-world-2015/discarding-democracy-return-iron-fist

Friedman, T. *The World is Flat: The globalized world in the twenty-first century*, Allen Lane, New York, 2005

Fukuyama, F. 'The end of history', *National Interest*, 16 (1989)

Fukuyama, F. *The End of History and the Last Man*, Free Press, New York, 1992

Fukuyama, F. *Political Order and Political Decay: From the Industrial Revolution to the globalization of democracy*, Farrar, Straus and Giroux, New York, 2014

Funke, M., M. Schularick and C. Trebesch. 'Politics in the slump: Polarization and extremism after financial crises, 1870–2014, Berlin, September 2015, available at: http://ec.europa.eu/economy_finance/events/2015/20151001_post_crisis_slump/documents/c._trebesch.pdf

Gilens, M. *Affluence and Influence*, Princeton University Press, Princeton, NJ, 2012

Glover, J. *Humanity: A moral history of the twentieth century*, Vintage, London, 2001

Góes, C. *Testing Piketty's Hypothesis on the Drivers of Income Inequality: Evidence from panel VARs with heterogeneous dynamics*, IMF Working Paper WP/16/160, Washington, DC, August 2016

Goos, M. and A. Manning. 'Lousy and lovely jobs: The rising polarization of work in Britain', *Review of Economics and Statistics*, 89:1 (2007), pp. 118–33

Gordon, R. *The Rise and Fall of American Growth: The US standard of living since the Civil War*, Princeton University Press, Princeton, NJ, 2016

Greenspan, A. *The Age of Turbulence: Adventures in a new world*, Allen Lane, New York, 2007

Hartshorn, P. *I Have Seen the Future: A life of Lincoln Steffens*, Counterpoint Press, Berkeley, 2011

Hatton, T.J. and J.G. Williamson. *Global Migration and the World Economy: Two centuries of policy and performance*, MIT Press, Cambridge, MA, 2008

Hausmann, R. 'Through the Venezuelan looking glass', Project Syndicate, August 2016, available at: https://www.project-syndicate.org/commentary/venezuela-destructive-belief-systems-by-ricardo-hausmann-2016-08

Hobbes, T. *Leviathan* (ed. J. Gaskin), Oxford University Press, Oxford, 1996

Hofstadter, R. 'The paranoid style in American politics', *Harper's Magazine*, November 1964, available at: http://harpers.org/archive/1964/11/the-paranoid-style-in-american-politics/?single=1

Humphrey, T.M. 'Lender of last resort: The concept in history', *Federal Reserve Bank of Richmond Economic Review*, March/April (1989), pp. 8–16

Huntington, S.P. *The Clash of Civilizations and the Remaking of World Order*, Simon & Schuster UK, London, 1997

Instituto Cervantes. 'El español, una lengua viva', available at: http://eldiae.es/wp-content/uploads/2015/06/espanol_lengua-viva_20151.pdf

James, H. *The End of Globalization: Lessons from the Great Depression*, Harvard University Press, Cambridge, MA, 2001

Jefferson, T. 'Letter to Joseph Priestley', 19 June 1802, available at: http://founders.archives.gov/documents/Jefferson/01-37-02-0515

Kane, T. *Global US Troop Deployment, 1950–2003*, Center for Data Analysis Report No. 04/11, Heritage Foundation, Washington, DC, 27 October 2004

Kennan, G. 'The charge in the Soviet Union (Kennan) to the Secretary of State', 22 February 1946, available at: http://nsarchive.gwu.edu/coldwar/documents/episode-1/kennan.htm

Kennedy, P. *The Rise and Fall of the Great Powers: Economic change and military conflict from 1500 to 2000*, Random House, New York, 1988

Keynes, J.M. *A Treatise on Monetary Reform*, Macmillan, London, 1924

Keynes, J.M. *The General Theory of Employment, Interest and Money*, Macmillan, London, 1936

Keynes, J.M. 'The economic consequences of Mr Churchill', in *Essays in Persuasion*, Norton, New York, 1963

King, M. *The End of Alchemy: Money, banking and the future of the global economy*, Little, Brown, London, 2016

King, S. *Losing Control: The emerging threats to Western prosperity*, Yale University Press, London, 2010

King, S. *When the Money Runs Out: The end of Western affluence*, Yale University Press, London, 2013

King, S. 'The alchemist's puzzle: The monetary threat to productivity growth', HSBC, London, November 2016

Kissinger, H. *World Order: Reflections on the character of nations and the course of history*, Allen Lane, London, 2014

Kurlantzick, J. *Democracy in Retreat: The revolt of the middle class and the worldwide decline of representative government*, Yale University Press, New Haven and London, 2013

Lakner, C. and B. Milanović. 'Response to Adam Corlett's "Examining an elephant: Globalisation and the lower middle class of the rich world" ', September 2016, available at http://www.gc.cuny.edu/CUNY_GC/media/CUNY-Graduate-Center/LIS%20Center/elephant_debate-4,-reformatted.pdf

Landes, D. *The Wealth and Poverty of Nations*, Norton, New York, 1998

Lane, P.R. and G.M. Milesi-Ferretti. 'The external wealth of nations mark II: Revised and extended estimates of foreign assets and liabilities, 1970–2004', *Journal of International Economics*, 73:2 (2007), pp. 223–50

Leech, D. 'Voting power in the governance of the International Monetary Fund', London School of Economics, 2002, available at: http://eprints.lse.ac.uk/648/1/ANOR109Leech.pdf

Lewis, W.A. 'Economic development with unlimited supplies of labour', *The Manchester School*, 22:2 (1954), pp. 139–91

Lucas, R.E. 'Macroeconomic priorities', *American Economic Review*, 93:1 (2003), pp. 1–14

Lyman, R. and J. Berendt. 'As Poland lurches to the right, many in Europe look on in alarm', *New York Times*, 14 December 2015, available at: http://www.nytimes.com/2015/12/15/world/europe/poland-law-and-justice-party-jaroslaw-kaczynski.html

MacMillan, M. *The War that Ended Peace: How Europe abandoned peace for the First World War*, Profile Books, London, 2014

Maddison, A. *Contours of the World Economy, 1–2030 AD: Essays in macro-economic history*, Oxford University Press, Oxford, 2007

Mann, T. *The Magic Mountain*, trans. J.E. Woods, Vintage Everyman's Library Edition, New York, 2005

Marshall, G. 'Speech at Harvard University', 5 June 1947, available at: http://www.oecd.org/general/themarshallplanspeechatharvarduniversity5june1947.htm

Mazower, M. *Governing the World: The history of an idea, 1815 to the present*, Penguin, New York, 2012

McCloskey, D. *The Bourgeois Virtues*, University of Chicago Press, Chicago, 2006

McCloskey, D. *Bourgeois Dignity*, University of Chicago Press, Chicago, 2010

McCloskey, D. *Bourgeois Equality*, University of Chicago Press, Chicago, 2016

Merriman, J. 'France since 1871: The birth of national identity and agents of modernization', Yale Open Courses Lecture, 17 September 2007, available at: http://oyc.yale.edu/transcript/357/hist-276

Mian, A. and A. Sufi. *House of Debt: How they (and you) caused the Great Recession and how we can prevent it from happening again*, University of Chicago Press, Chicago, 2014

Milanović, B., *Global Inequality: A new approach for the age of globalization*, Belknap Press, Cambridge, MA, 2016

Minsky, H. *Stabilizing an Unstable Economy*, McGraw Hill Education, New York, 2008

Mishra, P. *From the Ruins of Empire: The revolt against the West and the remaking of Asia*, Allen Lane, London, 2012

Mitta, R. *China's War with Japan, 1937–1945: The struggle for survival*, Allen Lane, London, 2013

Mokyr, J. *A Culture of Growth: The origins of the modern economy*, Princeton University Press, Princeton, NJ, 2016

Montesquieu, C. *The Spirit of the Laws*, ed. A. Cohler, B. Miller and H. Stone, Cambridge University Press, Cambridge, 1989

Moran, J. 'Defining moment: Denis Healey agrees to the demands of the IMF', *Financial Times*, 4 September 2010, available at: https://www.ft.com/content/11484844-b565-11df-9af8-00144feabdc0

Morgenthau, H. *Politics among Nations: The struggle for power and peace*, rev. K. Thompson, McGraw-Hill, New York, 1993

Murray, C. *Coming Apart: The state of white America 1960–2010*, Crown Forum, New York, 2012

Myers, N. and J. Kent. *Environmental Exodus: An emergent crisis in the global arena*, Climate Institute, Washington, DC, 1995

National Archives. 'Conclusions of a meeting of the Cabinet held at 10 Downing Street on Tuesday 23 November 1976 at 10.00am', available at: http://filestore.nationalarchives.gov. uk/pdfs/small/cab-128-60-cm-76-33.pdf

National Archives. 'The real choices facing the Cabinet, memorandum by the secretary of state for energy, 29 November 1976', available at: http://filestore.nationalarchives.gov.uk/ pdfs/small/cab-129-193-cp-76-117-7.pdf

Nordhaus, W. 'Two centuries of productivity growth in computing', *Journal of Economic History*, 67:1 (2007), pp. 128–59

Nye, J. *Soft Power: The means to success in world politics*, PublicAffairs, New York, 2004

Obstfeld, M. and A.M. Taylor. *Global Capital Markets: Integration, crisis, and growth*, Cambridge University Press, New York, 2004

OECD. 'Programme for International Student Assessment', available at http://www.oecd. org/publications/pisa-2015-results-volume-i-9789264266490-en.htm

Office of Immigration Statistics. *2013 Yearbook of Immigration Statistics*, Department of Homeland Security, Washington, DC, available at: http://www.dhs.gov/sites/default/files/ publications/ois_yb_2013_0.pdf

Passari, E. and H. Rey. *Financial Flows and the International Monetary System*, National Bureau of Economic Research Working Paper No. 21172, Cambridge, MA, May 2015

Petri, P. and M. Plummer. *The Economic Effects of the Trans-Pacific Partnership: New estimates*, Peterson Institute for International Economics Working Paper 16-2, Washington, DC, January 2016

Pettis, M. *The Great Rebalancing: Trade, conflict and the perilous road ahead for the world economy*, Princeton University Press, Princeton, NJ, 2013

Piketty, T. *Capital in the Twenty-First Century*, trans. A. Goldhammer, Belknap Press, Cambridge, MA, 2014

Pinker, S. and A. Mack. 'The world is not falling apart', *Slate*, 2014, available at: http://www. slate.com/articles/news_and_politics/foreigners/2014/12/the_world_is_not_falling_ apart_the_trend_lines_reveal_an_increasingly_peaceful.html

Rachman, G. *Zero-Sum World: Politics, power and prosperity after the crash*, Atlantic Books, London, 2010

Rachman, G. *Easternisation: War and peace in the Asian century*, Bodley Head, London, 2016

Reputation Institute. '2015 Country RepTrak': The world's most reputable countries', available at: https://www.reputationinstitute.com/CMSPages/GetAzureFile.aspx?path=~\ media\media\documents\country-reptrak-webinar-2015-forweb.pdf&hash=3e386f19a7 37277500c8c2c5f651f5810028665ad3c2af218dccc1e5856eacfd&ext=.pdf

Rhodes, C. 'Public sector employment and expenditure by region', House of Commons Library, London, July 2014, available at: http://researchbriefings.parliament.uk/ ResearchBriefing/Summary/SN05625

Rodrik, D. *The Globalization Paradox: Why global markets, states and democracy can't coexist*, Oxford University Press, Oxford, 2011

Rodrik, D. 'The abdication of the left', Project Syndicate, July 2016, available at: https://www. project-syndicate.org/commentary/anti-globalization-backlash-from-right-by-dani-rodrik-2016-07

Rodrik, D., 'The false economic promise of global governance', Project Syndicate, August 2016, available at: https://www.project-syndicate.org/commentary/global-governance-false-economic-promise-by-dani-rodrik-2016-08

Rogoff, K.S. *The Curse of Cash*, Princeton University Press, Princeton, NJ, 2016

Rose, N. *Churchill: An unruly life*, Tauris, London, 2009

Rothwell, J. 'Explaining nationalist political views: The case of Donald Trump', Gallup, August 2016, available at: http://papers.ssrn.com/sol3/papers.cfm?abstract_id=2822059

Salmond, A. 'Free to prosper: Creating the Celtic Lion economy', speech to Harvard University, 31 March 2008, available at: http://www.gov.scot/News/Speeches/Speeches/First-Minister/harvard-university

Schuman, R. 'The Schuman Declaration', 9 May 1950, available at: http://europa.eu/european-union/about-eu/symbols/europe-day/schuman-declaration_en

Seidentop, L. *Inventing the Individual: The origins of Western liberalism*, Allen Lane, London, 2014

Sen, A. *Identity and Violence: The illusion of destiny*, Allen Lane, London, 2006

Shaw, G.B. et al. 'Social conditions in Russia: Recent visitors' tribute', Letters to the Editor, *Manchester Guardian*, 2 March 1933

Silber, W. *Volcker: The triumph of persistence*, Bloomsbury, New York, 2012

Steil, B. *The Battle of Bretton Woods: John Maynard Keynes, Harry Dexter White and the making of a new world order*, Princeton University Press, Princeton, NJ, 2013

Stiglitz, J. 'A split euro is the solution for Europe's single currency', *Financial Times*, 17 August 2016, available at: http://www.ft.com/cms/s/0/dbbd151c-62f4-11e6-8310-ecf0b-ddad227.html#axzz4HY4gzCzn

Stockholm International Peace Research Institute. 'Military Expenditure Database', available at: http://www.sipri.org/research/armaments/milex/milex_database

Turner, A. *Between Debt and the Devil: Money, credit and fixing global finance*, Princeton University Press, Princeton, NJ, 2015

United Nations. *World Population Prospects: The 2015 revision*, Volume II: *Demographic Profiles*, United Nations Department of Economic and Social Affairs/Population Division, New York, 2015

Varoufakis, Y. 'Imagining a New Bretton Woods', Project Syndicate, May 2016, available at: https://www.project-syndicate.org/commentary/imagining-new-bretton-woods-by-yanis-varoufakis-2016-05

Williamson, J. (ed.). *Latin American Adjustment: How much has happened?*, Institute for International Economics, Washington, DC, 1990

Wilson, W. 'Address to a joint session of Congress requesting a declaration of war against Germany', 2 April 1917, available at: http://www.presidency.ucsb.edu/ws/?pid=65366

Winder, R. *Bloody Foreigners: The story of immigration to Britain*, Little, Brown, London, 2004

Wolf, M. *Why Globalization Works*, Yale University Press, New Haven and London, 2004

Wolf, M. *Fixing Global Finance: How to curb financial crises in the 21st century*, Yale University Press, New Haven and London, 2009

Wolf, M. *The Shifts and the Shocks: What we've learned – and have still to learn – from the financial crisis*, Penguin, London, 2015

Wolf, T. *Bonfire of the Vanities*, Random House, New York, 1987

Wolff, E.N. *Household Wealth Trends in the United States, 1961–2013: What happened over the Great Recession?*, National Bureau of Economic Research Working Paper No. 20733, Cambridge, MA, December 2014

ACKNOWLEDGEMENTS

In a parallel universe, I might have been tempted to thank Donald Trump and Nigel Farage. The ideas for *Grave New World* originally crystallized in 2015, long before the extraordinary political upheavals of 2016. I jokingly suggested to a number of people that the book would seem a lot more relevant if UK citizens were to vote in favour of Brexit and US citizens were to elect Donald Trump. Whilst I certainly hadn't ruled out either development, I was very much aware that the majority of pundits in 2015 and the early months of 2016 thought UK 'Remainers' would triumph and that the battle for the White House was most likely to be between Hillary Clinton and Jeb Bush (or, at a pinch, Mario Rubio). As it turned out, however, 2016's political shocks only served to reinforce the messages contained within *Grave New World*.

I shall nevertheless resist the temptation to express gratitude to Messrs Trump and Farage. After all, they didn't go out of their way to help me. Others, however, I absolutely must thank. I am particularly indebted to those who generously managed to find the time to read and comment on the whole manuscript as it went through various drafts: Peter Frankopan (author of the masterful *The Silk Roads*); John Llewellyn (at his eponymous consulting company) and his colleague, Russell Jones; Janet Henry, Doug Lippoldt and Chris Brown-Humes (all at HSBC); and Helena Nathan-King (whose sage advice on climate change was invaluable).

I have benefited from conversations with people who, at one time or another, served (and, in one case, still serves) at the IMF: Jim Boughton, for many years the IMF's official historian, offered a wealth of advice on the Fund's development; John Lipsky (the former deputy managing director of the Fund and, for a while, its effective head after Dominique Strauss-Kahn's fall from grace) made important points about the IMF's role during the Bretton Woods era, a period in which capital didn't flow across borders particularly freely; and Maury Obstfeld provided me with important data about the growth of cross-border capital flows in recent decades.

The book's opening speech – a piece of Victorian bombast – was, funnily enough, inspired by James Baker III, the former US secretary of state. At a conference in April 2016, Baker gave a very good – and upbeat – speech about America's enduring global role in the twenty-first century. Following his remarks, I had the pleasure of interviewing him. I asked whether he thought a British politician in the Victorian era might have offered similar sentiments regarding the UK's prospects in the twentieth century. He admitted that, yes, it could well have been the case. I couldn't resist the opportunity to prove him right.

Given the amount of history contained within *Grave New World*, I inevitably had to stand on the shoulders of historians or, at the very least, their books: many such volumes are listed in the bibliography. Those who have offered me advice and inspiration in equal measure on the economic aspects of globalization include Martin Wolf, Gideon Rachman, George Magnus, Shamik Dhar, David Bloom, Simon Williams, Murat Ulgen, Robin Down and Simon Wells. I also owe a debt of gratitude to the various anonymous referees who provided comments at various stages during the book's progress. Policymakers on both sides of the Atlantic (and the Pacific) have been enormously helpful (although I suspect they would rather be thanked in spirit rather than in name).

I have also benefited a great deal from the various conferences and roundtables I have attended in recent years, including regular gatherings at the Bank for International Settlements, the Oesterreichische Kontrollbank and the Centre for European Reform at Ditchley Park.

I have had tremendous support from HSBC. Stuart Gulliver immediately understood that my book-writing ambitions would require a more flexible arrangement with the Bank: he had no hesitation in agreeing to my request for a part-time role. Stephen Moss and Neelesh Heredia have offered encouragement throughout, as have Samir Assaf, Katja Hall and Jezz Farr. Debbie Falcus has, once again, organized my working life in ways that, left to my own devices, would have simply been impossible.

My editor at Yale, Taiba Batool, has been a constant source of wisdom. I have also received tremendous support from Ruth Killick, Clive Liddiard, Noel Murphy, Rachael Lonsdale and Heather Nathan.

Finally, and as always, I wish to thank my family for their love, support, patience and inspiration: my wonderful wife, Yvonne, and my three talented daughters, Helena, Olivia and Sophie. I sincerely hope that theirs will not be a grave new world.

London, January 2017

INDEX